Culture and Democracy

"We are not free because of what we statically are, but insofar as we are becoming different from what we have been."

John Dewey

To Mum and Dad

Culture and Democracy

Media, Space, and Representation

Clive Barnett

Edinburgh University Press

© Clive Barnett, 2003

Edinburgh University Press Ltd
22 George Square, Edinburgh

Typeset in Sabon
by J&L Composition, Filey, North Yorkshire, and
printed and bound in Great Britain by
MPG Books Ltd, Bodmin

A CIP record for this book is available from the British Library

ISBN 0 7486 1400 1 (hardback)
ISBN 0 7486 1399 4 (paperback)

The right of Clive Barnett to be identified as author of this work
has been asserted in accordance with
the Copyright, Designs and Patents Act 1988.

Contents

Preface

> Everybody gets told to write about what they know. The trouble with many of us is that at the earlier stages of life we think we know everything – or to put it more usefully, we are often unaware of the scope and structure of our ignorance. Ignorance is not just a blank space on a person's mental map. It has contours and coherence, and for all I know rules of operation as well. So as a corollary to writing about what we know, maybe we should add getting familiar with our ignorance, and the possibilities therein of ruining a good story.
>
> (Thomas Pynchon)

I have always liked this idea, which captures my own experience of how learning works, as an ever-expanding horizon of new areas and topics you don't know much about. Writing this book has been very much about coming to terms with the scope and structure of my own ignorance. My main aim in writing it has been to try to think through the terms of evaluation and judgement by which one might decide that certain situations are more or less democratic, more or less just, more or less justifiable. I don't pretend to have solved any fundamental political philosophical puzzles in this book. I have just wanted to take a step away from some taken-for-granted attitudes that characterise critical academic analysis, in human geography and beyond. This has primarily been about trying to resist a rush to judgement, to take things slowly, to be deliberate, to take care, and to show respect.

A long time ago, as a graduate student, various people helped me along the way to thinking seriously about ideas, including Gargi Bhattacharyya, David Harvey, Andy Merrifield, Adrian Passmore and Mike Samers. The main impetus for the focus of this book on issues of democracy has come from various research visits to South Africa (funded by the Leverhulme Trust, the British Academy and the University of Reading). This experience has stimulated an effort to think about how formal democratisation is related to the more elusive subtleties of creating a liberal culture. To acknowledge the range of hospitality, intellectual and otherwise, I have enjoyed on these occasions would take too long, but with respect to the research reported in the final chapter of this book specifically, I must thank Costas Criticos and Di Scott for sharing with me their knowledge and expertise about kids and TV and about environmental activism, respectively. Much of the research and writing of this book was undertaken while I worked at the University of Reading, and I would like to thank my colleagues there for making my time there so rewarding. This book was first conceived during a year spent at Ohio State University and a good deal of the research was also carried out there. I would like to thank Kevin Cox for his support both then and since. I would like to thank John Davey of Edinburgh University Press for encouraging me to write a book about my favourite theorists in the first place, and for his patience while I wrote it. Thanks to Abbey Halcli, Murray Low, Mark McGuinness, Julie McLaren and Mike Samers for reading earlier drafts and commenting kindly but critically upon them. Special thanks to Murray Low, with whom I accidentally discovered a shared intellectual affinity at Reading, and whose influence on this book is considerable, although only on the good bits. Finally, I would like to thank Julie, for not allowing me to take book-writing too seriously.

Introduction: how is democracy?

I The promise of communication

This book is about the meaning of democracy, and how this is related to practices of mediation. It uses the media as an entry point to think about democracy, difference and representation. The last decade has seen a wave of real-world democratisation, which has coincided with increasing soul-searching about whether or not the ideals of democracy are in deep crisis. A number of commentators identify the media as bearing primary responsibility for the decline of active citizenship and the decay of democratic institutions. The media are charged with encouraging cognitive dependence, narcosis and the attenuation of critical faculties (Zolo 1992); with eroding the capacity of citizens to trust in public institutions and hold them accountable (O'Neill 2002a); with undermining the autonomy of science and a robust public culture of criticism (Bourdieu 1998); and with encouraging widespread civic disengagement and the withering of social capital (Putnam 1995).

These criticisms are all made in the name of broadly participatory conceptions of democracy. They present a rather unhappy picture of the connections between citizen engagement and mass-mediated cultural practices. It is easy to recoil from the implicit cultural elitism of such analyses, and embrace instead the ordinariness of popular media cultures as inherently democratic. But the problem with the commonsense populism of so much contemporary cultural analysis is that it rarely addresses the issue of who speaks for the popular, and with what authority (Garnham 1995). Overextended notions of cultural politics rarely address the relationship between the multiple senses of the popular in the sense of popular culture (where it refers all at once to the ordinary, the well-liked, and the size of the appreciative audience), and the distinct sense of the popular in modern understandings of democracy (defined in relation to the idea of popular sovereignty, which in turn implies a combined sense of equality, participation and the rule of the many). The value of popularity in both cultural evaluation and political debate is highly ambivalent. It is often invoked as a knock-down device to close off argument, but this only raises questions about the validity, extent and fidelity of any such claim to know the popular mind.

Another way of putting this is to say that concepts of the people, the public and the popular are traversed by the problem of representation. Representing is always in part a conjuring up of things (the will of the people, models of reality, images of the nation). The conjuring up that is representation accompanies actions that claim broader legitimacy, but it also invites the contestation of those claims with reference to norms of representativeness, accountability or authorisation. This book argues that representation is central to a *parasitical* analysis of the dynamics of democratisation. The reference to a parasitical analysis (Derrida 1988: 135–6) is meant to capture the idea that democracy does not have a single pure form against which one can assess its actual manifestations. It suggests that democracy is not best approached in terms of the degree of purity and impurity of its proper expression, but rather in terms of a promise that will always exceed any particular effort at redemption (Derrida 1994: 64). In this respect, representation is central to the internal complexity of concepts of democracy, which combine emphases on equality, participation, and the binding authority of all of the people. In different forms, representation is the supplementary activity that is simultaneously invoked and tamed to juggle these different emphases. As such, representation inhabits the heart of the 'essentially contested' quality of democracy (see Gallie 1956). This means that democracy can be understood as a boundary concept, whose meaning is inherently connected to movements of translation and recontextualisation (Connolly 1993). The meanings, values and risks of democracy are most clearly exposed and problematised when applied to new contexts. With this in mind, the first four chapters of this book develop a differential sense of democracy and its relationships to mediated spaces of public communication. The final three chapters analyse three different examples of the grafting of democracy into new contexts, including the legal infrastructure of new communications regulation, the development of transnational cultural democracy, and the emergence of liberal public culture in a new democracy.

The focus on representation and democracy in this book might raise the objection that new technologies make the need for representative forms of political action redundant. We live, it seems, in an age of informational abundance, freeing human activity from the constraints of scarcity and necessity through the infinite proliferation of harmonious freedom and choice. This is the utopia of the weightless knowledge economy, matched by utopia not just of direct but of instant democracy. One lesson of thinking about media and democracy is to cast doubt on the utility of idealising communication as a meeting of minds, a transcendence of division or difference. The celebration of new technologies like the Internet as ideal for direct, plebiscitary democracy assumes that democracy is primarily about the expression and registering of personal preferences outside of any context of deliberative justification (Sunstein 1992). It is essential to confront the persistent elision of the problem of representation that characterises New Right discourses of freedom, corporate celebrations of choice and left-leaning celebrations of resistance. They all present new communications technologies as mediums for the direct expression of a unitary popular will. Each of these political visions assumes that political issues can be reduced to a question of more or less effective communication. Politics as communication is simultaneously a highly idealistic image, which holds out the promise of agreement and consensus, and a cynically realist one, in which politics is reduced to a zero-sum clash of opposed principles and interests.

For all their apparent populism, images of digitally mediated democracy easily flip over into anaemically administrative visions of democracy, in which the role of technology is reduced to aggregating individual preferences in order to facilitate more efficient political management (Schudson 1992). Rather than opposing inauthentic forms of representation, in which politicians, bureaucrats and journalists all come to be seen as usurping intermediaries, to the enhanced communicative potentials of digital interactivity, we should beware of the underlying assumption that political representation could or should ever be perfected and complete. At its worst, this assumption can be turned into a defence of fascist or totalitarian politics. Media and communications are neither obstacles to genuine participation and authentic representation, nor the potential solution that can reconnect rulers and ruled in harmonious union. The significance of TV or the Internet or radio is not best understood in terms of linear models of civic engagement or decline. The relationship between media and democracy is an internal, constitutive one, not an external, causal one. Following Martin-Barbero (1993), understanding media processes requires a decentring of the media, towards a broader analysis of the processes through which social life is mediated. This book is most concerned with patterns of mediation, rather than with the media *per se*, and with how this issue connects to normative political theories of democracy.

Roger Silverstone (1999: 26) has observed that contemporary debates about new media often do not just present technological change as having implications for politics, but equate technology directly with politics. Electronic town halls, on-line voting and instant referenda are all seen as providing problem-free, value-neutral means for more participation and better, more direct political expression. These sorts of claims erase the differential capacity for organisation and representation in public forums. Silverstone reminds us that the sorts of politics that go on within media, as it were, are shaped by the sorts of politics that go on around the media – the politics that determines patterns of access, ownership and regulation. The realisations of the varied hopes for new forms of politics invested in media technologies are, he suggests, 'themselves dependent on a more conventional politics which will, or will not, produce policies for access, defining and guaranteeing some form of universal service, protecting privacy and freedoms of speech, managing the concentration of ownership and in general securing the fruits of electronic space for the general social good' (ibid.). It is this more conventional sort of politics that this book addresses. Of course, the politics of interest group organisation, lobbying and policy-making is itself being reshaped by new media and communications practices. None the less, this does not invalidate a concern with analysing the politics that goes on around the media as the key to understanding the sorts of politics that go on within media. Understanding the role of media as mediums of political and cultural democratisation requires an appreciation of the ways in which media are themselves problematised as objects of politics and policy, and of the ways in which these two aspects are folded together. This book explores how particular public philosophies of citizenship are embedded in media policy debates, and how these are connected to a broader politics of interest group representation, mobilisation and lobbying.

The guiding theoretical influences discussed in this book all address questions of power not merely in terms of *who* exercises it, but in terms of *how* it is exercised. Taking seriously the 'how-of-power' that distinguishes democratic publicity underscores the point that, as a regime of power, democracy is not simply defined by the ascendance of a particular subject of power, the people. Democracy is often associated with the image of the assembly of a collective people to decide on matters of shared importance. Even if it is admitted that face-to-face deliberation cannot be practically implemented, the continuing idealisation of one territorial scale or another as the proper container of democratic politics is indicative of a conception of democracy which presumes that the scope and identity of participants, actions and consequences can be more or less easily delineated. The extension of democracy to the scale of the territorial nation-state depends historically, of course, on the institutionalisation of all sorts of mediating mechanisms, such as electoral systems, representative assemblies, a free press and so on. But political philosophy is deeply ambivalent about the mediated nature of political action without which modern democracy could not be imagined in the first place. It is still common to present democracy as an ideal that is at the very best menaced, if not negated, by the intercession of intermediaries in processes of deliberation and decision-making (see Hindess 1991).

The unsettling normative implications of the empirical fact that democratic rule relies on human and non-human intermediaries are frequently contained by conceptualising democracy in terms of undifferentiated communication. This involves pulling off the pretence that technologies of spatial and temporal mediation are simply ways of extending interaction over space and time without fundamentally altering the character of that interaction. At the same time, certain sorts of mediation are marked out as dangerous threats, diverting communication from its rightful path towards completion. But what if democracy, rather than being menaced by difference and distanciation, is in fact dependent in its very definition on them? The rule of the people, of the many rather than the few, is indissoluble from the exercise of power through a certain medium, the medium of publicity. It follows that the public and the people are not necessarily synonyms for one another in democratic theory. Whereas the notion of the people suggests an image of the collective assembly of real people, the notion of the public is characteristically insubstantial and elusive, as discussed in detail in Chapter 1. We need to question the value of an overly concrete sense of the people, if this implies the collective association of self-identical subjects, bearers of clearly defined interests. The public is not a subject, not unless one understands it as something like Julia Kristeva's subject-in-process, one that could never appear fully in a delimited place, securely speaking in its own name. The public, in democratic theory and practice, is constitutively disembodied, in a very particular sense. It is the figure for the uncertain addressee of communicative acts oriented towards universality. The emphasis on the public as a ghostly figure, only ever made present through various proxies, is not meant to deny the importance of embodiment in politics; quite the reverse. The ubiquity of embodied identities in contemporary cultural politics is always already representative; that is to say, the embodiment of actors in public spaces (on screen, in the street) is performed as standing for something more, as being representative, in ways that open up the contingent status of this excessive signification. The lesson of feminist theory, critical race theory and postcolonialism is that acknowledging the difference that embodiment makes to social practice requires a critique of overly unified and expressive images of subjectivity. Disembodying the figure of the public in democratic theory is crucial to broadening the understanding of democratic communication beyond a narrowly defined, highly cognitive understanding of rational-critical discourse (see Chapter 3).

The distinction between the people and the public points up the extent to which the irreducible problematic of representation inhabits the very heart of democratic theory and practice. Throughout this book, representation should be understood to be hinged on an invisible hyphen that registers the idea that democracy depends upon a logic of substitution and delegation that promises more than it can ever deliver. Political representation enables certain sorts of responsible action, but representation is also a two-way movement that opens a space for an exorbitant demand for the immediate presence of rulers before the judgement and direction of the ruled. This is a demand that can only ever be partially met, because representation is also the space and the movement that remind us that full presence and immediate expression are both an empirical impossibility and an ethically and politically suspect ideal.

II Democracy's shadows

All of the chapters in this book seek to address one or other aspect of what Robert Dahl (1989: 3–5) has called the 'shadow theory of democracy'. Dahl identifies four recurring themes that are normally consigned to the background in discussions of democracy. First, in so far as democracy refers to a norm of rule by the people, there is the assumption that the people exists as a substantial, singular collective entity. The argument of this book is that the value of the popular in democratic theory is irreducibly connected to the mediated character of all political action. Second, there is the question of political competence: just who is qualified to exercise the rights and responsibilities of democratic citizenship? This is perhaps the most contentious issue in democratic theory, since it indicates that the universalising ideals of equality and inclusiveness that democracy supposedly relies upon might be conditional. The question of competence has historically been associated with explicit discrimination on the grounds of class, gender, race and other lines of social division. But Dahl is surely correct that the question of competence is an unavoidable one in democratic theory, in so far as democracy is understood to involve rule-governed behaviour of certain sorts. The history of modern democracy turns upon a tension between extending equal political rights irrespective of status or qualifications, and the expanding efforts by a range of agencies to oversee the inculcation of appropriate norms, habits and skills amongst citizens.

Third, democratic theory is haunted by the problem of scale: what difference does the size of a polity, in numerical and spatial terms, make to the form and quality of democratic rule? This is not just an empirical issue, but one that raises fundamental questions concerning the value ascribed to practices of representation in democratic theory. Media practices are particularly important here, in so far as modern print and broadcasting media have served as technologies for social integration over extended territorial scales, and have therefore been key to the institutionalisation of democracy at expanded spatial scales encompassing large populations. But more than simply stretching social life and politics, different media practices articulate and rearticulate different sociospatial scales: the nation-state and the home, everyday life and formal public realms.

Finally, there is the perpetual problem of whether democracy is to be understood in procedural or substantive ways. It is common to criticise both actually existing democracies and resurgent democratic theory as narrowly procedural, as ignoring substantive issues of social and economic rights and questions of social justice (see Katznelson 1996). The theorists critically discussed in this book are all associated with a re-evaluation of the relationships between substantive and procedural conceptions of democracy, between process and outcome. Thinking about the how-of-power is connected to a strongly procedural understanding of democracy, one that presumes a non-foundationalist, open-ended and pragmatically grounded approach to political judgement that does without teleological hopes of an ideal end state.

Thinking of procedural and substantive justice as folded in on one another, rather than opposed, is crucial to the analysis pursued in this book. The early chapters develop a theoretical account of the practical difference that principles of deliberation, communication and representation make to the way power is exercised upon and through practices of mediated public communication. Later chapters address this same relationship by examining how principles are practically implicated in the development of concrete institutions, regulations and policies towards mass media. The contemporary restructuring of media and communications industries, in so far as it is played out through a political debate that counterposes global markets to national polities, has

emerged as a real-world arena for the conflict between different understandings of the relationships between media, markets and citizenship.
John Elster (1986) distinguishes between two broad understandings of
democracy and the public realm: a forum model, strongly associated
with civic republican traditions, that privileges values of collective
deliberation and norms of public debate; and a market model that privileges a classical liberal understanding of the expression of individual
rational choices. In large part, both academic and policy debates about
the future direction of media restructuring turn on these broad distinctions. Defenders of public interest standards invoke the norms of the
forum model, understood to be embodied in particular traditions of
national public service broadcasting. Proponents of globalisation, the
information age and convergence invoke a market-liberal model of free
choice and individual autonomy. These competing discourses of democracy and scale posit different understandings of the nature of citizenship and of the proper role of technological and institutional
infrastructures in supporting it. The later chapters in this book track the
ways in which this basic division has been worked out in different
policy-making contexts. While these chapters illustrate the ascendancy
of the market model of democracy in various realms, they also indicate
the limitations of the forum ideal as a critical lever with which to
address this phenomenon. The forum model of collective participation
and deliberation smooths over fundamental puzzles of autonomy and
rule, pluralism and decision, which are explored in the first four chapters. The treatment of these puzzles requires a reconsideration of the
values of diverse practices of representation in giving life and meaning
to democratic aspirations.

1

Spaces of representation: where is the public?

The difficulty of understanding democracy resides precisely in the need to grasp the people as an absent presence, that is, as neither a compact body nor a nullity.

Fred Dallmayr (1993: 94)

I Redeeming representation

This chapter explores the relations between the concept of representation and the value ascribed to the figure of the public in democratic theory. In particular, it asks where the public makes its presence felt. Rather than starting in what might be the expected place, with a discussion of Habermas' concept of the public sphere, in this and the next chapter I discuss the significance of representation, mediation and media for understanding democratic publicity. This will serve as the preliminary for a consideration of Habermas' work in more detail, and with more sympathy than might be expected, in Chapter 3. There is a widespread tendency to presume that the public is a collective social subject. This is related to thinking of the public sphere in an overly concrete fashion, appealing to exemplary material spaces and institutional configurations. In contrast, public spaces might be better thought of as more or less durable networks of communication. Furthermore, the virtuality of the public is not as new as is often supposed. It is an idea that runs through modern democratic theory, and one that calls into question the rhetoric of immediate, unmediated communication that often accompanies the emergence of new communications technologies.

Defining democracy is notoriously difficult. Democracy might be an essentially contested concept, but it is not an entirely empty signifier. A degree of family resemblance between different usages allows certain core values to be ascribed to democracy. An obvious starting point is the notion that democracy refers to rule by the people. But this only opens up a further set of questions: who are the People? And just what is Rule? (Birch 1992: 47–9). Historically, the definition of who qualifies as a citizen of a democratic polity (defined by gender, property, education, race and ethnicity, nationality, age) has varied enormously. Likewise, the

definition of just what constitutes rule has varied: is this limited to simply choosing rulers, or does it imply broader participation in public
debates and policy-making aimed at actually influencing decisions? It is
important to emphasise both elements of this definition, because the
value of communicative practices of public deliberation cannot be
properly grasped if detached from the objective of arriving at binding
decisions. What distinguishes democracy is that it refers to a system of
procedural rules that have normative implications. Primary amongst
these implications is the acknowledgement of irreducible conflict and
the institutionalisation of compromise (Bellamy 1999). Various institutional features are commonly ascribed to democratic systems of rule:
provisions for equal and/or universal suffrage; the balancing of majority rule with the protection of minority rights; the rule of law; freedom
of expression and dissent (Bobbio 1987: 65–6). These are all indicative
of a form of rule that enables binding decisions and effective public
action in the absence of final agreement. Democracy, in short, is characterised by a distinctive future-oriented temporality, in which institutional procedures guarantee 'the legitimacy of a debate as to what is
legitimate and what is illegitimate – a debate which is necessarily without any guarantor and without any end' (Lefort 1988: 39).

There is a long tradition of imagining forms of participatory democracy in terms of direct involvement by citizens in both discussion and
decision-making. This is an ideal model of the self-presence of the people to itself through the medium of public debate. It rests on the
assumption that the same social subjects, gathered together in a forum
of mutual communication, should participate in deliberation and carry
out decision-making. This ideal underwrites the opposition between
participatory democracy and representative democracy, in which the
latter is understood to be a lesser, indirect derivation of the former. At
best, representative mechanisms are understood to be empirical supple-
ments to direct, participatory practices. Representative democracy is
understood as a truncated shadow of proper, direct forms of democracy, a shadow which, by virtue of the intercession of various intermediaries, contains within it the source of deceitful usurpation of the
popular will. Preferred mechanisms of direct democracy include referenda and plebiscites, popular assemblies, and arguments for binding
mandates for delegates. Participatory democracy is often associated
with idealised images of communication as the means through which
diverse interests and opinions can be reconciled into actionable consensus. New technologies are often presented as the means of overcoming
the distance between the people and political elites. It is the apparent
time-space shrinking qualities ascribed to communications technolo-

gies that are identified as the source of their inherently democratic potential. The ideal of the instant communication of the will of the people without intermediary, and the running together of the sense of spatio-temporal transcendence with the sense of overcoming social division, reveal an image of the public as a unitary collective subject with a singular political will (see Low 1999).

The problematic relationship between representation and scale underlies the tendency of political theory to see modern democracy as having an essentially tragic trajectory, whereby the ideal of universal participation is undermined by its practical realisation in the form of mass democracy. From this perspective, demands for more areas of life to be opened up to democratic accountability and decision-making generate more and more *bureaucracy*, which curtails participation. Technological change leads to the increasing dominance of professionalised *expertise* in decision-making. The impacts of *massification*, in the form of generalised commodity consumption and the mass media, reduce the space for critically informed deliberation (see Bobbio 1987: 68–77). While the first two of these allegations refer to the monopolisation of knowledge in the hands of intermediaries, the third asserts that the flipside of this is a decline in the critical capacities of citizens. This sort of criticism turns upon a contrast between different scales of social interaction. As democracy expands *numerically* (with the extension of the franchise), *spatially* (with the inauguration of modern democracy at the level of the nation-state) and *functionally* (with the extension of the number of areas opened up to democratic scrutiny), the actual quality of democratic rule is threatened. The presumption is that there is a sort of quantity/quality ratio beyond which the universal promise of democratic ideals begins to negate itself. The idea that democracy is haunted by this paradox of scale rests on particular understandings of the subjects, forms and competencies that distinguish democratic practice. Above all, it is the messiness and indeterminacy of mediation that recur as the most problematic characteristics of actually existing representative democracies. Representative mechanisms are simultaneously understood as the cure for practical problems of scale, and the poison that undermines the very ideals they are meant to sustain. This construction of representation as a dangerous supplement (see Derrida 1981) in turn installs a particular understanding of participation as the ideal against which representative practices should be judged. If the mediation of opinions or interests by means of human or non-human intermediaries is understood to be a secondary, empirical expedient, then this implies that interests and opinions are the properties of pre-existing social groups. Acts of representation will always be subjected to a correspondence test, to check whether they accord with the real interests and viewpoints of the represented. In this way, the concept of representation is contained within a logic of identity. It is this identitarian understanding of representation that has become the target of poststructuralist cultural criticism and political theory.

Representation has a highly ambivalent status in democratic theory. Political mobilisations by subaltern social groups often take the form of struggles to have organisations and spokespersons recognised as legitimate representatives of oppressed and marginalised social groups. This politics of representation in turn provokes two forms of conceptual criticism. First, successful inclusion through representative procedures prompts the argument that the very success of struggles for political representation undermines broad-based participation. The second, more strongly theoretical criticism of the politics of representation is associated with theories of so-called agonistic democracy. From this perspective, the politics of representation closes down the essential instability of political subjectivities, by making claims about the identity between representatives and those in whose name they speak (see Mouffe 1994). There are three points worth making in response to this argument. First, it is worth emphasising that claims of identity in the politics of representation are just that – claims. They invite responses from those whose consent is invoked by them. There is no reason to suppose that political representation is necessarily a zero-sum game in which the claim to represent others renders those others silent (Barnett 1997). Second, arguments around agonistic democracy tend towards a purification of the political, which contrasts the closure of instrumental decision-making to the infinite semiosis of subject-formation. More generally, the appeal of agonistic models of democracy depends upon the maintenance of a series of hierarchical oppositions between openness and closure, contingency and necessity, freedom and constraint. In contrast, this chapter argues that a deconstructive understanding of democracy works by holding in tension the different temporalities of identity-formation, deliberation and decision. Third, the agonistic conceptualisation restricts the conceptualisation of representation to an order of identity, in order to reject it. The preferred conceptual alternatives to representation, such as articulation (Laclau and Mouffe 1985: 67) or performance (Honig 1992: 226), are deployed in ways that present authentic political action in terms of pure inventive creativity. The characteristic oppositional derivation of the political means that agonistic models of democracy set up an impossible distance between their preferred normative models and the pragmatic complexities of actually existing democratic systems (Dietz 1998). Democracy, understood as a

certain sort of politics (ibid.), is defined by holding together stable identities and transformation, decision-making and contestation, consensus
and dispute in a pattern of deferred resolution of conflicts. The peaceable negotiation of this sort of politics has institutional and socio-
cultural conditions that cannot be either established or maintained
through agonistic, performative modes of conduct alone. Agonism is an
end, and only one element, of democratic political action, not its
essence. With this in mind, the rest of this chapter develops an alternative reading of the poststructuralist problematisation of representation,
arguing that it is imperative to redeem the concept and practice of
representation to understand the distinctive normative dimensions of
democratic rule.

II *The double session of representation*

Representation has become a recurrently problematic theme in cultural
and political theory. Cultural studies has drawn attention to the abiding
political significance of constructing class, ethnic, racial, gender or sexual identities through the deployment of images and narratives, and this
critique is related to a problematisation of the modes of authority
embedded in practices of cultural representation. However, to see representation as just the usurpation of the proper expression of marginalised actors depends on a clear-cut purity of categorisation that allows
one to distinguish between representation and action (Spivak 1988). The
orthodox anti-representational prejudice in contemporary cultural theory rests on a very narrow concept of representation. The standard critique of the duplicitous qualities of representative signs (in politics,
epistemology or aesthetics) presupposes the capacity to distinguish
clearly between representation and the represented, between the event
and its repetition, allowing for an analysis of misrepresentation in the
name of the authentic identity of the represented (Derrida 1976: 296).
Understanding representation as a movement of restoration of original
presence is closely related to philosophical understandings of centred,
self-present subjectivity. An important reference point here is Heidegger's
analysis of the dependence of conceptions of autonomous subjectivity upon representation. Here, representation is the setting of an
object in place before a subject (Heidegger 1977: 120), a process that
secures the centred and sovereign subject as the measure of objective
reality (ibid.: 127). Heidegger's claim to move beyond this model of
subjectivity in the direction of authenticity accepts at face value the

simplicity of the concept of representation. Representation continues to be understood as the means of re-establishing presence, that is, of reinstalling an object before a subject and so securing the subject's identity. And it is worth noting that this sense of representation as the medium of subject-predication privileges a particular image of space. Representation as placing-before 'involves a determination of space and place such that a subject can take its place as the focal point of such "placing-before" ' (Weber 1996: 123). A deconstructive redemption of the multi-faceted concept of representation therefore involves a rethinking of the space of representation, necessarily traversed by the disruptive movement of repetition.

Heidegger's critique of representation shows that what is at stake in the critique of the philosophical determination of representation is the value ascribed to the supposed unity of the self-positing subject. The implications and limitations of this purely philosophical consideration are drawn out in Derrida's (1982b) deconstruction of Heidegger's account of representation, in which he affirms the irreducibility of representation in politics as in philosophy. Derrida establishes distinctions and makes connections between the notion of representation as the objective reality of the idea before a subject, and the political sense of representation as delegation, agency and substitution. His main point is that it might not be as easy to transcend representation as Heidegger supposes. Nor might it be politically or ethically commendable to suppose that it is. For Derrida, representation in the sense of presencing, or of presenting before a subject, is irreducibly related to other senses of representation: first, to representation as differential repetition, as a re-presentation which modifies a presence; second, to representation as what takes the place of, what occupies the place of, another (Derrida 1973: 49). In representation, the process of rendering present is 'a repetition which restitutes thanks to a substitute' (Derrida 1982b: 309). Taking representation as *repetition* and *substitution* together implies that the possibility of pure representation, in the sense of a movement that restores to full presence, depends upon and is therefore ruined by having to pass through a modifying intermediary. The deconstructive affirmation of representation asserts that repetition and difference make and undo identities, subjects and truths. In short, the exteriority of representation to presence, its derivative status, is called into question. The re- of representation is not a simple reduplication that is added to an already constituted identity: 'The presence-of-the-present is derived from repetition and not the reverse' (Derrida 1973: 52).

The deconstruction of representation does not therefore reject the concept altogether. The end of representation is a vain hope: 'Because it has always begun, representation therefore has no end' (Derrida 1978: 250). The different usages of representation in philosophical discourse all attest to the general characteristic whereby self-sufficient entities carry within themselves the possibility of being repeated, reproduced, represented. After deconstruction, representation is one term for the contaminating movement of infinite repetition that inhabits all structures of identity, expression and presence (see Gasché 1999). Thus, the temporal and spatial extension indicated by representation is rethought as a constitutive movement without reference to a still point of self-sufficient original presence. Deconstruction leads us to think of representation as a movement of differential repetition (Derrida 1973: 82, 1982a: 1–27). It draws out the irreducible spacing and temporalisation of processes of representation.

An affirmative, deconstructive critique of cultural and political representation depends on working through the double resonance of the term representation. First, representation has the sense of *depiction*, as standing for. Second, representation also has the sense of *delegation*, of speaking or acting on behalf of others. Both senses imply a process of substitution between the element represented and the representative intermediary. The sense and meaning of representation, understood as both depiction and delegation, turn out to be much more complex and problematic than is often supposed (see Birch 1964: 13–17; O'Neill 2001). Representation as standing for can be achieved by human actors or by objects, and it may be based on imitation or may be entirely conventional. Either way, representation in this sense of depiction depends upon a material intermediary of some sort, a medium whose substance cannot be fully reduced. Likewise, representation as acting for others, as a practice of delegation, raises a set of problems concerning the relationships between agents and those for whom they act. In both cases, the process of substitution introduces a degree of difference between representative and represented that is inherently unstable. Some element, a person, an object or an image, is made to stand in for the person, thing or theme represented. Successful acts of representation therefore depend on pulling off the fiction that something or someone is present when it is actually absent. Representation works (and is unworked) by a movement of spatio-temporal presence and absence. Hannah Pitkin's analysis of the usage of representation in political philosophy captures the (un)working of representation in her succinct definition of representation as 'the making present *in some sense* of something which is nevertheless *not* present literally or in fact' (Pitkin 1967: 8–9, original emphasis). Her account emphasises the essential impurity of any act of representation, an impurity that derives from the fact that the medium of representation, the

body of the representative, cannot be wholly reduced in the shuttling
between the representative and represented. The irreducible embodiment
of representation in a medium of some sort indicates the impossibility
of perfect transmission of ideal contents. That would, in principle, be
the end of representation, consumed in a circuit of pure, unmediated
expressive communication.

The irreducibility of the medium in processes of representation
points towards a deconstructive understanding of representation as a
supplementary concept. The 'strange logic of the supplement' refers to
the way in which the addition of the secondary element reveals 'the orig-
inality of the lack that makes necessary the addition of the supplement'
(Derrida 1976: 214). Thinking of representation as supplementary in
this sense involves radicalising the significance of the movement of repetition implied by understanding representation as making-present-
again: 'Representation is an ambivalent process that implies the absence
of what is being made present again, and this absence cannot be
assumed to be merely contingent' (De Man 1983: 123). If technological
devices can represent identities and interests, then this means that they
are incomplete from the very start. In short, there is no pure relation of
representation, 'because it is of the essence of the process of representation that the representative has to contribute to the identity of what is
represented' (Laclau 1993: 280). The prosthesis of representation reveals
an original non-identity, or lack of self-sufficiency, in the identity of the
represented (ibid.: 291). This is why it is important not to conflate a
deconstruction of representation with an anti-representational stance.
Rejecting representation as a mere supplement is to suppose that the
identities of the represented and the representative are self-sufficient
and not in need to further augmentation, 'which is precisely the
assumption that the whole critique of the notion of representation was
questioning' (ibid.: 280). Representation is possible because pure representation is impossible, and this is not only because representation as
mimesis is ruined by its dependence on difference, but more fundamentally because representation reveals there to be no pure anterior identity
waiting to be restored to presence.

Rather than restoring the value of authenticity, the deconstruction
of representation is better thought of as being animated by a deep-
reaching critique of identity thinking, and of associated norms of
immediacy and spontaneous expression. The analytics of voice and
subject-positions in cultural theory does not privilege a directly expressive relationship between a speaker and a social group. 'Speaking' is not
understood as equivalent to the expression of pre-formed interests or
identities. Rather, 'speaking' depends on a position within regulated

systems of discourse. Therefore, in asking the evaluative question 'who speaks?', which is called forth by practices of representation, it is always useful 'to keep the emphasis on "speaks" – on technologies and techniques of persuasion' (Morris 1998: 230). The deconstruction of representation leads, then, to a differential understanding of representation that keeps open the distance between *speaking for* others and *speaking as* another, in which the latter supposes a complete substitution of one party for the other (Young 2000: 127).

III Indeterminate representation and performative publicity

The classical deconstructive manoeuvre is to question the assignment of conceptual and normative privilege to living speech as the preferred medium of accurate self-representation and rational discourse. The images of community, self-presence and identity erected upon concepts of speech and dialogue betray a recurrent ethical and political imaginary that is intolerant of difference, pluralism and conflict. Characteristically, it is writing that carries the weight of ambivalent judgement ascribed to non-identity, dispute and difference (Barnett 1999b). The thematic of writing bears directly on questions of political theory, given the close relationship between concepts of dialogue, writing, and understandings of democratic publicity. Thus, Derrida's deconstruction of the narrow concept of writing has broader political significance. Conventionally, writing is understood in the Western philosophical tradition as the exemplary representative medium, a medium of spatial and temporal extension that maintains living speech but also betrays and corrupts it. The prioritisation of speech as a medium of self-presentation without deferral or repetition, without difference, determines the conceptualisation of genuine (political) community as unified and purified (Low 1999). In turn, such understandings are underpinned by a spatial imaginary of bounded communities made up of self-conscious, self-identical speakers communicating within the immediate proximity allowed by the range of the voice (Derrida 1976: 136). Logocentric theories of language underwrite conceptualisations of political community in terms of an essentially singular popular will. The denigration of writing is the index of a normalising impulse that reduces the differential openness of space and time to an order of essence, punctuality and identity. But the characteristics ascribed to writing keep recurring in the thematisation of the supposedly pure category. Writing, as a figure of non-identity, spatial extension and temporal repetition, turns out to inhabit two places at once: it is a secondary, external element that also inhabits the very centre of the conceptual space from which it is constantly expelled.

Derrida universalises writing by freeing the concept from its containment within a closed circle of origin and return. He does so to indicate that the power of dispersal usually reserved for this concept actually inheres in all communicative practice: 'That language must traverse space, be obliged to be spaced, is not an accidental trait but the mark of its origin' (ibid.: 232). The generalisation of writing prevents any categorical separation between the pure punctuality of acts, events and identities on the one hand, and representation and repetition on the other. Deconstruction reads the substitution implied by representative delegation as the principle of a necessary non-identity of any political community to itself. If the norm of democratic publicity implies a principle of accessibility and openness that establishes the conditions that enable the encounter with different points of view (Young 1990a: 240), then writing rather than speech, representation rather than presence, difference rather than identity might serve as more appropriate analogies for conceptualising such publics. Writing is constitutive of a public space of indeterminate address, and there is a necessary element of chance involved in any successful communicative act. Holding on to a revised concept of representation, understood after the deconstruction of the speech/writing opposition as a movement of differential translation, affirms a distinctive understanding of politics: 'Politics must be conceived as a relationship of strangers who do not understand one another in a subjective and immediate sense, relating across time and distance' (ibid.: 234).

To develop this understanding of democracy as instituting a community of strangers, it is worth considering Claude Lefort's distinctive analysis of democratic legitimacy. His account of democratic public space departs from the tendency to present this concept by reference to particular spatial archetypes. For Lefort, democracy is distinguished by a specific symbolic configuration of power. Legitimacy is located in the people, but this popular sovereignty is linked to a notion of power being an empty place:

> The legitimacy of power is based in the people; but the image of popular sovereignty is linked to the image of an empty place, impossible to occupy, such that those who exercise public authority can never claim to appropriate it. [...] Democracy combines these two apparently contradictory principles: on the one hand, power emanates from the people; on the other, it is

the power of nobody. And democracy thrives in this contradiction.

(Lefort 1986: 279)

This understanding of the empty place of power informs a conceptualisation of democracy as a social form in which

> power, law and knowledge are exposed to a radical indetermination, a society that has become the theatre of an uncontrollable adventure, so that what is instituted never becomes established, the known remains undermined by the unknown, the present proves to be undefinable, covering many different social times which are staggered in relation to one another within simultaneity.

(ibid.: 305)

Lefort therefore rejects an image of democracy that would privilege values of unity, identity and cultural integrity (ibid.: 270).

For Lefort, democracy is instituted by a distinctive mode of staging power that transforms the nature of political subjectivity:

> The modern democratic revolution is best recognised in this mutation: there is no power linked to a body. Power appears as an empty place and those who exercise it as mere mortals who occupy it only temporarily or who could install themselves in it only by force or cunning. There is no law that can be fixed, whose articles cannot be contested, whose foundations are not susceptible of being called into question.

(ibid.: 303)

This mutation has philosophical significance, Lefort argues (2000: 268), in so far as it marks the point at which democracy is instituted 'by challenging the notion of an ultimate reference'. Democracy has philosophical significance because, as a regime of power, it does away with the notion of a transcendent authority that can be made manifest in organisational or personal form. Lefort installs a 'metaphysics of absence' at the heart of democratic theory (Critchley 1992: 209), so that democracy is understood to depend upon the holding together of apparently irreconcilable principles. Democracy thrives in the gaps between the idea of law and positive laws, between the idea of truth and the contingencies of actual knowledge, and between the idea of true representation and the necessarily reserved appearance of the public. Representation is just one figure for this paradoxical play of presence and absence that distinguishes democracy as a regime of power (Dallmayr 1993: 77–105).

The sense of something being held in reserve whenever the public makes an appearance is underscored in Derrida's commentary on Carl Schmitt's (1996) conceptualisation of the political. Rather than thinking of democracy and liberalism, identity and representation, as contradictory opposites as Schmitt does, Derrida echoes Lefort in asserting that it is the perpetual oscillation between different imperatives that distinguishes democratic norms: 'There is no democracy without respect for irreducible singularity or alterity, but there is no democracy without the "community of friends", without the calculation of majorities, without identifiable, stabilizable, representable subjects, all equal' (Derrida 1997: 22). For Derrida, the promise of democracy inheres in the disjunction between these two imperatives, a disjunction which 'bears the chance and the future of a democracy whose ruin it constantly threatens but whose life, however, it sustains, like life itself, at the heart of its *divided virtue*, the inadequacy to itself' (ibid.). In insisting on holding together different imperatives in paradoxical relationship, Derrida and Lefort both positively affirm the indeterminate scope and identity of political communities.

In Lefort's account, one of the paradoxes of democracy derives from the fact that legitimacy is supposed to move upward from the people, but the image and identity of the people are constitutively uncertain. The people only appear in and through the symbolic staging that constitutes the identity it purports to re-present. In turn, democracy is always haunted by the possibility of its own usurpation, if the image of the people is actualised in a real presence, if the place of power is appropriated. In Lefort's account, democracy is distinguished by the manner in which the exercise of power is articulated through an indeterminate symbolic regime of representation. The radical indeterminacy of the identity of the people is a condition of the legitimisation of conflict and dissent characteristic of democracy. In this postfoundational theory of democracy, representation is freed from subordination to the value of self-present identity, and affirmed for two related reasons. First, democratic representation refers to a mode of rule in which power is disembodied, only ever held temporarily in the name of the people who are structurally non-identical with any given event of their manifestation. Second, practices of deliberation, debate and representation are understood not as expressions of identity or will, but as mediums for the remaking of identities.

The dislocation of power under democracy shifts authority from a fixed and determinate position into an unstable and indeterminate space 'whose existence is indicated by the incessant work of its enunciation', such that power 'moves into the impalpable, universal and essentially public element of speech' (Lefort 1988: 110). This deliberative speech is not the property of any individual or collective subject, but is the subjectless medium for the contingent articulation of political subjectivity. The significance of public discussion is attached to practices of representation, rather than opposed to it. This coupling enables the paradoxical identity of popular sovereignty to be given force without taking up full presence:

> The people, the nation, equality, justice and truth in fact only exist by virtue of the speech which is assumed to emanate from within them and which at the same time names them. In that sense, power belongs to the individual or individuals who can speak on their behalf or, to be more accurate, to the individual or individuals who appear to speak on their behalf, who speak in the name of the people and give them their name.
>
> (ibid.: 109–10)

On Lefort's account, democracy installs the people as the highest sovereign authority, but the exercise of this sovereignty is necessarily *staged* through the representational medium of public debate. Democracy is therefore understood as a regime that institutes the scope of political concerns by simultaneously *assigning meaning* and *staging power* in a public forum (ibid.: 11). The interests and identities of the subjects of democratic politics are constituted through this doubled-up setting into form of political space. Democracy is, in this account, representative in a fundamental, foundational sense. But this founding representation is properly thought of in performative terms. Representation here refers to a form of enactment that is constitutive of its own space, as a surface of spectacle displayed for spectators (Derrida 1978: 237). A performative is an act that produces the identity or state of affairs it appears merely to re-present. Democratic representation is performative in so far as it involves reiterative acts of description that bring into existence the identities that they appear to be merely re-presenting. At the same time, this framing of the space of politics is itself concealed, opening up in turn the possibility of subsequently contesting its scope and dimensions. Political discourse characteristically presents identities as pre-existing any act of representation, maintaining the sense of representation as mere re-presentation. But this trick works only by the portrayal of a state of affairs (an image of the people), so that the persuasive force of any such representation is both secured by its dependence on a portrayal and always potentially undone by it: 'there is no performative which does not also involve an at least implicit description of the shape of affairs it produces' (Butler 1993: 233). Splicing together performativity and representation in this way underscores the point that while democracy's foundations may be performative, they are not merely fictional, since they turn upon an undecidable play between invention and discovery. In discourses of democratic representation, the sovereign people are invoked in the descriptive register *as if* they were an already existing, independent collective subject who authorised the actions of those who speak on their behalf (Derrida 1986). Yet the people are constituted as an independent entity only through the performative register of the enunciation itself (Honig 1991; Lee 1997). Democratic representation therefore takes the form of a call that anticipates a response from the people whose identity is invoked in the descriptive register, a response that takes the form of subsequent authorisation and calling to account.

Understanding democratic political communication as taking the form of a claim for recognition addressed to others that invites a response indicates the central importance of publicity in securing the value of representation. The success of a performative is not guaranteed in advance, and it is not secured by the adequacy of its descriptive elements. It depends upon being recognised as authoritative by an audience. The notion of performative representation implies that the illocutionary force of democratic discourse (its qualities as discourse that commits, promises and can be held to account) depends upon its being made public. In short, democratic representation is an effective but uncertain mode of subject-predication. Public discourse takes the form of an invitation, an offering of sorts: 'a "we" signed by the few but putatively supported by the many is empowered largely by its indeterminacy. An unspecified "we" denotes and affords participation, on the part of its interpellated subjects, in a provisional community whose power is located in a potentially infinite constituency' (Lyon 1999: 26). Publics are, therefore, constituted by a structure of communication that is characteristically scattered and dispersed, lacking determinate address. This analysis points beyond accounts of democratic deliberation that privilege a prior horizon of shared interests or teleology towards rational consensus. Democratic political representation presupposes an understanding of communication as a precarious process set in motion by promises and gifts (Young 1993; Calhoun 1997). From this perspective, public communication is constituted by a postal logic (Derrida 1987). The deconstruction of the speech/writing opposition indicates that communication is not dependent on the precise containment of messages within enclosed channels of exchange, but always contains the chance of interception by unanticipated addressees in unanticipated places. Deconstruction exposes difference, disjuncture, and uncertainty as necessary conditions of communication: 'Communication occurs only insofar as the delivery of the message *may* fail: that is, communication takes place only to the extent that there is a separation between the sender and the receiver, and this separation, this distance, this *spacing*, creates the possibility for the message *not* to arrive' (Chang 1996: 216; original emphasis). The inscription of meaning in a technological prosthesis, that is, representation, opens up a public realm of spatial extension and temporal duration whose dimensions cannot be fully anticipated.

The flip-side of this underdetermined publicness is that communication is always premised on a reserve of meaning. It is, of course, common to remark on the extent to which the public only exists in and through its representation. The modes of appearance of the public include a range of technologies such as elections, statistical surveys and censuses (see Herbst 1993). But it would be unwise to dismiss public opinion as a mere fiction, usurping the genuine popular will with a deadening layer of intermediaries. Rather, this mediation suggests that the public can give no sign of life 'without a certain *medium*' (Derrida 1992: 88). The public only appears in moments of representation that hold in reserve its full manifestation:

> Exceeding electoral representation, public opinion is *de jure* neither the *general will* nor the nation, neither *ideology* nor the sum total of *private* opinions analyzed through sociological techniques or modern poll-taking institutions. It does not speak in the first person, it is neither subject nor object ('we', 'one'); one *cites* it, one makes it speak, ventriloquizes it.
>
> (ibid.: 87; original emphasis)

The dependence of the public and public opinion on mediation by technical prostheses underscores the constitutive paradox of democratic representation. The public cannot represent itself, make itself present, because it is not a unitary subject waiting to be represented. It is a figure *par excellence*, only ever spoken for, instantiated in different guises in different contexts. As a consequence, if it can never be made fully present, then nor does it have a proper place: 'Does it take *place*? Where is it given to be seen, and *as such*? The wandering of its proper body is also the ubiquity of a specter' (ibid.; original emphasis). If the conventional conceptualisation of representation is connected with a strong sense of presentation in a here and now, a delimited place and moment, then rethinking representation according to a deconstructive logic of translation, writing and dissemination necessarily problematises the stable emplacement of subjectivity (Lyotard 1991: 108–18). It follows, then, that the public spaces of modern democracy need to be conceptualised in ways that give credence to the spectral sense of excessive representation through which the very appearance of the public is made possible.

IV *The deferral of public space*

Maintaining the sense of representation as a relation without collapsing the gaps between the terms is the key to understanding the normative significance of practices of representation in democratic practice. Affirming representation disrupts any sense that democracy involves simply the delegation of authority by stable interests or identities, or that deliberation should be judged primarily in terms of a hypothetical one-to-one correspondence between those who speak and those who are spoken for. This ethico-political principle of the irreducibility of representation (its unavoidability, certainly, but also the irreducibility of representation to identity, presence or punctuality) calls into question notions of the public as a subject. In turn, this principle should lead onto a critique of arguments that persist in privileging bounded, areal spaces (the agora, the street, the nation-state) as the models of public space. The temptation to nominalise the public or the people as a collective subject is related to the tendency to develop excessively concrete images of the spaces of public action and political representation. In fields like human geography and urban studies, there is a persistent tendency to translate concepts from political theory into literal spatial archetypes. This is based on the presumption that social, cultural and political theories are marked by an excessively metaphorical usage of spatial categories. As a consequence, the resurgence of interest in normative political theory in other fields is registered in these spatial disciplines by the identification of exemplary forms of material, typically urban, spaces. More generally, it leads to arguments that democratic norms of equality, pluralism and justice need to be translated into real, material spatialities. Space is assumed to be the medium in which multiplicity, heterogeneity and plurality can co-exist on a single temporal plane of appearance (Massey 1995, 1999).

Conceptualising pluralistic difference in spatial terms alone fails to capture what is most distinctive about the norms of democracy. Contrary to this sort of argument, the significance of categories of the public in democratic theory requires us to resist overly literal determinations of public space. The value of publicity in democratic theory refers as much to the temporal dimension of political action as to the spatial. The notion of differential representation combines a sense of spatial dispersal with a temporal register of revision. The determination to spatialise principles of democratic publicity fails to register the extent to which deliberation, decision, action and accountability are irreducible temporal moments of politics that democratic procedures fold together. This means, most simply, that the public is neither a subject, nor has a proper place or spatial configuration. The geography of democratic public space is best captured by reference to the theme of the parasite in deconstruction. The parasite is the exemplary figure of the constitutive movement of mediation, defined by its apparently paradoxical spatial location – proximate and distant, similar and different, this side and that of a threshold (Miller 1991: 145). It is a figure of non-closure, of openness or, one might also suggest, of a certain understanding of publicness. Performative representation is one example of the parasitical undoing of norms of proper place that characterise traditional theories of subjectivity, action and politics. Thinking of democratic publics according to the logic of parasitical representation implies that the identity of a democratic public is not defined by a relationship to a proper place. Furthermore, the parasitical qualities of publicness also affirm the radical non-closure of public space. This understanding is oriented by a deconstruction of the straightforward critique of liberal representative democracy that holds that proper democracy requires a clear-cut delimitation of a polity, contained within boundaries of a deep horizontal cultural commonality and expressed politically within the bounds of the territorialised nation-state.

The errant qualities of democratic representation call for a concept of the public in terms of temporal deferral as much as spatial gathering and differentiation. The consideration of temporality leads to a recognition of the extent to which public space is constituted as a network of communicative practices, such as printing, publishing, broadcasting, reading, writing, watching, performing and listening. This sense that the media constitute the space of politics is often considered either an affront to the privilege accorded to older notions of real public space, such as urban forums and assemblies, or, just as often, a distinctively new phenomenon. There are strong normative grounds for being wary of the privilege accorded to material spaces of interpersonal contiguity as the paradigms of democratic publicness. This focus downplays some of the defining features of democracy as a system of rule and binding public action. There is a strong strand of social and political commentary that defines democratic publicity primarily in terms of sociability.

For example, Hannah Arendt's account of political action has been presented as offering a grounded material basis for a normative geography of the public sphere (Howell 1993). Arendt's account of pluralism rests on an image of the public sphere as a space of appearance and of visibility, that is, of spatial and temporal co-presence between subjects able to recognise each other as equals (Arendt 1958). It is a model of public space that is starkly counterposed to modern democratic practices, not least because the latter are representative in character: 'the notion of representation is alien and repugnant to her' (Lefort 1988: 55). Arendt defines politics as an essentially aesthetic practice of self-transformation, sharply distinguished from instrumental practices of work and labour, calculated strategic action and administrative power (Pitkin 1998). This detachment of the essence of public life from the pragmatics of rule is often seen as a positive feature of Arendt's work, informing an agonistic conceptualisation of the political as the practice of making and remaking cultural identities (Honig 1992).

The problem with Arendt's account, and with similar agonistic models indebted to it, is not the emphasis on the cultural dimensions of political action *per se*. The problem is the self-righteous purity of this nostalgic definition of the political as the pure action of self-creation detached from instrumental concerns. It is, in the final analysis, a self-defeating concept of politics (Elster 1983: 91–100). Essentialising public space as a realm of pluralist sociability puts the normative cart before the pragmatic horse, in so far as the qualities of public sociability that come to define the essence of public life actually depend on 'a range of decisions, actions, and policies that cannot emerge from the flow of everyday sociability alone' (Weintraub 1997: 24). The definition of the public by reference to sociability, to the exclusion of the dimension of problem solving, leads onto an unsustainable ideal of political action: 'we cannot exclude the element of strategic action from the concept of the political' (Habermas 1983: 181).

The continuing primacy accorded to material spaces of contiguity in definitions of public life underplays the distinctive relationship of temporal non-coincidence implied by the understanding of performative representation outlined above. Public spaces like squares, parks, streets might be material in the bluntly obvious sense, but they are not material in the sense of serving as practicable and effective spaces of deliberation and decision. The relationship between pluralistic difference, conflict, and the instrumental dimensions of democratic political action finds its clearest practical realisation in mechanisms that institutionalise contingency, reversibility and accountability in decision-making procedures. The folding together of different temporal registers enables legitimate binding decisions to be made in contexts of non-assimilable difference and fundamental substantive conflict, facilitating the formation of consensual decision-making freed from a horizon of transcendence. It is crucial to hold in tension this doubled sense of representation as a process of both spatial differentiation and temporal deferral. The crucial difference that a differential understanding of representation makes is to detach the notion from concepts of identity, emphasising instead the constitutive gaps and intervals of space and time that make representation possible, and finally impossible in any purity. This emphasis upon the temporal stretching of authorisation and accountability that the deconstruction of representation implies has been most fully developed by Iris Marion Young. For her, political representation is understood as a mediated relationship which is extended across a series of distinct occasions that are separate but related to one another: 'As a deferring relationship between constituents and their agents, representation moves between moments of authorisation and accountability. Representation is a cycle of anticipation and recollection between constituent and representative, in which discourse and action at each moment ought to bear the *traces* of the others' (Young 2000: 129).

On this understanding, questions of legitimacy, authority and accountability are thrown forward. Authorisation is a contingent ceding of power as delegation, and in turn it is recalled and reassessed in a moment of subsequent accountability. The differential understanding of representation therefore enables us to understand the practical institutionalisation of paradoxical democratic legitimacy. In principle, democracy implies a government of impersonal rules legitimised in the name of the people but not exercised by anybody in particular. In practice, specific persons necessarily implement a government of rules. In any imaginable democratic order there is likely to be a division of labour between those who exercise binding public authority and those who are obliged to obey. Democracy is best thought of as a system of rule, requiring binding decisions, and not as an alternative to rule and public authority (Dunn 2000: 15). Or, to put it another way, democracy faces up to the constitutive paradox (another one) of all political action – of how to render possible the positive exercise of centralised collective action while at the same time guarding against the abuse of this power (Ricoeur 1965: 202–3). What is distinctive about democratic rule is that it depends upon practical measures that ensure that rule is exercised as a form of *agency*, on the model of speaking-for, keeping open the distance between representative and represented, rather than as *substitution*, on the model of speaking-as, which closes down that space in an assertion of identity. The practical conditions for acting in complex societies require that delegates are ascribed a degree of freedom from tight mandates, but this in turn requires the careful cultivation of free citizenship able to hold rulers to account. The freedom of representatives to act without being wholly bound by prior authorisation is thus squared with the norm of popular sovereignty, because '[d]emocratic accountability is inherently retrospective' (Dunn 1999: 340). The concept of differential representation implies that democracy is best understood in terms of a play between anticipatory authorisation and retrospective accountability. Democratic representation takes the form neither of pure delegation nor of pure trusteeship. It folds elements of both into a differentiated temporal relationship of authorised delegation, independent action, and subsequent justification and holding to account.

The inherently retrospective quality of democratic accountability is tied to an orientation towards the future, so that democracy can be understood to have the structural form of an unredeemable promise that none the less binds actions to an ethos of responsibility (Derrida 1992). This orientation, referring action to a projected future occasion for holding rulers accountable and thus regulating their conduct in the present, is the index of a characteristically democratic acknowledgement of the irreducibility of conflict between different identities and interests: 'By using the future as a space in which to vindicate and enforce our judgements that we did not deserve to lose, democratic political accountability assuages the bitterness of political defeat, and gives those who would otherwise have little motive to do so a reason to stay in the game' (Dunn 1999: 332). The structure of spaced-out democratic temporality is therefore, in principle, a means of preventing ongoing oppression as well as ensuring the peaceable resolution of irreconcilable differences. This understanding of the temporally deferred relations between representation, authorisation and accountability means that an effective system of public scrutiny and access to information for citizens is crucial to the articulation of these different moments. The democratically generated legitimacy of representatives established at one moment is rendered accountable only by 'the development and deepening of practices of public exposure' (ibid.). A process-based understanding of political representation indicates the centrality of principles of free speech in democratic theory, realised through the spatio-temporal dispersal of the public through networks of communication rather than its gathering together in a space of co-presence. In fundamental ways, the visibility of political action to a citizenry cannot be considered to be temporally coincident with action itself, but is dispersed into a chain of information, argument and deliberation that requires an effective system of public communication.

It is a commonplace that, in modern democracies, public deliberation is carried on by professional communicators (pundits, politicians, journalists) on behalf of the people (Page 1996). At one level, this can be seen as a necessary result of a pragmatic division of labour. More abstractly, however, it returns us to Lefort's argument that democratic power is an essentially empty place only ever occupied temporarily by proxies. The irreducibly mediated character of public debate works in principle to prevent the people's representatives from substituting themselves fully for the represented, thereby appropriating the place of power, by preventing representation taking the form of a zero-sum game of identity: 'The struggle of the orators on the platform evokes the struggle of the scribblers of the press; the debating club in parliament is necessarily supplemented by debating clubs in salons and ale-houses; the representatives, who constantly appeal to public opinion, give public opinion the right to speak its real mind in petitions' (Marx, in Marx and Engels 1979: 142).

If accountability is retrospective and authorisation something anticipated in the form of a promise, then the normative role of mediums of public opinion in underwriting the legitimacy of democratic representation is multi-faceted (Dunn 1999: 335–9). They serve as the means of recording and recalling the promises and claims of representatives, enabling the later assessment of intentions and consequences. They also provide a basic source of information for citizens to track the course of political action. And they serve as important agents of public scrutiny and visibility. Principles of free expression, embodied in effective plural systems of media and communication, are therefore critical both to effectively maintaining the relationships between the different moments of representation, and also to maintaining the gaps and intervals between representatives and constituencies in which contested representations and claims to legitimacy can proliferate: 'Freedom of public opinion keeps open the possibility that the represented might at any time make their own voices heard' (Manin 1997: 174).

V Conclusion: trust in representation

This chapter has argued that the representative mediums of democratic publicity open up and maintain relations between claims of representation, broad-based deliberation and accountable decision-making. This might sound like a highly idealistic interpretation of a rather murky, compromised reality. The important thing is not to suppose that the media do automatically function in this way in actual empirical contexts, or to construct an impossible ideal against which to judge actual systems of mass media and journalism. To underscore the point made at the outset, democracy is a system of institutionalised procedural rules that have normative significance. By emphasising the spatial and temporal dispersal of moments of democratic authorisation and accountability, this chapter has elaborated a counterintuitive, deconstructive analysis of the geographies of democratic communication. These should be understood as stretched out across various spaces of deferred representation, rather than being modelled on spatial gathering and containment. This argument is related to the principle that the appearance of the public is always held in reserve. This is the condition of ongoing challenges to the legitimacy of particular patterns of representation. In short, the understanding of democratic representation developed here supports the contention that the public sphere should be thought of as 'structurally elsewhere, neither lost nor in need of recovery or rebuilding but defined by its resistance to being made present' (Keenan 1993: 135).

Democracy and representation are closely connected, not least through the affirmation of pluralism and difference as the means of squaring norms of autonomy and participation. In practice, principles of popular sovereignty have been realised by establishing the right of ordinary citizens to organise and to choose their own representatives. The organisational mediums of representation can take various forms – parties, social movements, trade unions, interest groups, various forms of media. The right to self-representation is empty without the countervailing right of free expression, which ensures that representatives are freely chosen on the basis of citizens' own opinions, and that they can be held to account. Thus, representative mediums of various sorts are fundamental to any workable principle of democracy. Representation is a practical instrument, but in turn it enshrines a commitment to the irreducibility of value pluralism. The role of representative mechanisms in maintaining democratic politics will not disappear with the advent of new media technologies. It is not uncommon to present communications technologies as promising the end of representative democracy. They seem to offer the hope that opinions will be instantly transmitted without delay or intermediary. Ironically perhaps, the allure of direct digital democracy rests on appealing to an image of a unified social whole finally able to express itself. However, the proliferation of information that results from communication innovations only intensifies age-old problems of representation, accountability, and trust (see Barnett 1998).

The analysis of communications innovations should, then, be shifted away from an oppositional staging of idealised participation and usurping representation, towards the question of trust. Trust is a concept intimately related to the dynamics of representation and accountability, and as a recurrent theme in political theory it testifies to the irreducibility of mediation in actually existing democracies. The issue of trust also underscores the main argument of this chapter, concerning the distinctive temporal register of democratic communication. It is a modality of action that is concerned with two related factors: the freedom of other actors to act (Dunn 1990: 33), and the uncertainty of actions and outcomes over time (ibid.: 26). As a condition and potential problem for social action, trust relations are haunted by betrayal and failure, since trust becomes an issue only in contexts of uncertainty (O'Neill 2002b: 12–13). In so far as democracy is intimately related to issues of trust, we might therefore characterise democratic action as being premised on a strictly undecidable structure of action and responsibility: 'the instant of decision must remain heterogeneous to all knowledge as such, to all theoretical or reportive determination, even if it may and must be preceded by all possible science and conscience' (Derrida 1997: 219). As a regime of rule that is oriented to a future calling to account, democracy requires modalities of action that cannot, in the final analysis, be based on or legitimised by reference to predictable or reliable calculations of consequences or on metaphysically robust accounts of what is right.[1] This is not a barrier to, but the very condition of, responsible action. It implies recasting the problem of democratic legitimacy, now understood not in terms of rationally justifiable obligations to obey laws, but in terms of the broader cultural infrastructure of establishing effective relations of responsibility and accountability between those who exercise power and those over whom it is wielded but to whom it is answerable. In so far as trust is central to democratic legitimacy, this legitimacy is constitutively unstable and paradoxical. It has the same temporal patterning as that ascribed earlier in this chapter to a deconstructed concept of representation. The capacity of actors to act on behalf of those from whom power has been legitimately ceded depends on a degree of freedom from control by those who are governed. The scope and form of their actions cannot be wholly determined in advance. This paradox of legitimacy is the site where accountability and trust are bundled together and thrown forward. Representation appears as a variegated medium for tying actions to a retrospective holding to account, and by extension, the very medium through which trust relations are reproduced and/or undermined. The

1   For more on this theme, see Derrida (2002: 295–314), or, for a similar argument of older vintage, Weber (1970).

undecidable structure of relations between trust, representation, and the spacing and temporalisation of democratic legitimacy does not mean that democracy can never be given real form. It does mean that democracy has no completely stable foundations (which is not the same as having no foundations at all), but that it is instead best approached as a mode of political action that takes on different appearances. Practices and claims of legitimate representation are fundamental to democratic political action, and do not recede in significance just because received theoretical understandings of both representation and legitimacy have been complicated. The theoretical insufficiency of both representation and legitimacy calls for an analysis of their empirical and normative significance in underwriting how democratic politics actually gets done.

The shift in the locus of representational truth marked by the historical movement from an absolutist to a democratic regime installs the people as the highest authority of political wisdom and authority. The populist reaction to this distinctive staging of power is to declare the modern public to be an abstracted fiction, invoking an authentic unified people in its place (Dostal 1994). Another response, characteristic of melancholic post-Marxism and ludic poststructuralism alike, is to find the notion of popular democratic legitimacy theoretically incoherent, thereby reducing the appearance of democracy to the pure play of power between forces. Neither response is very satisfactory, for both normative and empirical reasons. The first returns us to claims of authority and truth that are beyond contestation. The second fails to register the normative difference that democratic modalities of politics make to the ways in which power is practically exercised. The problem with both forms of critique is that they cling to all-or-nothing ideals of democratic legitimacy, collapsing the tension between theory and practice that defines this regime of power. Rather than finding representation abhorrent to or ruinous of democratic norms of legitimacy, a deconstructive affirmation of representation leads us towards a more considered understanding of the peculiar figure of the public in democratic theory and practice. The purely theoretical inadequacy of ideals of popular sovereignty, democratic representation and legitimacy might be the point at which democracy's pragmatist philosophical content becomes evident. In the next chapter, I want to pick up this idea, that democracy needs to be understood in strongly pragmatist terms, by considering the relations between technologies of mass mediation and the emergence of new forms of public life.

2

The production of communicative spaces: formations of the public

The personal and social consequences of any media – that is, of any extension of ourselves – result from the extension of scale that is introduced into our affairs by each extension of ourselves.

Marshall McLuhan (1964: 23)

I Speed, distance and democracy

Modern political theory connects the legitimacy of democratic rule to the capacities of citizens to exercise reasonable political judgement through the medium of public communication (Ferree et al. 2002; Splichal 2002). Melodramatic narratives of the decline of democracy often argue that the acceleration of processes of media communication and information transfer undermines the norms of reasoned debate and discussion upon which democratic participation depends (see Connolly 2000). The speeding up of communication is often associated with an extension in the scope of economic processes beyond the nation-state, rendering them beyond the reach of effective regulation by concerted public action. The communication-and-speed argument does contain the germ of a potentially rich understanding of the knowledge-conditions of democratic citizenship, referring attention as it does to the theme of styles of political communication. In particular, it dramatises the extent to which norms of democracy are implicitly premised on a distinctive modality of time:

> Political time, especially in societies with pretensions to democracy, requires an element of leisure [. . .] in the sense, say, of a leisurely pace. This is owing to the needs of political action to be preceded by deliberation and deliberation, as its 'deliberate' part suggests, takes time because, typically, it occurs in a setting of competing or conflicting but legitimate considerations. Political time is conditioned by the presence of differences and the attempt to negotiate them.
>
> (Wolin 1997)

This argument captures something very important about the notion of deliberation that has been so central to recent theoretical debates about democracy, namely the distinctive sense of pace and rhythm that under-writes taken-for granted norms of communication, participation and citizenship. Unfortunately, it is also a rather static image, and it leads to a somewhat pessimistic diagnosis about the possibilities of democracy in the contemporary context. It leads inevitably to a narrative in which the speeding up of activities through communications innovations leads to the replacement of reasoned, deliberate judgement with spectacular display and appeals to emotion.

There is a counterargument that holds that the acceleration of communication is the very essence of the democratising potential of new media technologies. In this argument, increasing speed is used to signify the overcoming of distance. This relationship between speed and distance is best revealed in the recurring motifs of publicity campaigns for multinational media and communications corporations. In the age of digital technology, constraints of distance will be overcome, facilitating extended social interaction across vast stretches of physical space. In turn, the worlds of work and leisure will both be utterly transformed, extending the range of choice of possible occupations and lifestyles. Technology is presented as having the potential to alleviate socio-economic inequality and political divisions by transcending the materi-alities of space and time (Robins 1997). Moving beyond these populist clichés requires us to rethink the plasticity of space and time that is implied by analyses of the increasing speed of social life and the death of distance. Time and space are not compressible forms moving towards a teleologically determined vanishing point. Communications technolo-gies do not obliterate time and space. They recast the organisation and production of the spatial and temporal scenes of social life. And they open new possibilities of public action.

II *Communications and the formation of public life*

John Dewey provides an interesting counterpoint to the overly opti-mistic and unduly pessimistic idealisms often associated with discus-sions of communications innovations and public life. He gives an account of communication as the very medium of public social life. His discussion of the fate of the public was developed within a context of debates about the significance of new communications technologies (the telephone, broadcast radio, new forms of print culture) in a rapidly urbanising, crisis-ridden round of capitalist restructuring (see Splichal 1999). Dewey understood democracy in a very broad sense, as a mode of associational living shaped by openness to new experience. Accordingly, democracy is characterised by two conditions: shared interests within society, and the freedom to develop new interests (Dewey 1980: 89–93). Understanding democracy as an orientation to enlarged experience is connected to a conception of social life as inherently communicative. This conceptualisation leads Dewey to a distinctive account of the relationships between the spatial scale of social processes and the possibility of democratic public life. The spatial extension of the communicative conditions of society through transport developments, economic development and trade are seen as positively expanding the conditions for democratic public life: first, by developing 'more numerous and varied points of shared common interests' (ibid.: 92), and second, by facilitating 'freer interaction between social groups' (ibid.). By breaking down social barriers and freeing up social interaction, the 'physical annihilation of space' (ibid.) through developments in communications stimulates an opening up of individuals to wider horizons:

> The extension in space of the number of individuals who participate in an interest so that each has to refer his own action to that of others, and to consider the action of others to give point and direction to his own, is equivalent to the breaking down of those barriers of class, race, and national territory which kept men from perceiving the full import of their activity. These more numerous and more varied points of contact denote a greater diversity of stimuli to which an individual has to respond; they consequently put a premium on variation in his action.
>
> (ibid.: 93)

Dewey's optimism is conditioned by a clear understanding that transformations in communications infrastructures do not necessarily lead to changes in the communicative ethos between persons and groups. Communication is more than a process of transmission. It is the medium for a set of practices of sharing, expectation and response (ibid.: 7). Communication is understood as 'the establishment of co-operation in an activity in which there are partners, and in which the activity of each is modified and regulated by the partnership' (Dewey 1981: 141). Communication in this sense of action-in-concert is required to transform the material extension of social interaction into effective public association.

Dewey's philosophy of democracy, communication and education was applied to the debate of the 1920s and 1930s over whether the rise of mass society rendered democracy impracticable as a form of government. The key reference point for Dewey's engagement is Walter Lippmann's elitist theory of democracy and public opinion (1925). Lippmann stands as just one example of a broader liberal elitist critique of democracy, one associated with figures as various as Weber, Michels, Schmitt, Schumpeter and Hayek (see Bellamy 2000). Lippmann's rationalist epistemological critique of normative democratic theory argued that the complexity of modern life, the psychology of mass audiences and the problems of information gathering combined to render public opinion a highly unreliable guide to the proper course of action. For Lippmann, democratic government is understood in terms of a narrow definition of efficient outcomes. The epistemological impossibility of citizens establishing rationally what is in their common interest leads on to an argument that democracy needs to be redefined as government for the people by enlightened and responsible elites. Dewey identified Lippmann's critique of 'the romantic notion of democracy' as turning upon the problem of the scale of social life (1984a: 213–20). Dewey did not reject the necessity for a division of labour in modern society or for practices of mediation in the formation of public opinion. He did reject Lippmann's narrow understanding of public opinion and instrumental vision of expert intelligence, arguing instead that public opinion was formed and transformed through social interaction and deliberation. Dewey's philosophy depended on a strong sense of the educational role of academic institutions in conjunction with the media as key agents in the reinvigoration of the public. He held to a broad, participatory conception of radical democracy as a process of debate, discussion and persuasion in public, an understanding that saw democratic participation as inherently transformative: 'popular government is educative' (1927: 207).

In *The Public and its Problems* (1927), Dewey reiterated his earlier argument that material transformations laid down the possibility of an expanded public life, but also refined his understanding of the obstacles facing the realisation of this potential. The vital question, he argued, was how to transform the 'great society' wrought by industrialisation into an effective public. Dewey's definition of the public combines an emphasis on self-transformation with a focus upon instrumental and purposive collective action. A public involved 'conjoint, combined, associated action' that addressed the problem of how to control certain phenomena: 'publics are constructed by recognition of extensive and enduring indirect consequences of acts' (ibid.: 47). While the public is not identical to the state for Dewey, the state is not understood to be inimical to democracy. Publics depend on the perception of consequences; states depend on the deployment of instrumentalities to address consequences. The emergence of publics is intimately tied to the material organisation of space and time through networks of economic trade, migration and transport. Herein lays the ambivalence in Dewey's account of industrial modernity. A public only emerges through a certain degree of abstraction from social contexts of face-to-face interaction, when the extent to social life requires combined action to address issues that stretch beyond the scope of small communities. The creation of a democratic state at a continental scale during the nineteenth century was tied together socially and politically through 'railways, travel and transportation, commerce, the mails, telegraph and telephone, newspaper' (ibid.: 113). The 'elimination of distance' through technological change had achieved integration, but continuing economic development in turn led to the 'eclipse of the public' it had originally ushered into existence: 'In spite of attained integration, or rather perhaps because of its nature, the Public seems to be lost; it is certainly bewildered' (ibid.: 116). The scope of indirect consequences has become so intensified, complicated and extensive that the ability of citizens to perceive and know them, rather than simply feel and suffer them, has been undermined. There was now, Dewey argued, 'too much public, a public too diffused and scattered and too intricate in composition' (ibid.: 137). Dewey's diagnosis of the eclipse of the public therefore turns on the contradictory relationship he discerns between the pluralisation of publics necessary to address the complexity of modern life, and the imperative for some co-ordination and channelling of this plurality to enable effective public action. The balance of this relationship was, he intimated, increasingly out of kilter.

The eclipse of the public is not simply a matter of functional diversification, spatial and temporal extension, and epistemological complexity. For Dewey, the problematic of modern democracy is fundamentally cultural (West 1989: 105). The proliferation and fragmentation of publics is associated with the increase in the amount of distracting amusements in the form of movies, radio and cheap transport. All of these divert attention from political concerns (Dewey 1980: 138–9). This analysis of popular culture is connected to a particular understanding of the relationships between material communications, spatial extension and mobility. Dewey's analysis turns upon a dualism between well-regulated movement and the overintensification of mobility that leads to social and psychological instability. This relationship is summed up in the opposition between two modes of identification:

attachment and affection. The main problem, for Dewey, with modern popular culture is that it encourages forms of identification that are shifting and unstable. 'The very things which stimulate and intensify affections may undermine attachments', he argues, going on to define attachments as being 'bred in tranquil stability; they are nourished in constant relationships. Acceleration of mobility disturbs them at their root. And without abiding attachments associations are too shifting and shaken to permit a public readily to locate and identify itself' (ibid.: 140–1). In creating the conditions for an expanded public, capitalist industrialism has also facilitated excessive geographical mobility and encouraged a flourishing of cheap and accessible popular culture that, taken together, undermined the stable conditions required for a public to come into existence.

In the final analysis, despite his expansive account of democracy, scale and experience, Dewey's is a fundamentally sedentary understanding of the relations between space, time and public life: 'How can a public be organised, we may ask, when literally it does not stay in space?' (ibid.: 140). His account of modern public life is underwritten by an implicitly gender-coded theory of popular culture that distinguishes between genuine engagement and mere distraction, expressed in the opposition of visual mediums to spoken ones: 'vision is a spectator; hearing is a participator' (ibid.: 219). This evaluation illustrates an understanding of communication as essentially a medium for the sharing of meanings, one that overcomes divisions and brings life to the deadened materiality of physical means of transmission (ibid.: 184). In Dewey, the ideal of communication stands as a norm of shared understanding and mutually beneficial self-activity that transcends the divided world of capital and labour. This is related to his naturalisation of technological change and industrialisation as mechanical processes, the social potential of which will be redeemed through communication. The elision of the social relations of capital and labour underwrites the image of a great society being reconstituted as a self-governing public of shared interest through the medium of educative communication. The presumption is that in conditions of undistorted and equitable communication, everyone will come to identify a common interest in shared concerns, rather than identifying fundamental conflicts of interest over issues to which they are related through a chain of indirect consequences. The evaluative opposition between labour and communication enables the latter to be presented as a properly reciprocal arena of shared understanding. Through this opposition, the question of what sort of structural inequalities of power might be embedded in practices of communication, not least in the realm of education, falls from view in Dewey's account (Schiller 1996: 33–9). It therefore ends up in a double idealisation of communication, understood as both an ideal of shared interest to be aimed at, and an essentially educative medium through which this end can itself be achieved.

Dewey develops a complex sense of public life that connects three distinct but related themes that it is important to distinguish in order to understand better the normative significance of this category (see Pitkin 1981: 239–330). These are the sense of public in terms of access, contrasted to issues dealt with in secret; a sense of public in terms of the scope of the impact of actions – the public defined by reference to the indeterminate range of consequence of actions; and a sense of public in terms of concerted, decisive action by a public authority. In his treatment of these related themes, Dewey's understanding of public life emphasises the overriding value of openness. The universal dimensions of publics are understood not by reference to transcendent rational principles, but through a pragmatic calculation of the scope of actions and consequences, and in turn publicness is ascribed value as a medium for the transformation of subjectivity through exposure to new experiences. It is this commitment to an expansive sense of self and an openness to unanticipated encounters that accounts for Dewey's characteristic optimism about the democratising potential of the enlarged range of interaction facilitated by time-space adjusting communications technologies. However, in Dewey, the distinctive emphasis upon the ways in which modernity is shaped by changing spatio-temporality of communications is associated with an intimation of loss. He thus rejoins a broader tradition in which new patterns of association are evaluated by reference to the idealised being-in-common of a genuine community, a norm that privileges substantive identifications between subjects. From such a perspective, the abstract relationships of modern democracy (rights, equality, contract) can easily appear as pale imitations of the forms of deep cultural unity that are presumed to underlie a genuine political community (Nancy 1991: 1–42). With this in mind, the next section turns to consider less melancholic considerations of the public-forming qualities of modern communications.

III *Phenomenologies of media culture*

Dewey's analysis of the historical formations of public life anticipated more recent conceptualisations of media and communications technologies as mediums for time-space distanciation, that is, for the stretching of social life and social systems over time and space (Giddens 1981). Time-space distanciation refers to a process of constitutive mediation, shaped by the institutionalisation of different mediums for articulating relations of spatial and temporal presence and absence. The notion is indebted to Paul Ricouer's philosophical hermeneutics (1981: 131–44). Distanciation (the archetype of which is the written text) moves the analysis of communication beyond an evaluative dualism between the alienating effects of distance and the participatory belonging of face-to-face interactions. In Giddens' usage, distanciation is expanded beyond strictly interpretative mediums of linguistic communication to include media such as money, commodities and surveillance technologies. He also introduces an explicit consideration of power into the analysis of distanciation. Time and space are understood not as neutral mediums for social and system integration, but as plastic configurations related to the constitution and transformation of unequal relations of power, exploitation and domination (Giddens 1984: 256–62). Processes of time-space distanciation are generative of a dialectic of control that stimulates the emergence of modern forms of political contestation, social movement mobilisation and representative citizenship (Tilly 1990).

The disembedding and re-embedding of institutions and interactions over extended times and spaces that distinguishes capitalist modernity implies that there is a distinctive phenomenology of modern, mediated public cultures. The building blocks of experience are shaped by temporal and spatial configurations of communications media, understood in the broad sense (Ferguson 1990; Tomlinson 1994). The horizons and forms of personal and social experience are shaped by combinations and recombinations of the proximate and distant, the intimate and the impersonal, knowledge and trust. In turn, this implies that everyday life is reshaped through new patterns of privatisation and public engagement that no longer refer to a neat separation between delimited spaces of conduct and action. There is a long line of thought that points to the ways in which media technologies enable new forms of integration over expanded spatial scales. The paradigm for this understanding is the rise of print capitalism and print culture, which have been central to understandings of modern democracy, political parties, social movements and nationalism. The combination of low cost, high durability and high mobility accounts for the impact of print in reshaping culture and politics over scales, typically that of the territorial nation-state. The capacity of print media to detach symbolic forms from local contexts and to reinscribe them in new ones depends on the physical transportation of material objects over material infrastructures. Nationalism, as the paradigmatic modern mass-mediated cultural form, is a product not just of newspapers and novels, but also of postal systems and railways. This doubled sense of communication and transport is captured in geographical work on time-space convergence (see Brunn and Leinbach 1991). This tradition focuses upon the role of so-called space-adjusting technologies in improving transport efficiency, with cultural change understood to be a more or less automatic function of these changes.

Telecommunications and broadcasting mark a decisive break with previous communications media, and cannot be easily contained within the paradigms developed around print culture, precisely because of the altered relationship between communication, infrastructure and transportation that distinguishes them. They detach communication from transportation, in that the communication of messages is separated from the actual physical movement of objects over space (Carey 1989: 203–4). Telecommunications and broadcasting fundamentally reorder the dimensions of public life, and attendant forms of privacy, because they serve as means of extending 'presence-availability' beyond contexts of physical proximity and the immediate corporeal limits of the body (Giddens 1984: 122). As such, electronic media and communications produce virtual spaces of para-social interaction, characterised by more or less rudimentary forms of co-presence (Horton and Wohl 1956; Samarajiva and Shields 1997). This understanding leads beyond a consideration of communications networks as conduits for the transmission of information, redirecting attention to the distinctive forms of communicative action and subjectivity that different mediums open up (Hillis 1998).

Analysis of the distinctive qualities of electronic media as means of time-space distanciation has been most developed in the work of John Thompson (1995). He identifies two related characteristics that define the spatiality and temporality of electronic communications technologies. They uncouple time and space, so that the transmission of information or symbolic forms over space can take place without the physical transportation of objects. Thus, spatial transportation is no longer dependent on temporal distanciation, giving rise to the sense of immediacy associated with the telephone, radio, television and now the Internet. The flip-side of the reduction of transmission time to close to zero is that the experience of simultaneity is detached from conditions of shared spatial locale with persons or events. Thompson calls this despatialised simultaneity, referring to the way in which the experience of 'now' is detached from shared locales, and how the sense of distance is detached from physical movement and travel. Both are now shaped by the available means of communication.

Thompson's analysis suggests that media practices rearticulate spaces of public and private action, by extending the presence-availability of actors and events into new contexts and locales. They can be understood as mechanisms for what Raymond Williams rather elusively referred to as mobile privatisation. This refers to a double movement that Williams diagnosed as being characteristic of the social changes wrought by new communications technologies in the twentieth century: 'Socially, this complex is characterised by the two apparently yet deeply connected tendencies of modern urban industrial living: on the one hand, mobility, on the other hand the more apparently self-sufficient family home' (Williams 1974: 26). This new form of social life is characterised by the simultaneous localisation of social interaction into the regulated spaces of the domestic sphere and an accompanying imperative for new kinds of contact. For Williams, this process is a matter not simply of public life being diverted by the attractions of popular culture, but of people finding consolations in realms of life over which they still retain some discretion given the overwhelming, immovable presence of both state and market. As a structure of feeling, mobile privatisation is thus seen as a means of finding 'a new kind of freedom in that area of our lives that we have staked out inside these wider determinations and constraints' (Williams 1989: 171). The dominant sense of Williams's usage of mobile privatisation is of a movement away from engaged forms of public association, and an extension of a private attitude. But one can just as easily argue that the rearticulation of spaces and mobilities might extend publicness into new areas, not least that of the home, so fundamentally transforming the meaning of what counts as public. Detached from a melancholic analysis of modernity, the concept of mobile privatisation directs attention to the ways in which cultural technologies bring individuals and groups into contact with people, places and events that are distant, enabling identifications with dispersed communities of interest, affiliation and feeling. There is in this idea the kernel of an essentially geographical conceptualisation of media such as radio and television, in so far as Williams approaches media as a set of institutionalised practices that organise and give meaning to the spatial and temporal dimensions of modern social life (see Moores 1993).

An obvious example of mobile privatisation is the case of the Walkman, which takes the personal consumption of media products (music) into the public realm of the street, bus or office (Du Gay et al. 1997). The Walkman blurs a distinction between a private-individual and public-social conduct and space. Laments about the Walkman as an exemplar of a broader privatisation of public culture away from collective provision towards individualised consumption prefigure those associated more recently with the proliferation of the mobile telephone. Mobile phones have been similarly associated with the intrusion of private conduct into the spaces of the public, and have similarly elicited moves to regulate the spaces of their use (see Katz and Aakhus 2002). One of the more notable things about the cultural discourses and regulatory manoeuvres around both the Walkman and mobile phones is that the eruption of private tastes and personal intimacies reveals particular understandings of what constitutes public space. The regulation of personal communications technologies routinely works to construct publicness not as a space of interaction, much less as a space of openness to the unanticipated, but primarily as a space in which the primary imperative is to allow people to be free of unwanted interactions if they so choose. The inscription of these cultural technologies, as both objects of desire and objects of regulation, in terms that privilege norms of individual autonomy is indicative of a particular determination of the meaning and scope of public life, the implications of which are discussed in more detail in Chapter 5.

The framing of communication by reference to norms of public civility and personal propriety has a long history. In particular, communications technologies have been central to modern constructions of the meaning of the home. Radio and television are amongst a range of domestic technologies through which the process of mobile privatisation has been sustained. The domestication of media technologies and their re-embedding of everyday life in broader spatial and temporal contexts transforms the relationships between what is considered public and private in significant ways. Communications technologies mediate between the public and the private, connecting domestic spaces with broader realms of information, culture and public life in ways that detach the meanings of public and private from associations with specific spaces of action. Broadcasting in particular has been pivotal in reshaping relationships between public and private, developing distinctively new forms of intimate publicity. The scrambling of categorical divisions between private domesticity and public realms accounts not only for the centrality of gendered meanings in shaping the development of broadcasting, but also for the sense of broadcasting as a technology for gendering public life in particular ways. This does not just refer to the ways in which meanings of femininity and masculinity are shaped by broadcast cultures, but directs attention to the ways in which the gendering of broadcasting has informed much broader debates about the meanings of public culture. Women's entry into the public life of formal politics in early twentieth-century Europe and North

America coincided with the development of broadcasting, which was understood as an inherently public medium projected into the sanctuary of a domestic sphere coded as feminine. Historically, the rise of concerns over massification, in politics, society and culture, was related to the political and economic enfranchisement of women, leading to a paradigmatic form of analysis that saw the decline of serious public culture as following on from a feminisation of the public sphere. The meanings of masculinity, femininity, public and private, and media are indissolubly connected to each other (Lacey 1996).

The gendered inscription and reinscription of public and private space through cultural technologies such as radio and television therefore requires a revision of highly abstract, rationalist conceptualisations of the forms through which proper public action and political mobilisation should be conducted. Rather than thinking of radio and television in terms of mass communication, Paddy Scannell (1992) argues that in fact they mark the end of mass communications, if mass is meant to refer to forms of communications that constitute and address audiences as a singular mass subject (see also Corner 1998: 35–44). The understanding of the audience for broadcasting on the analogy of the crowd fails to address the spatial and temporal dispersal of address that defines this medium, and the associated impulse towards an individualisation and personalisation of address associated with the historical emergence of broadcast cultures. In contrast to arguments that associate mass media with the decline of public life, Scannell produces a redemptive account of the salvation of public life through the characteristic care structures of broadcasting practice. The historical significance of broadcasting in reshaping the meanings of public life follow from its distinctive spatiality and temporality. Broadcasting creates the possibilities of being in two places at once, and two times at once – the time and place of the event, and the time and place of the context of viewing and listening. This doubling up and spacing out of the spaces of broadcasting in turn implies a revision in how the cultural power of media is conceptualised. The gap between the place of production and/or transmission on the one hand, and the multiple places of reception on the other, means that the relationships between broadcasters and their viewers and listeners is unenforceable (Scannell 1996). For broadcasting to work as a communicative medium, broadcasters have had to adjust to the rhythms and norms of the situated contexts in which programmes are received.

The historical development of broadcasting has therefore been shaped by the institutionalisation of a particular mode of address that is both personal and public. This amounts to a distinctive communicative ethos, best illustrated by the characteristic modes of address associated with broadcast talk, which is modulated as simultaneously intimate and authoritative (Scannell 1991). A for-anyone-as-someone structure of address defines modern media forms: 'They are heard, seen or read by millions (by anyone and everyone) and yet in each case, it seems, they speak to listeners, viewers, or readers personally, as individuals' (Scannell 2000: 5). The for-anyone-as-someone structure of radio and television repersonalises public life according to norms of sociability, sincerity and authenticity: 'Broadcasting transposes the norms of everyday interpersonal existence into public life' (Scannell 1996: 172). Broadcasting makes the world of public events available in a regularised way within the routines of everyday life, so that public life is no longer a separate realm from everyday life, but is brought within the scope of ordinary care relationships. This is more than a mere technological matter of making events available through radio and television. In fundamental ways, the characteristics of broadcasting transform the norms of those events that it transmits. Media events are no longer best thought of as events that take place and then are transmitted. The doubling of media space is inscribed within the organisation and regulation of media events, including symbolic national occasions, routine political communication, and forms of social protest and mobilisation (Scannell 2001a).

Scannell presents broadcasting as a means by which modern life has been re-enchanted and made meaningful, acting as a medium for the repersonalisation of public life. The communicative ethos of broadcasting presents public events as relevant to personal worlds: 'The world, in broadcasting, appears as ordinary, mundane, accessible, knowable, familiar, recognisable, intelligible, shareable and communicable for whole populations. It is talkable about by everyone' (Scannell 1989: 152). By reconstructing the immanent principles of publicity, accessibility and participation that distinguish this cultural technology, Scannell directs our attention to the public significance of a broad range of media culture. The democratic potential of media is thus located not at the level of content, but in the organisational articulation of dispersed sites and different rationalities. In rendering public life accessible to all, broadcasting cultivates a form of reasonable subjectivity, characterised by a willingness to listen and openness to other viewpoints that is essential to the maintenance of a shared public life. Private life and public events are now intermingled in new spatial configurations, and public life is as much about pleasure and enjoyment as about reason, information and education. On this account, popular media culture is embedded in wider social transformations through which the virtues required to engage in public life are reordered around a set of traditionally feminine-coded characteristics, including personalised modes of address (Hartley 1996). And the kinds of politics that new media forms make possible are likely to be most vigorously developed by those social groups excluded by the norms of participation in established public forums. From this perspective, then, it becomes possible to recognise that 'the development of mass communication and broadcasting in particular, rather than being a nail in the coffin of the public sphere, represented its extension and reinvigoration' (Lacey 1996: 235).

The distanciated geographies of mediated public intimacy associated with radio and television highlight the ways in which different media enable the extension of modes of moral action across time and space. The dependence of patterns of interaction, identification and subjectivity upon particular configurations of time-space adjusting technologies is suggestive of a social theory of the flexible spatial and temporal formation of trust, interest, empathy, belonging, care and so on. The scope of human care and feeling is dependent on the variable institutionalisation of technologies and social organisations. The forces that once stretched and embedded culture at the national scale might well now be 'steering it beyond the scale of the nation' (Robbins 1999: 21). Robbins point outs the crucial role of media institutions in mobilising what he calls global feeling, and is keen to avoid the tendency to present mediated forms of identification as modes of alienated, vacuous attachment by virtue of the intercession of distance. There is a particular ethical and political stake in insisting that proximity and distance not be thought of in terms of an opposition between concrete presence and alienating absence. This opposition allows media technologies to be both chastised for fostering inauthentic forms of identification and celebrated for reconstituting a lost sense of community. The disruption of clear, two-dimensional divisions between proximity and distance suggests not an understanding in terms of alienation, but rather one in which media are understood as cultural technologies of welcome and hospitality.

The distinctive phenomenology of broadcasting culture suggests that the 'where' of public life needs to be rethought in terms of the spaces opened up by spatially extensive networks of media communication. This implies more than a simple stretching, but also a fundamental transformation in the norms of public action and conduct. For Scannell, as we have already seen, broadcasting takes place in two places, those of the transmission and those of reception. More pertinent is Samuel Weber's characterisation, according to which mediated communication actually takes place across three spaces: the place from where images and sounds are recorded and produced; the places where they are received; and the spaces in-between, through which images and sounds are transmitted (Weber 1996: 117). This sense of the space in-between through which any communication must pass points towards the fact that even despatialised simultaneity depends on putting in place a complex material infrastructure that enables the uncoupling of time-space. The rhetoric of the death of distance works to hide practices of intermediation from view, whether these be policies, regulatory systems, corporate structures or social practices. Communications technologies do not overcome distance and separation, they render them invisible:

> Transmitted vision and audition 'contain', as it were, distance and separation while at the same time confounding the point of reference that allows us to define what is near and what is far, what is connected and what is disconnected. For those points of reference involve precisely the unequivocal determination of place and of bodily situation that the television transmission tends to undermine.
>
> (ibid.: 122)

As mediums for the phantasmogoric reordering of time and space (Giddens 1990: 18–19), modern media like television introduce a peculiar sense of vertigo into the phenomenology of everyday life. Television is 'a medium that deprives distance as well as proximity of their traditional stability and hence their power to orient. What is distant is set right before us, close up; and yet what is thus bought close remains strangely *removed*, indeterminably *distant*. And what is traditionally proximate is *set apart*, set at a distance' (Weber 1996: 124–5; original emphasis). This argument suggests that taking into account the spatiality and temporality of media practices has significant implications for established ways of thinking about identity, subjectivity and experience. The experience provided by radio and television is divided across multiple spaces and times, and extended beyond the immediate emplacement of the sensuous body. This implies that the supposed unity of place as the site of experience is shattered, and 'with it the unity of everything that defines its identity with respect to place: events, bodies, subjects' (ibid.: 125). Considering the phenomenologies of media practices requires us to reassess the normative value ascribed to ideas of identity, authenticity and place in ethics and politics, suggesting instead a practical philosophy of dissemination and displacement (Peters 1999).

The social-theoretic phenomenologies of media culture discussed in this section underscore the ways in which the dimensions and meanings of public life are shaped by the spatial and temporal relationships opened up by media practices. They do so without recourse to the narrative of loss that connects analysis of communications to a diagnosis of the eclipse of community. There is still, however, in the work reviewed here, a persistent tendency to conceptualise space as a gap, as a distance bridged through different media, a tendency indicated by the routine recourse to a grammar of interaction (Gregory 1994: 117–19; 1989). The focus upon the interactional potentials opened up by different media tends to ignore the significance of the production of the material and organisational infrastructures that enable such communication.

IV *The production of communicative spaces*

The phrase 'the production of communicative spaces' is meant to suggest a double emphasis upon both the production of new spaces of communicative sociality through social practice, the sense already discussed, and the institutional production of the material and organisational infrastructures of communication. This latter theme draws on David Harvey's conceptualisation of the production of capitalist spatiality. The contradictory relationships between fixity and mobility are central to Harvey's geographical imagination (see Harvey 2000). The dynamism of capitalism is understood to be dependent on the contingent stability of co-ordinating mechanisms that its own development perpetually undermines. According to this argument, if capitalism resolves tendencies to crisis through the perpetual production of space, then this means that space is not progressively overcome, but perpetually reorganised. The production of space and time is a process of unstable, uneven and unpredictable stabilisations of temporal rhythms and spatial patterns. It is a process that opens up new possibilities for interaction and circulation only by laying in place fixed material and organisational infrastructures that are characterised by their own forms of inertia. This conceptualisation depends on a narrative of capitalist development in terms of a series of communications innovations (turnpikes, canals, railways, the telegraph, telecommunications) that reduce the costs of circulating commodities, labour, money – value – through space and time (Harvey 1990).

The recurring theme in Harvey's conceptualisation is the contradictory process of creative destruction through which the material configurations of accumulation laid down in one period of development are transformed in a subsequent period of crisis. The twin imperatives to expand the spatial extent of markets for commodities while reducing the turnover time of capital leads to the investment of capital of long turnover time in the production of space. Thus, the more capitalism develops, the more it embeds tendencies to geographical and temporal inertia: it takes a specific organisation of space to annihilate space; and it takes capital of long turnover time to facilitate the more rapid circulation of the rest (Harvey 1982). The material and organisational mediums through which space and time are co-ordinated eventually come to serve as a brake for the further expansion and speed-up of accumulation, leading to a reorganisation of spatial and temporal configurations.

Harvey's conceptualisation of the crisis-dependent dynamics of the production of capitalist spatiality has been consistently linked to analyses of socio-cultural change and political mobilisation. Innovations in the means of communication associated with waves of investment in the built environment not only enable new phases of capital accumulation, but are also associated with new political forms, new forms of cultural expression, and new forms of social experience. There is an implicit phenomenology of modernity in this understanding of capitalist space, one most clearly expressed in the notion of time-space compression (Harvey 1989). This should not too readily be assimilated to other, similar-sounding formulae, such as time-space convergence or time-space distanciation, precisely because it is derived from a conceptual analysis that explicitly breaks with the friction-of-distance understanding of time and space implied in both those notions. Time-space compression refers to the idea that the expression of capitalist crisis in the periodic restructuring of the spatial and temporal configurations of everyday life disrupts stabilised patterns of meaningful social action. Thus, crisis at one level of a social totality is mediated through the changing material dimensions of space and time, triggering changes in structures of cultural expression and individual consciousness that are also experienced in crisis mode. In particular, time-space compression shrinks time-horizons while extending the immediacy and spatial scope of consequential action. It therefore renders it difficult to apprehend the totality of actions and effects, either conceptually or aesthetically, an apprehension that is considered essential to effective political action (Harvey 1996). This diagnosis of contemporary cultural and political change stakes political representation, political action and public decision-making on highly rationalist, cognitive models of the collective monitoring of actions and consequences. Where Harvey sees a retreat from political critique and a failure of critical imagination in contemporary forms of cultural politics, others see the emergence of new modes of representation and

new forms of expression related to the rethinking of the forms and
objectives of progressive political action.

Compared to the accounts of spatiality and temporality discussed
earlier in this chapter, Harvey's conceptualisation of the production of
space is distinguished by a greater sensitivity to the extent to which the
restructuring of communications involves both the convergence and
divergence of differentially situated actors (see Leyshon 1995). This
emphasis has been most developed in critical elaborations that have
challenged the sense that material transformations lead to a uniform
shift in modes of consciousness. Massey (1994) argues that greater
attention should be paid to the power-geometry of contemporary spatial and temporal restructuring. This refers to the ways in which different groups and individuals are placed in distinct relations to flows,
interconnections and mobilities. Time-space compression is socially
stratified by class, gender, race and ethnicity, and other unequal social
relations. Placement within these relations will determine crucial differences in degrees of movement and interaction, and differences in the
forms and degrees of power deployed in relation to such networks
(Bridge 1997; Kirsch 1995).

Information and communications technologies are certainly given an
important place in materialist accounts of the production of space.
Improvements in information transfer are seen as fundamental to the
co-ordination of capital investments, credit-money systems and the circulation of commodities. In these narratives, communications technologies are understood primarily as vectors for the heightened
mobility of capital and for the organisational restructuring of corporations and markets. But the production-of-space approach continues to
present media and communications as having a derivative relationship
to the key dynamics of accumulation, by facilitating the circulation of
commodities. It thus reiterates an older blindness to the ways in which
media are themselves sectors for the accumulation of capital through
the production of commodities (Smythe 1977). Media can be understood as having a dual role in the production of surplus value: indirectly,
through advertising and other forms of promotion, in a circuit of distribution and exchange; and directly, since media programmes are produced as commodities, and are also used to produce audiences as
commodities (Garnham 1990). Once this second point is acknowledged,
then the difficulty with a purely economistic analysis of media commodity production becomes clear. Broadcasting is again paradigmatic
here. Historically, the commodification of broadcasting has followed
one of two ideal types. The 'British' model was to make broadcasting a
public monopoly, so that commodification was primarily facilitated

through the production of hardware (radios and televisions). The 'American' model was to use programming to construct audiences as commodities to be sold to advertisers. The idea of the production and exchange of audience-commodities illustrates the importance of knowledge in constituting media as arenas for accumulation (Gitlin 2000: 19–30). Audiences are determinative fictions, constructed through mechanisms such as audience ratings (Meehan 1986), and constituted according to a range of identity characteristics, including gender (Streeter and Wahl 1995), ethnicity (Rodriguez 1997) and language (Collins 1994). Media commodification is, then, an area where a wholly class-based, economistic form of analysis just will not suffice, since the political economy of media is shaped by a set of cultural practices relating to the construction of identities, the production and circulation of expert knowledge, and the routines of everyday life.

The constitutively cultural and political nature of media commodification follows from the combination of the distinctive formal, technological and spatio-temporal characteristics of informational products such as books, newspapers, radio and television programmes, films and recorded music. These all share two related characteristics (see Garnham 1987; Edelman 1979; Miège 1987). First, they are all produced by distinctive technologies of reproduction. One important consequence of this dependence on technologies of reproduction is a particular cost structure, whereby the marginal costs of producing extra units rapidly approaches zero. Second, however, the potentially huge return on initial capital investment is rendered uncertain because the commodification of music, films, television, books and so on is subject to the vagaries of taste. A further feature of media products being *reproduced* is that they are not destroyed in consumption, giving rise to the recurrent problem of piracy and unauthorised copying in the history of modern media, from samizdat literatures to Napster (Frow 1994). The combination of easy reproducibility and durability means that media products are both indivisible, in so far as the consumption of a television programme or a magazine does not diminish the possibility of consumption by others, and non-excludable, since it is difficult to control free-riding.

The low incremental cost of media reproduction leads to an imperative to expand market share as the easiest avenue to expanding profitability and extending accumulation. The tendency towards economies of scale in media industries, expressed in frequent bursts of consolidation and conglomeration, is related to strategies of so-called spatialisation, reflecting the imperative to expand the spatial scope of the circulation of media commodities and communications services into new markets (Mosco 1996: 173–211). However, this imperative to expand circulation is dogged by the problem of maintaining the economic scarcity of commodities that are durable as well as cheap and easy to reproduce. These contradictory tendencies, between the drive towards expanding market share and extending the spatial scope of markets on the one hand, and the difficulty of maintaining price-regulated scarcity on the other, means that in media and cultural industries it is not production but distribution that is 'the key locus of power and profitability' (Garnham 1987: 31).[1] The contradictory characteristics of media commodification highlight the central role that the state, and in particular the politics around various state apparatuses, plays in the development of media economies. Any adequate account of the production of communicative spaces, understood in the double sense suggested above, requires an approach that can account for the constitutive role of political action in restructuring communications infrastructures and media markets (Schiller 2000). The state is an autonomous agent for the production of certain forms of spatial configurations, not least facilitating territorial consolidation through various modes of pacification and technologies of surveillance (Mann 1993). States have distinct interests in the spatial and temporal organisation of media and communications practices that cannot be properly understood as merely the outcomes of the functional requirements of a general logic of expanded capital accumulation. Economic processes and technological change in media and communications sectors are modulated by the contingencies of regulatory and institutional frameworks that are the outcome of political processes of alliance formation, lobbying and advocacy.

V Conclusion: public life and the ambivalence of commodification

Following on from the above analysis, we can understand the development of public media and communications as being shaped by a double movement of circulation and containment (Gaines 1991). The expansion and deepening of the scope of media commodity production depend on containing the circulation of media products (programmes and audiences) within formal boundaries of commodity exchange. This is a practical achievement that depends upon the construction and regulation of property rights (Streeter 1996). Copyright is the oldest

1　There is scope here for understanding the distinctive economics of media commodification in terms of an analysis of monopoly rent (Harvey 2001).

example of the institutional formation of this double movement. Increasingly, media and cultural commodification depends on the innovation of new forms of property rights which secure the same double movement in relation to images, ideas, codes, etc. (see Lury 1993). The central role that property rights plays in the development of media economies underscores the argument that the economics of media commodification is irreducibly *cultural* (involving constructions of identity, conceptions of the self) and *political* (involving the law, regulatory agencies, policy-making). In both respects, control over the production of authoritative knowledge is a central site of political conflict. This is the theme I will return to in later chapters. To close this chapter, I want to reiterate the dual sense of the production of communicative spaces it has developed. This idea connects up the emphasis on the contradictory production of material infrastructures of communication with the emphasis on the social production of new spaces of communicative sociality. It is an idea that resonates with Dewey's double emphasis on communication as both a material configuration of relations and shared action-in-concert. The idea of the production of communicative space underscores the sense that the social uses of modern communications technologies open up of new spaces of sociability that transform the ways in which ordinary people engage in a wider world of publicly significant processes and events, as well as transforming the nature and meanings of those processes and events themselves. But it also reminds us that the idea of the social production of the spaces of communicative action needs to be supplemented with an analysis of the production of the material infrastructures of communication. And this implies an analysis of the politically contested process of commodification, regulation and policy-making. And understanding media commodification in terms of the double movement of circulation and containment requires an acknowledgement of the extent to which the public availability of mass-mediated symbolic forms – the constitution of modern media publics and the meanings ascribed to them – has historically depended upon the institutionalisation of private property rights in various media products. Commodification is not something that befalls modern, democratic public culture from the outside. The politics of media commodification is therefore central to the construction and contestation of different understandings of publicness. With this in mind, the next chapter considers a central category of recent theoretical debates in cultural studies, media and communications theory, and political philosophy, namely the notion of the public sphere.

3

Media, communication and legitimacy: representing the public sphere

The public sphere cannot be conceived as an institution and certainly not as an organisation. It is not even a framework of norms with differentiated competencies and roles, membership regulations, and so on. Just as little does it represent a system; although it permits one to draw internal boundaries, outwardly it is characterised by open, permeable, and shifting horizons. The public sphere can best be described as a network for communicating information and points of view (i.e., opinions expressing affirmative or negative attitudes); the streams of communication are, in the process, filtered and synthesised in such a way that they coalesce into bundles of topically specified public opinions.

Jürgen Habermas (1996: 360)

I Deliberation, representation and the public sphere

This chapter applies the arguments developed in the previous two chapters to a critical consideration of the relevance of Habermas' conceptualisation of the public sphere for understanding the relations between media, culture and democracy. In so doing, the aim is not to dismiss Habermas, but to suggest that in certain fundamental respects, Habermas' work remains an unavoidable reference point for any consideration of a radical democratic vision of public life. His conceptualisation of the public sphere has become a ubiquitous reference point across the social sciences and humanities (see Calhoun 1992). The English translation of Habermas' (1989) *The Structural Transformation of the Public Sphere* (hereafter *STPS*) coincided with a wave of real-world democratisation that has stimulated a resurgence of interest in questions of democracy, citizenship and social justice for which Habermas' book has provided a ready-to-use set of analytical categories. The original account of the public sphere in *STPS* is a tragic narrative, which finds the seeds for the demise of the public sphere already present in the conditions of its historical emergence. The public sphere has a very precise meaning in Habermas' work. It is one element in a four-way division of the social field. The patriarchal family and the market economy belong to the private realm, while the state is the locus of public authority. The public sphere is defined as an intermediating zone between these two realms. The concept therefore refers to the set of practices through which public opinion is formed and articulated with concentrated power. In the terms of Habermas' later social theory, one can divide these four realms into a more complex pattern of cross-cutting relationships: a private realm of communicatively integrated *lifeworld* relations (the family); a private realm of *system* relations (the capitalist market economy); a public realm of *system* relations (the state); and a public realm of *lifeworld* relations (the literary and political public spheres). Public and private therefore refer to a distinction between practices governed by an orientation towards universal values (the state and the public sphere), and those governed by particularistic values (the family and the market).[1]

In *STPS*, Habermas argues that the emergence of an infrastructure of protected public discussion in eighteenth-century Europe was a key moment in the transformation of political power, legitimacy and sovereignty. The institutionalisation of popular sovereignty does not just mark a change in who holds political power, it also fundamentally transforms how power is exercised. The new form of democratic power depends upon the active participation of equal individuals in public discussion and debate. This replaces a form of representative public sphere, in which power is displayed before a passive people (Habermas 1989: 5–14). This mutation in the relationship between power, publicity and representation does not merely exchange one form of legitimisation for another, it transforms the very nature of power itself. Once the exercise of power passes through the institutionalised mediums of public deliberation, economic organisations and political institutions can be subordinated to the rationalising influence of public deliberation.

Habermas' original discussion provides the outlines of a cultural theory of democracy that puts considerable emphasis on the role of communications media in shaping the way in which political power is exercised. Conceptually, *STPS* privileges a particular set of cultural institutions that are shaped by inequalities of both class and gender. This specificity is reflected in the definition of particular literary capabilities as the conditions of democratic inclusion (Hohendahl 1987).

---

1   For a critical discussion of the implicit gender coding of these analytical distinctions, see Fraser (1989: 113–43) and McLaughlin (1993).

The emphasis on the cultivation of literary competencies is related to the consolidation of capitalist property relations. These not only define the autonomy of the private (masculine) citizens who engage in public deliberation, but also facilitate the circulation of a politically free, commercialised and competitive market for information and opinion, in the form of books, newspapers and pamphlets. This cultural theory of democratic competence underwrites the tragic narrative of the decline of the public sphere in the second part of *STPS*, in which the gendered subtext of Habermas' account becomes evident. The primary cause of the transformation of the public sphere is the interweaving of the public and private realms, as the modern state progressively takes on responsibilities for the reproduction of the social relations of commodity production and exchange. This is itself the expression of a deeper contradiction between the social relations of exchange, based upon equality, that underwrite the formation of civil society and the public sphere; and the social relations of production, based on inequality. As the contradictions of the social relations of production are increasingly expressed in the realm of political action, the ideal of equal participation in public discussion to arrive at a universal opinion and general will is replaced by forms of bargaining and compromise between special interests. In Habermas' narrative, the critical function of the public sphere is eroded as the media of public debate are transformed into mediums for the expression of particularistic interests rather than the formation of a universally agreed general interest. The increasingly commodified, as distinct from merely commercialised, mass media thus become arenas for winning mass approval, a process dubbed refeudalisation. This is associated with a process in which both the content of politics and the modes of public communication are implicitly presented as becoming progressively feminised, not least by the commodification of public communication with the rise of electronic mass media of radio and television. Popular literature, radio and television, cinema and popular music all come to stand as models of bad culture, wherein the autonomy of art is undermined by commodification, and the conditions for cultivating the critical capacities of citizens are destroyed.

The narrative of the refeudalisation of the public sphere is characterised by a deep distrust of representation (Peters 1993). Critical, democratic publicity should be fully participatory and non-representative (Saccamano 1991). The effective disenfranchisement of citizens from influence over decision-making is expressed in the rise of representative forms of public debate, exemplified by the scientification of politics and public opinion. Habermas' subsequent analysis of the crisis of mid-twentieth-century welfare capitalism diagnosed a dual crisis, of legitimacy of the state and motivation amongst citizens. These crises were ascribed to the increasing complexity of social systems, leading to the subordination of rational participatory debate to scientific and techno-logical expertise. When public opinion becomes a mere representation, embodied in intermediaries like opinion polls, pollsters and experts, parties, unions and interest groups, the critical role of the public sphere is undermined. Democratic participation is equated with involvement in highly rational forms of communication that are pre-oriented to uni-versality, requiring the exchange of ideas between subjects who should ideally be indifferent to their own particularistic interests and embodied identities.

The textuality of modern public communication is the source of the founding ambivalence of Habermas' original account of media and the public sphere (Lee 1992). On the one hand, the liberal public sphere depended upon various print media (pamphlets, newspapers and nov-els). However, these mediums are understood merely as conduits for the transmission of information between locales. In his account of the lit-erary forms of eighteenth-century public culture, Habermas explicitly subordinates the disseminating force of print to the bounded continu-ities of idealised conversation: 'The dialogue form [. . .] employed by many of the articles, attested to their proximity to the spoken word. One and the same discussion transposed into a different medium was continued in order to reenter, via reading, the original conversational medium' (Habermas 1989: 42). Habermas' understanding of the geog-raphies of the public sphere is thus governed by a particular postal prin-ciple, in which printed texts always arrive at their intended destination, completing a circuit of conversation without chance or change. The spatial and temporal extension enabled by print media is not allowed to disrupt a model of consensus formation through undistorted dialogue amongst an essentially homogeneous reading public. The conceptual reduction of print to an idealised model of conversation drastically restricts the forms of communication through which the problematisa-tion of the public interest and the delineation of politics are allowed to take place. Spectacle, display and other affective forms of communica-tion are understood to reduce citizens to passive spectators, rather than active participants in deliberation.

The value of Habermas' account in *STPS* lies in the insistence on treating the public sphere as a historical category with specific institu-tional conditions, but the use of a particular historical example to derive universal principles condemns the analysis of the transforma-tions of public life to find only degeneration and decline. The utility of the public sphere idea as a critical analytical concept therefore depends

on retaining the emphasis upon the historical variability of institutional
forms, while reworking the terms used in evaluating this variability
(Hohendahl 1979, 1995). In Habermas' work subsequent to *STPS*, the
contradictions between historicity and normativity are resolved by
developing a transhistorical foundation for the ideals of the public
sphere. His theory of communicative action continues to display a characteristic ambivalence towards practices of mediation. His analysis of
the trajectory of modernity turns on a distinction between two modes
of mediation. So-called steering media (money, expert systems and
administrative power), replace ordinary language as a medium for co-
ordinating action, and give rise to subsystems differentiated out from
the communicatively integrated lifeworld. On the other hand, what he
calls generalised forms of communication (media like newspapers,
radio and television) remain dependent on the lifeworld and condense
communicative action, simplifying complex patterns of communicative action, enabling the management of risks of misunderstanding
(Habermas 1987: 390).

The practical value of steering media lies in their being able to be
detached from lifeworld contexts and operate autonomously, reducing
impediments to co-ordination by eliminating the burdens of consensus
formation through communicative action. However, these delinguistified mediums of co-ordination harbour the potential of complete
autonomy, swinging back to 'colonise' lifeworld contexts, so further
undermining the communicative co-ordination of social systems. There
is thus a built-in dialectic whereby the rationalisation of action (the definition of the goals and objectives of action) comes to be shaped by the
independent rationalities of steering media rather than the rationalities
of participatory communicative action. It is important to emphasise
that Habermas does not oppose rationalisation *per se*. He sets up a tension between two alternative modes of rationalisation of social action:
the rationalisation of everyday communication which remains tied to
the structures of the intersubjective lifeworld, in which language is the
medium for reaching understanding; and the growing complexity of
subsystems where rationalisation is determined by delinguistified steering media. The colonisation of the lifeworld is not simply the intrusion
of a wholly external logic; it is the result of the separation of modes of
rationality that should be properly kept in relation, and the turning
back of one of these modes onto the other. This relationship between
system integration and social integration, between delinguistified co-
ordination and rationalisation through lifeworld practices, defines
democracy: 'The normative meaning of democracy can be rendered
in social-theoretical terms by the formula that the fulfilment of the

functional necessities of *systematically* integrated domains of action shall find its limits in the integrity of the lifeworld, that is to say, in the requirements of domains dependent on social integration' (ibid.: 345). Democracy is understood here a defensive modality against encroachment by administrative and commodified processes.

The distinctions between system and social integration, between steering media and generalised forms of communication, guide Habermas' analysis of the 'ambivalent potential of mass communications' (ibid.: 389). Mass media combine elements of both steering media and generalised communication. On the one hand, electronic media like radio and television expand the horizons of possible communication. On the other, in the form of broadcasting, they rest on a one-way flow of communication from centre to periphery, introducing hierarchy and strengthening the efficiency of centralised control over communication practices. But this possibility of control is always precarious. Habermas' post-*STPS* media analysis acknowledges the complex roles of professional journalism, public relations industries, the oppositional value of popular media cultures, and the subcultural initiatives of reception contexts in mediating the political impact of media, marking a clear break with the mass-culture hypothesis that informed the media analysis in *STPS*.

Nevertheless, the theory of communicative action remains limited as an approach to understanding the relationships between media, communication and the possibilities of democracy. The 'ideal speech situation', the counterfactual orientation towards impartial agreement built into the pragmatics of conversation, and the related understanding of ideological power in terms of systematically distorted communication are the proposed theoretical constructs with which to evaluate the actualities of communicative practice. It is indicative of a sustained commitment to understanding democratic legitimacy as an end point to a process of rational justification, rather than as a process of claims-making without end. This in turn reflects the residual theoreticism that characterises Habermas' work, in which an abstract set of criteria is deduced from general principles to substitute for what people *should* have decided *if* they had engaged in rational discourse (Canovan 1983: 111). Further, the conceptual formalisation of the conditions of rational consensus implies that democratic communication should be properly 'devoid of body politics, art, rhetoric, festivity, and disobedience' (Keane 1984: 190). This formalistic rationalism restricts democratic communication to a narrowly cognitive model of argumentative dialogue over validity. This restriction fails to register the extent to which marginalised and subaltern actors are often obliged to adopt non-traditional modes of communication because of the patterns of access that shape actually existing public spheres. Particularly in contexts of highly unequal social relations, the enforcement of abstract universalised conventions of political conduct and participation will tend only to reproduce patterns of exclusion and inequality.

II *The approach of democratic communication*

In the theory of communicative action, the mass media are understood as forms of generalised communication, which act as second-order mediums of consensus formation, still dependent on the same linguistic resources as first-order consensus formation. By continuing to contain the spatio-temporal dispersal enabled by mass media within the idealised contexts of intersubjective communication, Habermas prioritises the informational function of the media over other characteristics such as entertainment, display or affective identification. Reading against the grain of Habermas' own interpretation of the circulating media of the public sphere suggests an alternative understanding of public communication. Publics are bought into existence in relation to a temporally and spatially distanciated network of circulating texts, images and symbolic acts, and without any necessary orientation to closure (see Warner 2002). The exemplar of this sort of strung-out, open-ended public would be those publics constituted by the indeterminate address of various forms of electronic mass media (Scannell 2000). This understanding is implicit in Habermas' original discussion of a public constituted by circulating print media, but his account needs to be freed from the conceptual containment of print-writing within a closed circuit of dialogue. Lifting this restriction recasts the understanding of what sort of subject the public is. As argued in Chapter 1, acknowledging the irreducibility of differential representation suggests that the concept of the public is not best understood as a synonym for a social totality or a collective actor. Nor should it be immediately understood as referring to particular public spaces of bounded social interaction. A fully democratic theory of public life would acknowledge the value of a diverse institutional infrastructure of mechanisms of accountability and representation to encourage pluralism and guard against the atrophied concentration of power (Keane 1995). This is the full implication of Habermas' account of the institutionalised separation of the institutions of the state, the economy and the various intermediary agencies of civil society, but it is an implication not fully worked through in his original account of the cultural conditions of democratic publicity.

Understanding rational deliberation as the medium for the resolution of differences tends to imply that political conflicts can always be translated into matters of differing opinions (Phillips 1995). The procedural emphasis upon reaching consensus that is already built into norms of rational debate illustrates an unwillingness to acknowledge conflicts as resting on fundamental, substantive differences (Phillips 1991: 141). The principle of disembodied popular sovereignty, dissolved into the medium of public discussion, rests on the idea that only the force of the better argument should determine the course of deliberation. This assumption enforces a clear separation between the value of *what* is represented (an opinion or idea) and the identity of *who* is doing the representing. The assumption is that the content of public debate and political discourse, sharply distinguished from their form, is what is most significant. But if it is not in fact possible to disentangle the force of the better argument from the force of rhetorical devices, authority relations and desire, then this requires us to rethink the relationships between embodiment, deliberation and universalisation.

Iris Young's account of *communicative democracy* draws Habermas' critical theory into a productive engagement with deconstructive understandings of difference and representation. Importantly, it retains a sense of the institutionalised asymmetries of access to resources that shape participation by different social actors. Young reaffirms the principle that democratic deliberation is the best means of arriving at just outcomes. Participation is practically valuable because it ensures the inclusion of all relevant information in decision-making, but also normatively valuable because it contributes to the development of the capacities of participants as citizens (Young 1990a: 92–3). The idea of communicative democracy negotiates a path beyond the rigid choice between an interest-based version of democracy, understood as the expression of pre-existing preferences, and which has no role for the public formation of political preferences, needs or identities; and a deliberative/discourse model of democracy, understood as a process of gathering together to deliberate over collective issues and arrive at consensus (Young 1993: 126). The second model presupposes shared understanding or agreement over the common good as either the basis or the telos of deliberation. This posits the possibility of communication on identity, and therefore limits the possibilities of self-transformation through communication (Young 1997: 66).

Young's critique of deliberative ideals of public space turns on the argument that such conceptualisations often depend on a hierarchical opposition of rationality and affect, reason and desire. The exclusion of desire, affect and embodiment from the realm of the civic public is, she argues, the point at which homogeneity is conceptually imposed on the definition of the public realm (Young 1990a: 109). The extension of rights to participate to those previously excluded does not fundamentally alter the gendered norms of public life, which persist in the delimitation of the modes of conduct in terms of finding a universal and impartial perspective: 'This requires abstracting from the particularity of bodily being, its needs and inclinations, and from the feelings that attach to the experienced particularity of things and events' (Young 1990b: 97). For example, Habermas recognises the plurality of subjects in public life, but maintains an understanding of dialogic reason in terms of the expression of generalisable interests. The fundamental question is whether the notion of generalisable interests necessarily implies shared, universal interests that can be articulated in a universally shared language of justification (ibid.: 107–8). In answer to this question, Young positively asserts the normative value of plural modes of expression: 'when political dialogue aims at solving collective problems, it justly requires a plurality of perspectives, speaking styles, and ways of expressing the particularity of social situations as well as the general applicability of principles' (Young 1997: 73).

Young questions the assumption that rational debate needs to be based on demonstrable universal principles, not only on the grounds that ideals of impartiality falsely universalise particular positions, but on the more fundamental grounds that the inevitability of particular perspectives and local rationalities provides the positive basis for the comparative analysis of needs and values. In her model, difference should be understood as a resource that is drawn upon in public forums of needs interpretation and judgement (Young 2000: 81–120). A fully inclusive conception of dialogic reason must forswear the ideals of impartial universalistic reason, replacing the assumption that communication depends on *a priori* foundations of understanding with a notion of public deliberation in terms of translation. By virtue of being undertaken in a public medium, democratic discourse obliges actors to translate their particular needs and desires into *claims* for justice: 'The claim of justice does not presuppose agreement on principles of justice. Instead, it carries embedded in it an acknowledgement that we are together, socially bound to one another, whether we like it or not' (Young 1998: 41). This does not require a transcendence of particularity in favour of a universal perspective. It depends instead on a shift from a self-centred understanding of needs to the recognition of other perspectives and a commitment to negotiation. Principles of justice are the starting point of a process, rather than the cut-and-dried outcomes that will enable deliberation to be closed off in favour of decisive action. Injustice is not recognised by applying universal principles to actual situations. It appears as the result of the articulation of appeals to justice that are addressed to a broader public: 'Appeals to justice and claims of injustice are not a result, they do not reflect an agreement; they are rather the starting point of a certain kind of *debate*. To invoke the language of justice and injustice is to make a *claim*, a claim that we together have obligations of certain sorts to one another' (ibid.: 40; original emphasis).

Understanding democratic justice in terms of claims-making, translation and negotiation implies a reorientation of conceptualisations of democratic communication towards the articulation of promises, giving reasons, and a willingness to talk and listen. Justification is rethought in terms of an open-ended process of addressing and responding to others. This argument in turn informs Young's broadening of the range of modes of communication through which political action is practised. Norms of rational deliberation tend to elevate particular forms of discourse – those that are formal, general, dispassionate and disembodied. So defined, deliberation 'does not open itself equally to all forms of making claims and giving reasons' (Young 1997: 64). Young draws on Derrida, Levinas and Irigaray to argue that a consideration of the ethical and political claims of other actors does not depend on the idealised symmetries of rational dialogue. Communication is understood as a process of call and response without any guarantees of reciprocation. Young suggests that a range of non-deliberative modes of communication (such as gesture, jokes and poetry) is appropriate and necessary to enable people to acknowledge the concreteness of other subjects (see Oliver 2001). Young (1997: 60–74) argues that greeting, rhetoric and storytelling are as important modes of democratic communication as is highly rational argument.

Young proposes a notion of dialogue without assimilation, premising communication upon the maintenance rather than the transcendence of difference: 'Participants in communication are in a relation of approach. They meet across distance of time and space and can touch, share, overlap their interests. But each brings to the relationship a history and structured positioning that makes them different from one another, with their own shape, trajectory, and configuration of forces' (ibid.: 50). Communicative democracy does not presuppose reciprocity as either origin or telos of dialogue. The important element of a claim for justice is its illocutionary status as a claim, its trajectory as an appeal addressed to others: 'There must be an appeal to [. . .] a minimal consensus if anything at all is to be said. Whether this appeal corresponds, *in fact*, to a comprehension or an agreement, if only on the meaning of what is said, appears to us secondary with regard to the appeal itself' (Derrida 1997: 214).[2]

This conceptualisation of communication as call and response helps us to understand the normative relationship between democracy and media. The movement from self-centred claims of interest to the embracing claims of justice depends upon the institution of pluralistic mediums of publicity: 'only a democracy structured to foster public communication among diverse agents in the polity can be expected to transform citizens' interests form being merely self-regarding to being concerned with justice' (Young 1993: 140). It is not necessary to stake the realisation of democratic justice in this communicative sense on either an unrealistic transcendence of social position in favour of an impartial standpoint, or the shaky foundations of public virtue. Rather, one only needs to recognise the normalising effect of public debate on the calculation of consequences by purposeful social actors: 'the effect of an audience is to replace the language of interest by the language of reason and to replace impartial motives by passionate ones. The presence of a public makes it especially hard to appear motivated merely by self-interest. Even if one's fellow assembly members would not be shocked, the audience would be. In general, this civilising force of hypocrisy is a desirable effect of publicity' (Elster 1998: 111). Democratic claims to justice are distinguished by being forced through the medium of public debate, entangling opinions and interests with those of other actors, transforming them in the process into claims for justice and the common good (Young 1997: 65).

It is here that one can pinpoint the importance of media publics to the practical realisation of democratic justice. Even in highly unequal societies, media exposure remains a crucial resource for pressuring powerful institutions to act in accord with publicly accepted norms rather than from narrow private interest. The public exposure of injustices can serve as 'an important means of breaking the cycle by which social and

---

2   This account of democratic communication has clear affinities with Arendt's understanding of the public realm as a space between actors, not as a space of commonality or shared identity, but one of gathering *and* separation (Arendt 1958: 45–53). In this understanding, there are no firm foundations for acting in concert with others apart from those constituted and reconstituted through such action. Solidarities are not pre-formed and discovered, they are formed and transformed through the giving and keeping of promises. This understanding of communicative action maintains plurality by staking communication not on its constative or cognitive register, but on the performative orientation towards obligations, responsibilities and accountability.

economic inequality reinforces political inequality' (Young 2000: 176). Democratic publicity therefore implies channels of media communication that can effectively institutionalise a 'politics of shame', through which public promises and commitments can be monitored and held to account in the future (see Chapter 7). As one element in an institutional complex of plural representation, free expression and rights to participation, media institutions are therefore crucial to the instrumental realisation of normative principles of democracy, equality and social justice (Sen 1999).

Young's account of communicative democracy holds that effective agreements on general issues cannot be staked on the idealisation of communicative consensus. Her affirmation of difference as a resource to be drawn upon in democratic public deliberation is not based on a failure to acknowledge the persistence of structural inequalities. Quite the contrary: her defence of the legitimacy of mechanisms for group representation (Young 1990a: 183–91), for example, indicates a commitment to think through the practical conditions for broadening democratic principles in contexts of structural inequality and systematic discrimination. Furthermore, this acknowledgement of persistent structural inequality informs the argument for a plural conceptualisation of the legitimate forms of democratic representation. This is therefore both a pragmatic and a principled commitment. Rather than the choice between universal consensus and particularistic fragmentation, Young's deconstructive critical theory recasts universality and particularity in terms of translation. In so doing, universality is rethought not in terms of sameness, but in terms of openness, a value that presupposes plurality, implying an understanding of communication as a process of translation across difference (Calhoun 1996: 246–7). Along with other feminist political theorists, Young's work recasts rather than rejects the value of universality, now understood as an 'aspiration' (Butler 1997: 90–1) or 'impulse' (Phillips 1992: 26–8) towards which progressive political action is oriented without presuming that this requires complete transcendence of partial positions (see also Howell 1994).

III (Dis)embodying the public

The arguments of feminist theorists and others about the exclusionary effects of highly rationalist principles of deliberative democracy suggest that the relationship between abstraction and embodiment in conceptualisations of democratic public life needs to be rethought. Habermas' theory of democratic public life rests on a suspicion of forms of political conduct related to representation, where this involves the embodiment and display of personal authority in the presence of an audience. In his original account of the public sphere, abstraction and universality are opposed to embodiment and particularity. This opposition is illustrated by the containment of writing within a circuit of conversation. Representation is hence restricted to the representation of ideas. However, the historical example used by Habermas in *STPS* was dependent not just on books, newspapers and pamphlets as neutral mediums, but upon the formation of a particular culture of print (Warner 1990). This refers to an institutionally located set of dispositions and forms of conduct that enabled print to be incorporated into practices in which it supported the adoption of anonymous modes of disembodied subjectivity. The imaginary disincorporation of authors and readers via the medium of print was made the condition for the transformation of persons into a general public. This achievement depended upon the adoption of a particular rhetoric of personal abstraction, which determined the class-, gender- and race-based exclusivity of the classical liberal public sphere. Some social subjects were defined as irrevocably embodied, and therefore excluded from entry into the sphere of public deliberation: 'the ability to abstract oneself in public discussion has always been an unequally available resource' (Warner 1993: 239).

As already noted, Habermas' restriction of critical publicity to non-theatrical, non-representative self-expression through the medium of discussion implies that action in the public sphere is not constitutive of subjectivity as such. The conceptual separation of material reproduction from symbolic reproduction, system and lifeworld is indicative of an understanding of identity-formation as a process undertaken wholly in the private realm, prior to and outside of the public sphere of rational debate. Accordingly, any attempt to reshape identities through public action is looked upon with deep suspicion, as an index of a backsliding recourse to symbolic forms of representative publicity (Calhoun 1993: 274). In contrast, one can suggest that the role of media as mediums of cultural and political subject-formation can be better understood in terms of the performative generation of cultural identities and political subjectivities (Saccamano 1991: 697–8). This implies broadening out the sense of the public sphere and pluralising it to refer to public *spheres*. This is the task presaged by Negt and Kluge (1993), who develop an understanding of the public sphere as a diffuse medium of cultural democratisation. They extend the notion of the public sphere to include the relationships which constitute the very conditions of possibility for social and individual experience:

Public sphere refers to certain institutions, establishments, activities (e.g. public power, press, public opinion, audience, publicity work, streets, and squares); but at the same time it is also a general social horizon of experience, in which what is really and supposedly relevant for all members of a society is summarised. In this sense the public sphere is a matter of a few professionals (e.g. politicians, editors, officials or federations); on the other it is something that has to do with everybody and which is only realised in the heads of people, a dimension of their consciousness.

(ibid.: 1–2)

This emphasis upon multiple publics is linked to a pluralisation of the modes of public communication through which interests, needs, identities and desires can be legitimately articulated. The reconstitution of public spheres through the structural transformations of media systems has been associated with the emergence of new types of public and political action. The 'utopia of self-abstraction' has been supplanted by a politics of personalised, embodied subjectivity. This pluralisation recasts Habermas' focus on the literary formation of democratic competencies in terms of a cultural public sphere (McGuigan 1998). In contrast to narrowly cognitive and rational understandings of deliberation, this term directs attention to a wider array of affective communicative and expressive practices of popular culture, and to the institutional and social determination of the distribution of the cultural capabilities to engage in public culture.

This all implies that the relationship between abstraction and embodiment is less one of opposition, and more a matter of moving between two different registers. Mass-mediated, pluralised public spheres are characterised by communicative practices that involve a two-way movement between self-abstraction and self-realisation, between universalising and minoritising discourses (Sedgwick 1990). Democratic communication in the public realm cannot be conceptually detached from embodiment, affect or desire. Contemporary forms of identity politics simultaneously affirm particular embodied identities while reaching out to broader identifications in an orientation towards universality without transcendence (Warner 1993: 252). The critique of the ideal of a single public sphere thus disembodies *the* public, understood as a single collective subject made present in a space of assembly. At the same time, it opens up a cultural politics where the representation of ideas is supplemented by a 'politics of presence', in which the representative value of certain irreducibly embodied identities is asserted

(Phillips 1995). The media have become key sites for this sort of cultural action, in both formal politics and popular culture. With the ascendancy of so-called audience democracy, the nature and mediums of democratic accountability and trust have altered: 'Political appeals now depend on the claimed trustworthiness of the principal participants, a claim that displaces institutional trust in favour of trust based on characteristics' (Manin 1997: 123). Effective political communication increasingly depends upon the ability to embody and perform certain sorts of persona credibly (Corner 2000). This argument can, of course, confirm a self-righteous denunciation of the recidivist dumbing-down of rational political discourse. But it can be given an alternative inflection, as indicative of a fundamental cultural democratisation of formal politics that is reshaped by the most intimate characteristics of distanciated mediums of public communications discussed in Chapter 2, through which the norms of the everyday life take on a heightened significance in shaping the conduct of formal public life (Silverstone 1994; Thompson 2000).

The simultaneous disembodiment of a singular public and the heightened importance of the purposeful performance of embodied identities in plural public spheres suggest that contemporary forms of political mobilisation are illustrative of forms of democratic communicative action that are not best thought of by reference to ideals of rational deliberation (Young 2001). For example, the framing of contentious issues by social movements, in particular through tactics aimed at gaining and maintaining media attention, involves a keen awareness of visual and other non-verbal symbolic strategies (Tarrow 1998: 114–16). The dramaturgical dimensions of protest transform the role of public spaces into stages for the projection of movement messages. In addition to purely instrumental objectives, media-oriented protest has an important expressive function for participants, in which the symbolic representation of embodied identities is a crucial element (Halcli 1999: 136–7). In a stronger sense, modern social movements can be theorised not as groups or organisations, but as cumulative 'clusters of political performance' that are sustained by 'public displays of numbers, commitment, unity, and worthiness' (Tilly 1994: 7–8). On this understanding, the analysis of the relationships between popular political mobilisation and democratisation requires an investigation of the production and transformation of spaces for communication in public through which such political action can be pursued.

These arguments suggest the strong sense in which democratic political action might be understood to be 'cultural'. But we are here faced with a dilemma. While it is important to acknowledge that identity-formation is an integral element of public life, there is also the danger of positing this form of cultural politics as the essence of the political as such. For a number of contemporary theorists, culture is political because the formation and transformation of subjectivities are understood to be the very essence of politics. But there are good reasons for not taking solace in the cliché that everything is political (Staeheli and Mitchell forthcoming). The important question is how to understand the articulation of the distinctive rationalities of 'cultural politics' with those of 'political politics' (Gilroy 1996: 36). The importance of the public sphere concept lies in keeping in tension the different modalities of purposeful action without collapsing distinctions whose status is precisely what remains contested. The problem of how to reconcile irreducible imperatives of concentration and plurality, closure and openness, is constitutive of the theoretical problematic implied by the concept of the public sphere: 'Within the concept of the public sphere, there is an unresolved and perhaps unressovable tension, between a tight, authoritative singleness (the public as object of a quest for a universal collective subject or a privileged area of struggle) and a more relaxed, decentred pluralism (publicness as something spread liberally through many irreducibly different collectivties)' (Robbins 1993: xxi). Resolving this problem requires more than an oppositional staging of transcendent consensus versus mutually independent language games of dissensus. It returns us to the theme discussed in Chapter 1, of the deferral and reserved appearance of the public.

As already noted, Habermas' original formulation of the public sphere derived an ideal model from a context (that of historical struggles against the absolutist feudal state) in which the trajectory of democratisation involved the formation of counterpublics outside of the sphere of the state's influence. There is a continuing tendency to presume that the public sphere is properly external to both the state and the market. However, it is questionable whether this understanding can capture the multiple institutional sites through which contemporary public spheres might emerge: 'Given the complex interpenetrations of state and society in late capitalism, one can no longer postulate the ideal of a public sphere which can function outside existing commercial and state institutions and at the same time claim an influential and representative function as forum for oppositional activity and debate' (Felski 1989: 172). There is no *a priori* reason to suppose that public, political action is contained in particular spatial locations or institutional sites (Staeheli 1996). Publics can emerge in any number of contexts: 'they are brought into being not merely outside of and in opposition to the bureaucratic apparatuses of the state but also within those apparatuses

or in varying degrees of quasi-autonomous relations to state bureau-
cracies' (Keane 1984: 235). It is not necessary to imagine that public
spheres exist solely in external opposition to the state or market, or that
the public sphere must form a single unified political will. This is the
crux of Negt and Kluge's elaboration of Habermas' original account.
They argue that there never was one, single model of the public sphere,
but rather a number of contesting counterpublics. Rather than elevate
one model as an ideal, they analyse the contradictions between different
publics and their articulation with different social relations of production, distribution and exchange. The public sphere is extended beyond
mere rational communication, to include the diverse practical forms
through which the meanings of collective existence are expressed,
debated and challenged. The translation between plural counterpublics
and concerted action is, in this account, not guaranteed by formally justifiable principles, but understood as a practical matter contingent on
the machinations of politics.

Negt and Kluge's expanded, pluralistic sense of public spheres as the
formative horizons of experience provides an important impetus
towards addressing the relationship between 'cultural politics' and
'political politics'. To develop this further, it is worth considering
Nancy Fraser's (1997: 89–92) analytical distinction between *weak* and
strong public spheres. This distinction is meant to supplant the rather
static dualism between state and civil society. Weak publics refer to
those activities 'whose deliberative practice consists exclusively in
opinion-formation and does not encompass decision-making'. Strong
publics, more directly connected to institutionalised concentrations of
power, are those activities whose 'discourse encompasses both opinion-
formation and decision-making' (ibid.: 90). The distinction acknowledges the plurality of forms that a public might take, and the different
degrees of influence that they can be expected to exert over different
institutions of power: 'Some are large, authoritative, and able to set the
terms of debate for many of the rest. Others, by contrast, are small, self-
enclosed, and enclaved, unable to make much of a mark beyond their
own borders' (Fraser 1989: 167). Two points are relevant here. First, the
distinction is not meant to imply that so-called enclave publics are
unimportant. Feminist theorists, for example, have argued that counterpublics are crucial for the affirmation of marginalised identities, and
may in turn inform broader, more directly political forms of action. Second, this differentiation between different modalities of public action
guards against the temptation to model all forms of politics on the sovereign state (Brown 1995). To elaborate further the significance of the
distinction between weak and strong publics for an understanding of

the mediated dynamics of democratic politics, we need to return to Habermas.

IV *The withdrawal of the public*

In contrast to the temptation to think of the subjects and sites of democracy in overly concrete terms, Habermas' recently refined procedural vision of radical democracy is based upon an understanding of society as fully dispersed into networks of practices, not gathered together as a mass subject. He rejects the nominalisation of the public as a collective subject, the image of society as a large association, and thinking of society as a present social totality (Habermas 1992: 442–3). Society is only 'embodied' in 'subjectless flows of communication' (Habermas 1996: 486). This means thinking of the public as anonymous, and as having withdrawn into 'democratic procedures and the demanding communicative presuppositions of their implementation' (ibid.). Democratic procedures of opinion-formation, will-formation, binding decisions, and accountability take the vacant place of legitimate power, so that '[t]he idea of popular sovereignty is thereby desubstantialized' (ibid.).

Habermas' procedural turn has also explicitly reconsidered the relationships between civil society and public sphere. It is important not to conflate these two categories. Civil society is 'something like the societal basis for a vital form of communication operating between state and economy as a medium that preserves citizenship itself' (Habermas 1994b: 61). This basis takes the form of intermediary organisations, institutions and patterns of associational life. The public sphere refers more precisely to 'the specific organisation within civil society of social and cultural bases for the development of an effective rational-critical discourse aimed at the resolution of political disputes' (Calhoun 1993: 269). The great strength of Habermas' considerations of civil society and the public sphere is that, in contrast to classical republican models of politics, he does not privilege opinion-formation over the systematic and instrumental dimensions of political action. The importance of the public sphere concept lies not simply in analysing patterns of discourse and identity-formation, but in its implied emphasis on thinking through the ways in which opinions and discourses can be made influential. It is a concept that is primarily oriented towards understanding the conditions for effective leverage by citizens on the actions of the state and other powerful institutions (ibid.: 278).

Habermas' understanding of the relationships between civil society, the public sphere and the exercise of administrative and economic power has been significantly revised in the procedural turn of his recent philosophy of law and democratic legitimacy. He has explicitly taken up Fraser's distinction between weak and strong publics as a means to rethink the relationships between different forms of public discourse. In a more or less explicit acknowledgement of the force of feminist and other critiques of overly formalist and rationalist constructions of the public sphere and communicative action, Habermas now accords considerable importance to weak publics, understood as a 'wild complex' of informal processes of opinion formation: 'The opinion-formation uncoupled from decisions is effected in an open and inclusive network of overlapping, subcultural publics having fluid temporal, social, and substantive boundaries' (Habermas 1996: 307). Weak publics serve a crucial function as realms in which the boundaries between public and private are determined and contested. The distinction refers to two related dimensions of needs interpretation: the determination of the limits of public authority (that is, what will and will not be subject to regulation and policy-making); and the determination of the range of topics open to public debate (that is, what will and will not be thematised as a public issue) (ibid.: 313–14). This formulation is a concession to feminist critiques of Habermas' earlier formulations. The scope of public discussion should not be restricted to those issues considered within the proper purview of state action. Discussing an issue is not identical to interfering in private affairs, but those issues that are reserved for private decision are not necessarily withdrawn from public debate: 'every affair in need of political regulation should be publicly discussed, though not every legitimate object of public discussion will in fact be politically regulated' (ibid.: 313). This might be reformulated in terms of a distinction between political action and a broader sense of public action. Conflating the two dimensions either evacuates the sense of instrumental action and binding decisions from the meaning of the political, or it overextends the model of sovereign state action into all realms of public action.

Habermas' recourse to Fraser's analytical distinction informs a notably more optimistic conceptualisation of the possibilities for the effective democratic oversight of administrative and economic power. As already noted, the theory of communicative action underwrote a 'siege' model of the relationships between lifeworld and system. Lifeworld practices were defined as bulwarks against bureaucratisation and commodification, generating mobilisation to protect the lifeworld from further encroachment by system imperatives. Political mobilisation in this model was understood as a primarily defensive means of putting up 'a democratic dam' against further colonisation (Habermas 1992: 444). This siege model has been replaced by an argument that communicative action in dispersed publics articulates with centres of opinion-formation and decision-making through a series of 'sluices'. In principle, these provide effective critical leverage on economic and political systems (Habermas 1996: 354–9).[3] This sluice model of radical democracy is premised upon a decentred image of society. The category of the public sphere is now conceptualised as an anonymous network of 'streams of public communication' (Habermas 1994b: 92–3). There is no *a priori* restriction placed on the precise content, form or medium of these networks. This networked model of civil society and public life displaces the notion that the public is a concrete, collective subject. It thus forestalls the general objection raised against deliberative models of democracy, by dispensing altogether with the idea that democracy has to be imagined in terms of simulating the mass assembly of the people:

> a deliberative and proceduralist model of democracy does not need to operate with the fiction of a general deliberative assembly [because] the procedural specifications of this model privilege a plurality of modes of association in which all affected can have the right to articulate their point of view. These can range from political parties, to citizens' initiatives, to social movements, to voluntary associations, to consciousness-raising groups, and the like. It is through the interlocking net of these multiple forms of associations, networks, and organisations that an anonymous 'public conversation' results.
>
> (Benhabib 1996: 73–4)

In the course of developing this procedural account of radical democracy, Habermas' earlier suspicion of electronic media has been significantly revised. However, he is still prone to interpreting the detachment of public communication from the concrete presence of an audience in negative terms, as the unwelcome differentiation 'among organisers, speakers, and hearers; arenas and galleries, stage and viewing space'

3   The key to this argument is the claim that constitutional law provides the primary medium through which the different logics of social integration and instrumental system integration are connected, and through which the administrative and economic power is subordinated to the norms of democratic participatory oversight. This argument derives from a longer debate in critical theory concerning the relationships between democracy, law and legitimacy (see Scheuerman 1998).

(Habermas 1996: 363). This is indicative of a residual attachment to a dichotomy between active participation and passive spectatorship. Alternatively, we might instead consider media and communications as opening up spaces for *mediated deliberation* (Thompson 1995: 125–34). At its simplest, this refers to the re-embedding of mass-circulated symbolic materials into contexts of face-to-face dialogical interaction. In this way, modern media and communications technologies vastly expand the range of information, ideas and opinions made available to larger numbers of ordinary people than ever before. This is one of the main contributions of modern communications technologies in expanding the scope and power of public action. However, the concept of mediated deliberation suggests a stronger emphasis upon the necessarily mediated character of any and all deliberative practice (ibid.: 270). If we take the idea of networks of public communication seriously, there is no need to imagine that mediated communication installs a dichotomy between active deliberation amongst co-present actors and passivity: 'There are no good grounds for assuming that the process of reading a book or watching a television programme is, by itself, less conducive to deliberation than engaging in face-to-face conversation with others' (ibid.: 256). The decisive question is what sorts of practices different symbolic materials are embedded in. In large, complex societies,

> democracy depends on the possibility of a critical public discourse which escapes the limits of face-to-face interaction. This means, in part, finding ways to make the space transcending mass media supportive of public life. It also means developing social arrangements in which local discussions are both possible and able to feed into larger discussions mediated both by technology and by gatherings of representatives.
>
> (Calhoun 1989: 68–9)

One concrete example of this sort of mediating practice would be James Fishkin's (1995) deliberative polling, which combines public opinion sampling techniques with practices of participatory deliberation. Another is the form of multimedia educational broadcasting initiative discussed in Chapter 7. These examples indicate that the idea of mediated deliberation captures the extent to which the sort of civil, reciprocal, rule-bound talk often idealised by theorists of deliberative democracy is in fact dependent on the provision of an infrastructure of technologies, institutions and social and cultural norms that cannot be bought into existence through conversation alone (Schudson 1997).

The concept of mediated deliberation reminds us that the main emphasis when assessing different media practices should be upon, first, the availability of the technological means of communication, and, second, the determination of access to the capabilities required to engage in streams of discourse that effectively articulate with centres of decision-making (Garnham 1999). The analytical distinction between weak and strong public spheres, and the idea of mediated deliberation, both imply rethinking the modes of participation through which citizens engage in democratic deliberation, and in particular, they open up new ways of thinking about the spatialities and scales of the networked public sphere theorised by Habermas. It is to this issue that we turn in the next section.

V *The spatialities of mediated citizenship*

One of the fields where Habermas' emphasis on the linkages between the cultural conditions of citizenship and the strategic rationalities of political action has been most usefully developed is in media and communications theory. The public sphere concept has been used to analyse and evaluate the ways in which the organisation of mass communications, and broadcasting in particular, has served as a medium of political citizenship, for inculcating broader habits of sociability, and for expanding the scope of care networks (Dahlgren 1995; Murdock 1993; Scannell 1989). The notion of the public sphere directs attention to an analysis of media in terms of 'the range of information the media make available to individual human minds, the range of connections they bring to light, the particular social practices and collective rituals by which they organise our days and ways' (Schudson 1995: 25). Understood in this sense, the public sphere concept has been used to develop understandings of media citizenship that focus upon the relationships between media and the practical capacities of participation in public life, broadly conceived. Media citizenship is defined according to overlapping rights to information, rights to receive and register opinions, and rights to fair and diverse representation. This idea of media citizenship raises a set of questions concerning the structuring of access to material resources (money, free time), symbolic resources (languages, idioms, meanings), and social resources (membership of social relationships, or social capital) necessary for participation in the cultural practices (see Murdock 1992). The emphasis on media citizenship moves beyond binaries of production and consumption, textual meaning and creative use, to focus upon the institutional dimensions through which cultural value is produced, reproduced and contested. It fits in with a broader range of critical media analysis that deployed ideas about the public sphere in order to gain critical leverage on the institutional restructuring of British and European media systems and cultural policy in the 1980s and 1990s. However, there is a tendency in these debates to conflate the idea of the public sphere with a specific institutional, economic and regulatory configuration of public service broadcasting (Collins 1993; Curran 1996). In turn, media restructuring has often been understood in terms of an opposition between citizenship (where viewers and listeners are addressed as members of a public) and consumerism (where they are addressed as private individuals).

The most sustained application of theories of the public sphere to the analysis of the changing dimensions of media citizenship is in the work of Nicholas Garnham. His interpretation of media globalisation is premised on the assumption that the territorial scope of political and economic power must be matched by the territorial scope of a singular universal media public. The public sphere concept, he argues, necessarily implies a strong concept of universality, understood in a procedural sense as a minimum set of shared discursive rules necessary for democratic communication (see Garnham 2000). On these grounds, globalisation is seen as leading to a disempowering fragmentation of the public sphere, due to the combination of three related processes: the restructuring of the production and exchange of culture on a global scale; the restructuring of the social relations of cultural production and consumption, leading to the increasing privatisation of the provision and consumption of culture; and the restructuring of the relationship between political and cultural power, with the decline of public interest models of regulation and the transformation of citizenship around discourses of consumerism (Garnham 1997: 56–7). From the assumption that democratic citizenship requires a singular and universal public sphere coterminous with the territorial scale at which effective political power is exercised, Garnham deduces that 'the process of cultural globalisation is increasingly de-linking cultural production and consumption from a concrete polity and thus a realizable politics' (ibid.: 70). Consequently, globalisation not only disconnects media systems from the hollowed out nation-state, but in so doing also generates a feeling of powerlessness, expressed in the rise of identity politics, understood as a symptom of the evacuation of 'the field of established national representative democracy' (Garnham 1995: 373). Conceptually, Garnham's argument runs together an assumption about the spatial scope of power, which he considers to be universal on the grounds that capitalism is now a global system, with an argument for a universal set of norms embodied in a singular institutional structure of mass media:

> the problem is to construct systems of democratic accountability integrated with media systems of matching scale that occupy the same social space as that over which economic and political decisions will make an impact. If the impact is universal, then both the political and media systems must be universal. In this sense a series of autonomous public spheres is not sufficient. There must be a single public sphere, even if we might want to conceive of it as made up of a series of subsidiary public spheres, each organised around its own public political sphere, media system, and set of forms and interests.
>
> (Garnham 1993: 264)

Garnham's evaluative opposition between the ideal of a universal and singular public sphere versus the pluralistic fragmentation triggered by globalisation depends upon an unquestioned assumption that political power is naturally territorialised. It therefore presumes that the key issue in assessing discourses of globalisation is a choice between different areal scales at which power should be subjected to democratic oversight, rather than thinking of globalisation as the occasion for reassessing how we conceptualise the spatiality of scale – in networked rather than areal terms.[4] If the scales at which social integration and cultural engagement are modulated have increasingly become distinct from the scales of national political participation, then this might open up new possibilities for political action, not least at the national scale itself (Staeheli 1999). In order to avoid the rather glum prognosis that Garnham's analysis presents, we might follow Keane's (1995: 8) suggestion that the public sphere is best understood as 'a complex mosaic of differently sized, overlapping, and interconnected public spheres'. Elaborating on this, Keane distinguishes between three scales of public sphere: micro-public spheres, existing at a subnational level, and containing from just a handful to tens of thousands of people; meso-public spheres, at the national level and containing millions of participants; and macro-public spheres, at an international scale (ibid.: 9–16).[5] In

4   The argument here is heavily indebted to Low (1997).
5   There is a degree of inconsistency in Keane's schema, since he conflates spatial scale with numerical scale. This runs counter to the full implications of his networked model of communication. Spatially extensive public networks might include large numbers or small numbers of people. The key variables are the durability of networks, the extent to which they are institutionally embedded, and the ways they exercise influence.

contrast to the assumption that political power is always exercised within a territorialised power-container of one scale or another, Keane argues that the conceptual relationships between media and democracy should be based on a networked conception of political power. The power of large-scale organisations, like states and corporations, depends on 'complex, molecular networks of everyday power relations' (1991: 146). This means that power is much less consolidated, centred or coherent than is often supposed by areal conceptions of scale. And it follows that the 'often uncoordinated and dispersed character of state power makes it more susceptible to the initiatives of social movements and citizen groups, backed by countervailing networks of communication, which change prevailing codes and practice the art of "divide and rule" from below' (ibid.: 144–5).

From this capillary perspective on power, conceptualisations that idealise unified and territorially bounded media publics are ill suited to assessing the progressive potential of contemporary transformations in the spatial organisation of media and communications. They underestimate the potential of a multiplicity of networked spaces of communicative practice to induce changes in organisations and political institutions. This suggests that Garnham's oppositional formulation of the main questions facing theories of media and democracy needs to be rethought. The fundamental issue is not whether effective democratic media publics can be constituted at the same global level to match the jump of scale by capital and by administrative and regulatory authorities. It is, rather, whether and how actors embedded at particular territorial scales are able to mobilise support and resources through spatially extensive networks of engagement in order to pursue their interests and objectives at home, as it were (see Cox 1998). It is this issue that is explored in greater depth in Chapters 5, 6 and 7.

VI Conclusion: dissolving legitimacy

This chapter has argued that the constitutive relationship between conventions of democratic discourse and acts of representation requires a conceptualisation of the public sphere as a range of institutionalised processes of public communication. Stretching out the concept of the public implies that the media need, in fact, to be decentred from an evaluation of the relationships between the public sphere and communication: 'The media do not constitute the core of a critical media theory' (Negt 1978: 64). Habermas' procedural account of the subjectless streams of public communication redirects our attention to the fact that the vitality of any public sphere does not simply depend on structures of media organisation, ownership and use, but rests on the existence of a plurality of modes of social organisation and association. This also directs us away from the search for a theoretical resolution to the problem of democratic legitimacy, towards an analysis of the ways in which democratic politics is practised through contested claims to legitimacy.

The continuing salience of the public sphere concept depends upon revising some cherished assumptions that often shape academic discourses about media and democracy. These include assumptions about what counts as rationality, acknowledging the diverse modes through which public issues can be problematised and addressed. It is also important to affirm the practical existence of counterpublics with different norms of access, conduct, participation and representation. These challenge a class- and gender-biased model of publicity that continues to underwrite ideals of undistorted communication, disembodied reason and universalistic interests as the singular form of public discourse (Fraser 1997: 75). In this respect, the public value of popular media culture lies in making visible issues, identities and needs that are not readily aired in more formal arenas of public debate and decision-making. The great strength of the public sphere concept is that it broadens the definition of what counts as politics beyond a narrowly ends-oriented focus, to a wider conception of politics as a process of determining the subjects of concerted public action. This refers to a dual focus, on the subjects of politics in terms of *what* is problematised and contested, and on the subjects of politics in terms of the *who* of political action and debate (which identities, which collective actors, which forms of conduct). This latter sense is, in turn, divided, since subject-formation implies both a being-subject-of and being-subject-to. With this complex, doubled sense of the formation of public subjectivities we are, however, moving into a different conceptual terrain.

Habermas' radical thick proceduralism proposes an image of a society united around shared identification with a set of political rights, and still depends on a clear separation between the good and the right, ethics from morality, culture from politics. Issues of ethical substance are still supposed to be left at the door of public spaces of deliberation. They are crucial to the formation of the deliberating self, but not supposed to be thematised as a subject of public debate as such. It is open to question whether conceptions of the good and conceptions of right can be kept separate quite so easily as Habermas supposes (see Connolly 1999). Indeed, Habermas' proceduralism secretes a considerable slice of substantive content, not least the presumption of minimal economic and social equality as the prerequisites for participation. The presence of these substantive conceptions of the good in Habermas' procedural account of democracy does not invalidate this approach. It does, however, complicate his consistent argument that the lifeworld contexts out of which a liberal political culture emerges are spontaneously produced: 'Political culture is made up of a delicate fabric of mentalities and conviction that can neither be invented nor manipulated through administrative measures' (Habermas 1994b: 47). The assumption that the cultural conditions of citizenship cannot be properly managed or governed from above without irreparable damage being done to the cultural capacities and moral resources of citizens will be critically addressed in the following chapter, which works more fully through the normative implications of the doubled-up sense of democratic subject-formation alluded to here.

4

Technologies of citizenship: assembling media publics

What defines a relationship of power is that it is a mode of action which does not act directly and immediately on others. Instead it acts upon their actions: an action upon an action, on existing actions or on those which may arise in the present or the future.

Michel Foucault (1983: 220)

I Formations of autonomy

Habermas provides one way of thinking about democracy as a cultural project, dependent upon institutional practices that sustain particular patterns of social interaction and individual competencies. His social theory and political philosophy depend on holding fast to an understanding that coercion-free communication is, at least in principle, possible. He has suggested that the formal idealisation of communicative action should not be assumed to be a picture of actual social relations, but rather is a means of constructing methodological fictions. These are useful because they make visible 'the scarcity of those functionally necessary resources on which processes of deliberative opinion- and will-formation significantly depend' (Habermas 1996: 326). The key question facing Habermas' critical theory is, then, the extent to which actually existing patterns of power, communication and decision-making are best evaluated with reference to an ideal of undistorted, coercion-free communication oriented towards the reaching of consensus.

The strongest objection to Habermas' reconstruction of the principles of democratic legitimacy casts doubt on both the methodological and normative utility of his idealisation of communication, on the grounds that it represents a fundamental misunderstanding of the nature of power. This objection depends on reading Foucault's analysis of power as arguing that there are no coercion-free social relations, and that all forms of action, not least communicative action, involve power relations. Foucault and Habermas have become iconic figures for a fundamental dispute in contemporary social theory over whether or not conceptualisations of the public use of reason are rational ideals of democratic legitimisation, or ever so subtle forms of social control.

Foucault is often read as providing an unrelentingly pessimistic account of modernity, one which sees all social life saturated with power relations which are beyond legitimisation, and only liable to destabilisation through incessant acts of resistance. The saliency of this objection depends upon how power is specified as a concept. The dominant social science conceptualisation of power is a positive, descriptive sense of *power as a capacity* of actors to achieve certain ends. In this understanding, power is primarily thought of in terms of quantifiable amounts of material and symbolic resources held by individual or collective subjects. Distinct from this notion of power as a capacity is the more explicitly normative understanding of *power as a right* to rule over others, connected to the idea of power as action-in-concert. This idea is inherently tied to questions of how rule can be rendered legitimate. It gives significant importance to communication as the equitable medium through which the consent of those ruled to the authority of their rulers is mutually sought and secured. Hindess (1996) argues that Foucault's conceptualisation of power is distinct from both of these understandings, of power as capacity and of power as right. Foucault effectively brackets the question of the legitimacy of power, asking instead about the practices, rationalities and technologies of different power relations and the effects they produce. At the same time, this set of questions displaces the centred human subject from the analysis of power, no longer assuming power as a capacity wielded by subjects, but rather thinking of different forms of subjectivity as effects of the variable operations of power.

Foucault's perspective on power enables us to approach in new ways the problem of democratic competence, one of Dahl's shadows of democratic theory. In Habermas' work, the development of the competency to act as a free subject in the public sphere is dependent on the development and sustenance of a private realm where individuals are constructed as citizens through intersubjective interaction that is uncontaminated by systematic logics. Habermas is quite adamant that a liberal political culture cannot be organised. The resources upon which deliberative political communication depend 'form and regenerate spontaneously', and the lifeworld structures upon which a genuinely autonomous public sphere depends 'elude legal regulation, administrative control, or political steering' (Habermas 1996: 359). The fundamental disjuncture between a Habermasian conception of power and a Foucauldian one therefore lies in different understandings of the autonomy of ethical and political agents. In Habermas, consent is normatively valued when a free subject freely gives it. Foucault, amongst others, leads us towards a rather more ambivalent understanding of consensual practices, as combining the assertion of subjectivity with subjection to externally derived norms. If democracy is understood as requiring citizens who have learned to regulate their conduct as autonomous moral agents, and who can therefore be governed on the basis of their own informed consent, then there are good reasons to suspect that Habermas' account of the spontaneous formation of these capabilities is neither empirically nor normatively sustainable. What is needed is an account of how free and autonomous actors are formed and maintained (Calhoun 1993: 272). Foucault's work remains pertinent to these themes because it reinterprets the foundational relationship between freedom and obedience derived from Kant's account of the public use of reason (Kant 1970: 54–60). Foucault focuses upon the historical conditions of knowledge, power and ethical self-relation through which it is possible for people to be constituted as subjects of self-knowledge, as moral subjects, and as possible subjects of freedom (Foucault 1986: 32–50). That these are no longer considered innate capacities does not mean that they are ideological chimera. Rather, it implies shifting the analytical focus towards the contingent working up of these capacities, on analysing their conditions of possibility in a historical-genealogical register rather than a foundational one.[1]

Foucault is therefore useful for an analysis of the public cultures of democracy because he is concerned with the intersections between administrative power and the formation of modern forms of free subjectivity. In particular, he helps us approach in less tragic ways the fundamental 'paradox of autonomy' that haunts democratic theory (Post 1993: 672–3). This paradox turns on the intimation that, on the one hand, the value of autonomy is by definition dependent on being *attained* by a free subject through its own conscious effort, while, on the other hand, this autonomy is something necessarily *ascribed* to subjects in various institutional contexts (and not others). The ascription of autonomy *as if* it were an attainment is the paradoxical precondition of democratic self-government (ibid.).[2] Foucault's utility derives from his attention to this latter aspect, to the regulative character of modern practices of citizenship. This theme is developed most fully in recent

1 Rather than taking a static idealisation of the autonomy of moral agents as the measure of the legitimacy of actually existing arrangements, the positive norm governing Foucault's critical analysis is one that assigns value to the capacity to be normative in the sense described by Canguilhem (1991; Macherey 1992), that is, in terms of a capacity to adjust to new circumstances.

2 This paradox of autonomy cuts across a simple opposition between democracy and liberalism that informs other accounts of the paradoxes of democracy (for example, Mouffe 2000; Popper 1966).

work on Foucault's elusive discussions of governmentality. Governmentality-studies emphasises how the conditions of democratic citizenship and participation are regulated through an array of cultural technologies (Flew 1996). In this work, liberalism is defined as a political rationality characterised by the limitation of centralised, coercive power, opening up a separation between state and society (Bennett 1998). The delimitation of a sphere of autonomy is, however, matched by a persistent drive to govern-at-a-distance the conditions of this autonomous realm of the social. On this account, liberal forms of rule are characterised by a will to empower, illustrated by the proliferation of programmes and policies aimed at assembling populations into capable, self-governing democratic subjects (Cruikshank 1999).

One particular focus of the governmentality approach has been upon the forms of knowledge that make citizenship a knowable object of policy intervention and public deliberation. In this focus upon practices of imaginary representation, one finds the point at which governmentality studies can be reopened to a set of questions regarding legitimacy, accountability and symbolic power that a more fully political sense of representation provides, and which are too often closed down in this sort of approach. The predominant Foucauldian approach to understanding power tends to avoid analysis of any consideration of the normative specificity of democratic politics, a reduction implicit in the insistence on treating power only in terms of the materiality of its effects (see McNay 1998). Following this line of argument, this chapter pursues a re-reading of Foucault in relation to the problematic of indeterminate media power, arguing that this provides an entry point for developing an alternative understanding of the relationships between democratic citizenship, culture and norms of freedom and autonomy. Examining the distinctive liberal rationality of media technologies as mediums of citizenship might lead us towards a more fruitful understanding of the paradoxes and indeterminacies that define democratic rationalities of power, an emphasis too frequently lacking in extant Foucauldian analyses.

II *The dark side of liberal democracy*

Like both Lefort and Habermas, Foucault's understanding of modernity turns on the discernment of a decisive mutation in the structure of political authority in eighteenth- and nineteenth-century Europe.[3] This

---

3 See Slater (2002) for a critique of the tendency to locate this shift in political rationalities within a narrowly contained narrative of Western progress.

is the shift from kingly prerogative to popular sovereignty. However, the emergence of new regimes of visibility and publicity is given a much more sinister interpretation by Foucault. He reads modern forms of public culture not as an index of the rise of democratic egalitarianism and the emancipatory triumph of reason, but as the moment when new forms of surveillance and sequestration replace the spectacle of absolutist power with much more intimate, insidious forms of control. Foucault's earliest studies of the history of medicine, psychiatry and the human sciences provide an alternative history of the relationships between knowledge and modern ideologies of progress, enlightenment and reason. The focus of these studies is upon the practices that made possible the emergence of particular understandings of the human as a *subject* of scientific knowledge, political freedom and moral action as well as an *object* of scientific, political and moral programmes. In this work, Foucault developed an enormously influential account of the formation of rational subjectivity through the discursive identification and practical sequestration of various stigmatised populations (the mad, the delinquent and the criminal).

The relationship between conceptions of rational subjectivity and conceptions of political subjectivity is often only implicit in this early work. These connections become quite explicit with Foucault's turn to the analysis of power from the late 1960s, culminating in *Discipline and Punish* (1978; see also Foucault 2000). Foucault's account of the historical mutations in the forms through which power was exercised and represented in the course of modern penal reform reveals a distinctive understanding of the nature of modern liberal rationalities of rule. Modernity is inaugurated with the move from modes of power that directly apprehended the bodies of subjects through public spectacles of absolutist authority such as torture, to less obviously corporeal forms of power that depend on the intense calculation of a 'whole play of spaces' (Foucault 1978: 177). This interpretation of modern political enlightenment as turning on a decisive shift from the public display of power to the anonymous exercise of power is linked to an account of subject-formation in terms of the spatial containment of subjects, ensuring the relationship between surveillance and self-regulation. Discipline depends on the development of physical infrastructures in which people's activities can be monitored in minute detail. It partitions, encloses and codifies space, enabling the detailed management of conduct by organising the movement of bodies in space and through time. It is therefore exemplified by various spaces of enclosure (Deleuze 1992a), such as the school, the hospital, the factory, the asylum or the prison.

Foucault's genealogy of liberal reformist modes of punishment, rehabilitation and judgement is related to a broader questioning of models
of rational, deliberative and contractual social relations. He counterposes two views of power, a contract-coercion model that is concerned
with the normative relationships between legitimacy and illegitimacy,
and one which is concerned solely with relationships between struggle
and submission (Foucault 1980: 92). From the latter perspective, modern discourses of right appear not as realisations of inherent human
capacities for freedom, but as instruments of domination and subjugation. The consensual legitimacy of modern rule is seen as a ruse hiding
a more sinister transformation in the effectiveness of power (ibid.:
95–6). The shift from a form of power that is manifested before its subjects and applied directly to the body, to one based on norms of public
reason, marks a mutation that is all the more effective because of its
very invisibility (Foucault 1978: 131). *Discipline and Punish* provides an
unsettling interpretation of modern understandings of rights, justice
and law:

> Historically, the process by which the bourgeoisie became in the
> course of the eighteenth century the politically dominant class was
> masked by the establishment of an explicit, coded and formally
> egalitarian juridical framework, made possible by the organisation
> of a parliamentary, representative regime. But the development and
> generalisation of disciplinary mechanisms constituted the other,
> dark side of these processes. The general juridical form that
> guaranteed a system of rights that were egalitarian in principle was
> supported by these tiny, everyday, physical mechanisms, by all
> those systems of micro-power that are essentially non-egalitarian
> and asymmetrical that we call disciplines. And although in a
> formal way, the representative regime makes it possible, directly or
> indirectly, with or without relays, for the will of all to form the
> fundamental authority of sovereignty, the disciplines provide, at
> the base, a guarantee of the submission of forces and bodies. The
> real, corporal disciplines constituted the foundation of the formal,
> juridical liberties.
>
> (ibid.: 222)

What is most interesting about this interpretation is the extent to which it
echoes the classical Marxist distrust of bourgeois rights almost exactly,
seeing these as merely superficial coverings for deeper, more real power
relations. It is certainly quite plausible to read Foucault's account of disciplinary power in this vein, not least by conflating it with a Gramscian

understanding of hegemony, lacking the explicit class content perhaps, but still emphasising an essential continuity across different modes of domination. In *Discipline and Punish*, Foucault strongly implied that apparent changes in the mechanisms of power made no real difference to actual relations of subjugation. This erases any sense of significant change in the exercise of power, flattening all modes of rule to Manichean processes of domination and resistance. There are, however, reasons to suppose that the Gramscian recuperation of Foucault is a little too neat. Foucault's analytics of power does, after all, accord considerable importance to changing *forms* of power, and evacuates any specific content, in the shape of a particular social subject, from the operations of power. This complicates the superstructural tenor of the above citation. Rather than thinking of different modes of power as either direct substitutes for one another or essentially complementary, Foucault argued elsewhere that the task of political theory should be to 'cut off the King's head' (1986: 63), that is, to rethink the relationships between different modalities of power as essentially heterogeneous and contingent. Instead of supposing that the problematic of sovereignty can be replaced wholly by an analysis of discipline, Foucault proposed instead that there is a disjunctive relationship between the migration of sovereignty into the body of the people and the emergence of disciplinary techniques of power. Modern juridical notions of power and rights, in which power is understood negatively, are intimately related to a technical, positive and productive model of power (1980: 104–5). If the principal mode of sovereign power in modern societies is 'the people' and the 'delegative power of each citizen', then networks of disciplinary power 'assure the cohesion of this same body' (ibid.: 106). It is quite possible to read such formulations as arguing that all forms of resistance, dissent or opposition are always anticipated and co-opted by power. Hence, it is not unusual to find Foucault invoked, both positively and negatively, as a theorist of entrapment (Sinfield 1992: 38–51), where all forms of subversive activity are already anticipated by the system and therefore reinscribe the reproduction of power relations. This interpretation of Foucault tends to imply that the operation of power is always modelled on the absolutist state, assuming that it is centred, unitary and purposeful. Further, it assumes that power relations are shaped in the form of a tight circle of containment, rather than being fissured and open to new possibilities.

The dominant register of *Discipline and Punish* renders discourses of right and practices of discipline in terms of a simple dialectic, whereby the second term effectively negates the putative value of the former. The normative problems that this account raises, not least for Foucault's own critical practice, have been well rehearsed. I want to suggest that, from the perspective of subsequent work on ethics and government, it is more likely to be in the true spirit of Foucault's fugitive political imagination to suppose that in raising the question of the *relationship* between reason, right and modern discipline, he was recommending an analysis of the antagonistic dynamics of sovereignty and surveillance, rather than a surface and depth analytics (see Baker 1994). At the very least, and irrespective of Foucault's own vacillations on these issues, his consistent affirmation of the possibilities of resistance to power sits uneasily with the denigration of legal and political rights as illusory, since more often than not resistance and refusal take the form of rights-based struggles. Again, from one interpretation, the articulation of political struggles through the discourse of rights might only confirm the always already captured status of such struggles. However, such a self-confirming reading only works if one refuses to acknowledge the constitutively indeterminate nature of the democratic discourse of rights (see Lefort 1986: 239–306, 1988: 7–45). This indeterminacy derives in particular from the symbolic register of rights-talk. The ease with which Foucault's understanding of power can be reduced to a refined version of social control theory (see Lacombe 1996) is an index of his own inadequate acknowledgement of this dimension of modern power: 'While there is a submerged recognition of the symbolic indeterminacy of democratic forms in parts of Foucault's work, his conceptualisation of power primarily in terms of its material effects results in a reduction of democracy to its *de facto* functions and in an overestimation of its disciplinary effects' (McNay 1998: 225). The analytics of discipline too easily conflates the specifically *normative* dimensions of democratic rights (which involve the conditional definition of norms) with a generic model of automatically effective *normalisation* (understood as successful the enforcement of norms).

One way of saving Foucault's dark image of political modernity from itself, and in particular of resisting the implication that there is no significant qualitative transformation in the nature of power as its forms change, is by reference to Giddens' (1985: 10) analytic distinction between the scope and intensity of rule. On this understanding, the diffusion of disciplinary modes of power extends the scope of power: it enables superordinate actors to intervene in more and more areas of the lives of those subject to their rule. However, the intensity of rule is significantly diminished in the process: the sanctions that can be exercised to secure compliance to rule do not involve the direct application of repressive legal sanctions or physical force. This tension between the scope and intensity of rule draws out the extent to which, if disciplinary

power refers behaviour to norms and is exercised by positively governing conduct rather than constraining an essentially free individuality,
then it must be understood as open to unpredictable changes, rather
than always contained within a circuit of subversion and incorporation.

III *The loosening up of power*

Foucault's counterhistories of the Enlightenment reorient understanding of the changes in modes of publicity and representation that both
Habermas and Lefort consider to inaugurate democratic models of
legitimacy. Foucault provides a decidedly darker interpretation of these
changes. For him, the emergence of modern forms of democratic rule,
based on rights, the rule of law and putatively liberal state forms, is
underwritten by dispersed networks that discipline the subjects of
democratic rights. Rather than accepting the self-image of liberalism as
being founded by a retreat of power from civil society, science and personal life, Foucault presents an account in which the formal separation
of public and private spheres serves as the occasion for the multiplication of new modes of power and for their extension into all facets of
everyday life. Whereas for Habermas, subjects emerge fully formed out
of an integral lifeworld context of intersubjectivity untainted by administrative power, for Foucault the liberal division between public and
private, and the appearance of a self-limiting administrative mode of
power, is the effect of the operation of a generalised logic of disciplinary power that shapes the attributes and aptitudes of human
subjects in minute detail. However gloomy this image might appear, it
does contain an important corrective to the notion that the subjects of
modern understandings of citizenship are spontaneously formed in
intersubjective contexts, but without supposing that the shaping of
citizen attributes is solely a matter of conscious effort by the state.

While the Foucault of the mid-1970s seems to offer an image of rights
as merely formal, and essentially illusory, a means for more effectively
exercising domination, it is important to point up the limitations in the
disciplinary understanding of modern rule in order to grasp properly
what is most distinctive about the shift from discipline to the analysis of
governmentality in Foucault's later work (McNay 1994: 85–132). This
latter idea should not be collapsed into the disciplinary understanding
of power. Foucault's work subsequent to *Discipline and Punish*, on sexuality, ethics and government, is indicative of a move beyond the idea
that power is best understood in terms of the 'hostile engagement of
forces'. The post-disciplinary analytics of power focuses much more

upon power in terms of 'games of freedom', and shows a heightened
sensitivity to the differences that characterise different forms of power
relations. Emphasising the variable forms of power underscores the
extent to which understandings of power in Foucault's work are related
to the analysis of the variable configurations of subjects, spaces and technologies. Foucault's later work is marked by a differentiation of forms of
power according to the spatial and numerical scale of their operation,
and this implies a significant loosening up of the tightly contained model
of subject-formation that subsists in models of effective disciplinary
subjection.

The idea of governmentality connects the detailed regulation of individual conduct with the regulation of whole populations, linking the
micro-domains of individual behaviour to the macro-domains of large
institutions. It is crucial that this connection not be thought of simply
as the extension of disciplinary practices over larger scales. Governmentality implies a different spatial configuration of rationalities, technologies and subjects from that characteristic of disciplinary practices.
In turn, it is a concept that, in principle at least, implies a less coherent
fit between programmes and actual practices of subject-formation: 'I
intend this concept of "governmentality" to cover the whole range of
practices that constitute, define, organise, and instrumentalize the
strategies that individuals in their freedom can use in dealing with each
other' (Foucault 1997: 300). To understand the difference that governmentality introduces into understandings of power and subjectivity, it is
important to grasp the contrasting spatial imaginations that underwrite
Foucault's accounts of discipline and government. The exemplary figure
for the proliferation of the disciplinary of power is Jeremy Bentham's
design for a morally reforming prison, the Panopticon (Foucault 1978:
195–228). This is interpreted as indicative of a broader logic of
reformist rule, in which a precise arrangement of physical space secures
the automatic, depersonalised and anonymous operation of power-
relations through the structured arrangement of vision. The Panopticon
is a 'diagram' of practices for the training of individuals as self-regulating,
reforming masters of their own conduct.

The Panopticon is a model for governing-at-a-distance. Power operates through self-regulation rather than by the direct application of
force or coercion to the body. However, the disciplining of bodies as the
means of changing conduct is dependent on the continuous supervision
within the spatial and temporal range allowed by technologies of visual
surveillance. If hypostatised into a general theory of modern power, the
diagrammatic conception presents a far too simple picture of the seam-
less operation of coherent disciplinary effects. Rather than considering

'complete and austere institutions' as expressing the essence of disciplinary power, they might be best thought of as maximising disciplinary
power (Giddens 1984: 153–8). For example, outside of locales of sequestration, the activities of individuals are less prone to detailed regulation
and monitoring. It is also likely that the operations of disciplinary
power in any one context will be overdetermined by the trajectories of
subjects through different institutional sites in the course of everyday
life. The argument that the discourse of rights conceals domination is
dependent on a particular spatialisation of power, one that works
through the metaphorical extension of monitorial power, so that any
and all forms of apparently autonomous action are seen as the effects of
highly efficient mechanisms of surveillance. But the fact that the territorial consolidation of the modern state is associated with the emergence of rights of citizenship indicates that the extension of rule over
space involves a significant reordering of the relationships between
subjectivity and power (Held 1989a). The increase in state capacity
associated with disciplinary institutions and administrative procedures
implies a relinquishing of tight control over subjects and a more co-
operative form of power relations, opening up new forms of relationship between state and populations premised on the capacity of human
subjects to act as agents (Giddens 1981: 171). The emergence of disciplinary subjectivity is as much the contingent outcome of social
struggles and the adjustment to problems of co-ordination of rule as it
is the automatic unfolding of a panoptic logic or the dialectic of bureaucratic rationalisation (Giddens 1984: 145–61).

Rather than making the model of discipline into the general formula
for modern power, Foucault's focus on the historically variable relationships between subjects, spaces and technologies should direct attention
to the different ways in which power is exercised in particular configurations to different effects (Driver 1994). The effects of power are likely
to be differentiated according to the geographical scale over which sub-
jectification is organised; the levels of technological sophistication
characteristic of different modes of power; and the degree of spatial
confinement characteristic of different practices (Hannah 1998). The
spatial modalities of social practices constitute power relations differently, in terms of the reach, scope and intensity of actions that are made
possible (Allen 1999). The relationship between micro-regulation in disciplinary spaces and the extensive administration of whole populations
is unpredictable. Subsequent to *Discipline and Punish*, Foucault distinguished between two poles for understanding how 'power over life' is
deployed (Foucault 1979: 139). Disciplines exercise the precise, localised
and detailed management of individualised bodies (for example,

schools, barracks, prisons). They are mediums for an 'anatamo-politics of the human body'. On the other hand, regulatory controls are more extensive mediums of a 'bio-politics of the population'. Discipline and regulation are therefore differentiated according to spatial and numerical scale, and in turn according to a fundamental difference in the intensity and scope of rule characteristic of each. Anatamo-politics works in contexts where the number of subjects 'is small [. . .] and the space limited and confined' (Deleuze 1988: 72). Bio-politics, in contrast, aims not to impose conduct, but to administer life (ibid.: 137), and takes as its object a large and diffuse population dispersed in a space that is 'spread out and open' (ibid.: 72). The distinction underscores the point that any analysis of modes of rule should consider the difference that specific configurations of space, subjects and technologies make to the ways in which power realises effects.

The ideas of bio-politics and regulation indicate a step towards a more varied account of modern power, in which discipline is understood as one element in an array of political rationalities that distinguish modern societies (Foucault 1991: 101–3). Government does not refer to the direct regulation of subjects in specialised locales. It involves the attempt to shape the general conditions of daily life of whole populations. It is not the intensive management of bodies in time and space, but the general regulation of dispositions at an actual distance. The development of the theme of governmentality therefore marks a significant revision of the previous image of the self-policing subject wholly defined by the operations of a superordinate disciplinary apparatus. This is evidenced by Foucault's consideration of the theme of freedom in his later work on ethics, sexuality and political rationalities. The emphasis on rethinking the conditions of possibility of freedom is evident in the analysis of the historical emergence of various technologies of the self, 'which permit individuals to effect, by their own means, a certain number of operations on their own bodies, on their souls, on their own thoughts, on their own conduct, and this in a manner so as to transform themselves, and to attain a certain state of perfection, of happiness, of purity, of supernatural power, and so on' (Foucault 1993: 203). Foucault's excavation of 'modalities of the relation to the self' is explicitly distinguished from the earlier concern with punitive rationalities and the formation of domains of knowledge (Foucault 1985: 3–13). Government refers to a set of processes in which the operation of power over others is connected to the ways in which individuals conduct themselves as free subjects. Power is recast as 'a set of actions upon other actions' (Foucault 1983: 220). On this understanding, to govern 'is to structure the possible field of actions of others' (ibid.: 221). If government implies a conception of power as acting on the actions of others, then this implies a notion of power as predicated on freedom:

> Power is exercised only over free subjects, and only in so far as they are free. [. . .] By this we mean individual or collective subjects who are faced with a field of possibilities in which several ways of behaving, several reactions and diverse comportments may be realised. Where the determining factors saturate the whole there is no relationship of power.
>
> (ibid.)

Freedom is not seen as an intrinsic capacity of an innate self or consciousness. It is understood as an array of attributes ascribed to different agents that can only be realised in relation to specific institutional conditions of possibility.

As a concept, governmentality breaks with the imagination of power in terms of disciplines, so that freedom is understood to be neither illusory nor opposed to power. The conception of power implied by the analysis of governmentality is itself therefore a substantively liberal one. Consider, for example, the following definition of the notion of power underlying the idea of governmentality:

> A man (*sic*) who is chained up and beaten is subject to force being exerted over him. Not power. But if he can be induced to speak, when his ultimate recourse could have been to hold his tongue, preferring death, then he has been caused to behave in a certain way. His freedom has been subjected to power. He has been submitted to government. If an individual can remain free, however little his freedom may be, power can subject him to government. There is no power without potential refusal or revolt.
>
> (Foucault 1981: 253)

What is striking is how far this formulation resembles more straightforwardly liberal definitions of power: '*A* has power over *B* to the extent that he can get *B* to do something that *B* would not otherwise do' (Dahl 1969: 80). I do not want to push the analogy too far, but simply underscore that in Foucault's later work, power is understood by reference to regulatory practices that address individuals as autonomous agents 'and defines itself wholly in relation to them and to their freedom' (Halperin 1995: 18). Foucault certainly considers liberalism as a contingent historical achievement, rather than as a universal rationality. The rehabilitation

of freedom in Foucault's later work is premised on an understanding of
agency as an attribute of particular ensembles of subjectivity, knowledge and power. A subject can only be a subject if it is in a relationship
with power: 'the subject is constituted by power relations, and if the
subject is free, its freedom cannot be divorced from its ability to possess
its freedom as a form of power' (JanMohamed 1995: 55).

Foucault's work on governmentality, pastoral power and bio-politics
has stimulated the formation of a distinctive paradigm in social and
political theory concerned with reinterpreting modern political reason,
liberalism, the human sciences and the professions (see Barry et al.
1996). Following Foucault's lead, this work focuses on forms of power
where the populations who are subjects of rule are presupposed to be
free and autonomous citizens (Hindess 1997). Liberalism is rethought as
a set of rationalities and technologies for governing the conduct of subjects through cultivating practices of self-regulation. From this perspective, the notion of government refers attention to the inculcation of
those ethical competencies that are considered to be basic attributes of
modern citizenship. A particular emphasis of the governmentality literature is upon the role of knowledge and expertise in the administration
of complex social practices (Rose 1994). Rationalities of government
are understood to be related to practices and technologies which make
up apparatuses of power in the sense of Foucault's use of the term
dispotif, which refers to 'a thoroughly heterogeneous ensemble consist-
ing of discourses, institutions, architectural forms, regulatory decisions,
laws, administrative measures, scientific statements, philosophical,
moral and philanthropic propositions – in short, the said as much as the
unsaid. Such are the elements of the apparatus' (Foucault 1980: 194; see
Deleuze 1992b). This means that political rationalities are more than
mere discourses, in the narrow sense of a system of statements, but part
of broader institutional apparatuses for problematising and intervening
in defined fields of social action. The idea of governmentality therefore
directs attention to the analysis of 'contingent lash-ups of thought and
action' (Rose 1999: 27).

On this understanding, modern media practices might well be understood as paradigmatic liberal technologies of citizenship. Their distinctive institutional and symbolic forms have emerged in response to a set
of imperatives to govern the habits, desires and passions of dispersed
populations characterised by a considerable degree of discretion over
their engagement with media forms, and therefore various forms of
knowledge have been central to the dynamics of media practices. To
explore this understanding of media practices fully, however, it is necessary to move away from the purism of political-theoretic readings of

governmentality, which lean towards ascribing a high degree of system-aticity to Foucault's thoughts on modern political reason. They tend to be much less well developed in the analysis of the implementation of pro-grammes of rule, and display a tendency to overestimate the coherence of knowledge practices in realising their objectives. The next section dis-cusses the distinctive pragmatic appropriation of the idea of govern-mentality in cultural studies, which bears directly on conceptualisations of media, citizenship and democratic rule.

IV *The cultural pragmatics of democracy*

In cultural studies, the idea of governmentality has informed the reassessment of the ways in which cultural practices have historically served as apparatuses of democratic citizenship (Hunter 1988; Meredyth and Minson 2001; Miller 1993, 1998). Culture has been understood as a prime medium for acting upon the social while main-taining the separation between state and society (Bennett 1998). The understanding of autonomy that underwrites modern understandings of culture is given a central role in liberal conceptualisations of democracy, which is understood to depend in part on the internalised power of rational reflection by self-regulating individuals. The rela-tionship between practices of culture and notions of the autonomous self is fundamental to the deployment of culture as a political tech-nology concerned with empowering citizens. Herein lies the specific instrumentality of conceptualisations of culture as inherently non-instrumental (Bennett 1995b). The development of a Foucauldian paradigm of cultural-policy studies is not, in principle, limited to addressing the relationships between culture and policy in the narrow sense of state programmes or bureaucracy. Rather, the reference to policy signals an understanding of culture as inherently constituted in relation to institutionalised practices aimed at shaping conduct. Culture is understood as 'the institutions, symbol systems, and forms of regulation and training responsible for forming, maintaining and/or changing the mental and behavioural attributes of populations' (Bennett 1989: 10). Culture, understood in terms of practices and insti-tutions for the inculcation of values, beliefs, routines of life and forms of conduct, is variously deployed to administer conduct – in state agen-cies, markets, corporations, institutions of civil society such as schools, universities or broadcasting, or in the more informal but routinised practices of everyday life.

The turn to Foucault in cultural studies is in large part centred on a critique of notions that cultural politics remains anchored to a single axis of power. Foucault's formulation of power refers not just to multiple and diffuse sites of power, but to fundamentally heterogeneous forms of rule and contestation which do not presume any necessary overarching dynamic, sovereign will or singular rationality drawing them into a unified relation. There is no single logic of power behind the proliferation of governmental instruments for the management of individuals and groups (Hunter 1993: 131–2). Governmentality also implies breaking with the residual attachment to a problematic of consciousness (Bennett 1990: 270). Cultural power is henceforth understood neither in terms of psychological mechanisms of ideology or consent, nor in terms of unstable chains of signification. It involves instead the detailed regulation of social activity in particular institutional sites to particular effects, and is not taken to be a derivative form of power that necessarily reflects or refracts other dynamics of power.

Historically, culture has been institutionalised as a medium for regulating the forms of 'free subjectivity' that are constitutive of the autonomy of liberal understandings of the social field (Bennett 1998: 110). The utility of culture as a means of liberal rule, maintaining and bridging the separation of formally constituted political and social fields, derives from the defining antithetical structure of modern understandings of the term. Culture tends to be defined diacritically, in external opposition to nature, civilisation or anarchy. It is also internally divided into hierarchies of high and low, elite and mass. This discursive splitting of culture defines, first, a range of resources for governing (a body of cultural works and artefacts, as well as modes of interpretation, appreciation and judgement). Second, it defines a set of domains to which these technologies can be applied to change conduct. Culture is both a potential object and instrument of government:

> its object or target insofar as the term refers to the morals, manners, and ways of life of subordinate social strata; its instrument insofar as it is culture in its more restricted sense – the domain of artistic and intellectual activities – that is to supply the means of a governmental intervention in and regulation of culture as the domain of morals, manners, codes of conduct, etc.
>
> (Bennett 1992: 26; see also Hunter 1988)

This Foucauldian redefinition of culture as inherently governmental (Bennett 1995b: 884) directs attention to the ways in which cultural practices have been used to provide repertories of conduct and resources for organising the routines of everyday life. In the seminal Foucauldian genealogies of modern culture, the main institutional settings for this deployment of culture as a means of governing conduct include museums, galleries, libraries and schools (Bennett 1995a; see Hunter 1994). However, the argument has also been extended to the analysis of telecommunications, broadcasting, tourism and other spheres. And this conceptualisation has in turn been used to analyse shifts in the rationalities of governing culture from classically liberal forms of social democracy to neo-liberal forms such as the discourses of multiculturalism, consumer sovereignty and the culture industries (Barnett 2001a).

The central tenet of this approach is that (neo-)liberal government depends on the deployment of various forms of knowledge and expertise, in rendering aspects of existence thinkable and calculable, and thereby open to policy interventions. The rise of governmental rationalities depends on the proliferation of technologies of representation and inscription that produce various fields of positive knowledge: 'All government depends on a particular mode of "representation": the elaboration of language for depicting the domain in question that claims both to grasp the nature of that reality represented, and literally to represent it in a form amenable to political deliberation, argument and scheming' (Miller and Rose 1990: 6). In practice, the emphasis upon the rationalities of rule and on the role of knowledge in public and private administration tends to present the rationalities of government as univocal, systematic and coherent. This underplays the messiness of policy processes, institutional dynamics and subject-formation, a trait that is confounded by critical governmentality studies' self-conscious disdain for conventional forms of political-sociological analysis. If only by the omission of sustained consideration of how rationalities are played out in practice, governmentality-studies tends to be characterised by an overly administrative model of government, and an overly coherent model of subject-formation (O'Regan 1992). In its attention to internal rationalities, much of this literature has difficulty in acknowledging the agency of the governed in shaping practices of rule (O'Malley 1996). As a consequence, it does not adequately address the contradictions that beset practices of government. In particular, given the emphasis upon the role of knowledge and expertise in the governmentality literature, one might suppose that liberal and neo-liberal modes of rule are dogged by an endemic crisis of legitimacy and accountability that follows from the contradictions between the rhetoric of public participation and the actual monopolisation of expertise (Flew 1997). The struggle over definitions of the scope and actors of public participation is a basic feature of modern forms of administration, bureaucracy and policy making. The importance of legal rules, evidential criteria, and other forms of technical procedure in liberal modes of rule means that the role of expertise in governmental strategies needs to be conceptualised in terms of technologies of representation in the narrow sense of inscriptions of authority and meaning, but also in the broader sense of claims to speak in the public interest, a claim that invites counterclaims and thus generates the proliferation of counter-representations.

The need for a greater recognition of the agency of the governed in strategies of rule, of the indeterminacy of policy programmes, and of the complexity of subject-formation all suggest a rethinking of the preferred spatial models of power upon which much of the critical governmentality literature has depended. Much of this work, in cultural studies and political theory alike, continues to rely implicitly on an essentially disciplinary imagination of power and its effects, understanding diverse institutional and disciplinary forms as the Panopticon writ large. As already suggested, the paradigmatic analyses of the deployment of culture as a medium of liberal government take as their models various monitorial regimes of education and cultural instruction that inculcate new ethical practices of self-formation in distinctive spatio-temporal locales of co-presence – the school, the playground, the museum. Power is understood to refer to practices through which actions are cultivated 'in a distinctive milieu or habitus', one which 'presupposes supervision, instruction, sanctions and judgement' (Smith and Minson 1997: 193–4). In turn, there is a tendency to assume that the liberal deployment of culture is related to national programmes of citizenship formation. These two assumptions – of the tightly supervised contexts for the deployment of culture, and of the coherence of national-scale cultural policies – underwrite the polemical arguments in favour of pragmatic policy advocacy that distinguishes the cultural-policy studies approach (see Barnett 1999a). Both conceptually and empirically, the assumption of cultural power being contained within spaces of enclosure (from the school or museum up to the nation-state) needs to be questioned.

The ongoing restructuring of modes of government beyond the realms of the nation-state is associated with an institutional shift of government from state to market. The dominant rationality of contemporary neo-liberal modes of rule is directed towards the problem of 'the governability of the passions of self-identified individuals and collectivities: individuals and pluralities shaped not by citizen-forming devices of church, school and public broadcasting, but by commercial consumption regimes and the politics of lifestyle, the individual identified with one of a plurality of cultural communities' (Rose 1999: 46). From this perspective, circuits of culture, images and meaning are an increasingly important assemblage of contemporary freedom, where freedom is understood as 'a kind of power one brings to bear upon oneself, and a mode of bringing power to bear upon others' (ibid.: 99). This implies new, multiple and non-cumulative modes of citizenship, which can be actualised in relation to a variety of formal and informal institutional domains: 'Citizenship is no longer primarily realized in a relation with the state, or in a single "public sphere", but in a variety of private, corporate and quasi-public practices from working to shopping' (ibid.: 166). But the neo-liberal re-ordering of the 'territory of government' (Rose 1996), exemplified by shifts away from attempts to govern through a nationally constituted social sphere to myriad modes of government through community and culture, also involves a complex set of processes rearranging the material spaces and scales of citizenship formation (see Marston and Mitchell forthcoming). The desocialisation of public policy characteristic of neo-liberal governmentality indicates a shift away from a single unified national territory and a unified citizenry as the object of governmental regulation. The government of culture, as a result, is no longer institutionally or spatially contained within the nation-state. The transformation of the spatialities of subject-formation is associated with a multiplication of the spaces of democratic problematisation and the forms of political subjectivity.

The ubiquity of culture in the vocabulary of management, business, innovation policy and other fields in the 1980s and 1990s illustrates a distinctively neo-liberal framing of culture as something to be changed – the culture of work, the culture of public services, the culture of schools. This is indicative of a steady governmentalisation of politics and economy in which complex organisations and practices are reordered according to programmes aimed at changing the norms, values and conduct of those working in them (Morris 1998: 114–19). This relocation of cultural governmentality beyond the limited realm of formal cultural policy is, however, also associated with a literal re-scaling of the spaces through which cultural practices are organised. Culture, as the object and the medium of political rationalities of the state and civil society, is no longer contained within the nation-state, if it ever was. The contemporary reconfiguration of the government of culture beyond the state towards market mechanisms means that culture's articulation with the territorial scales of institutionalised democratic politics is being reordered, as it is articulated with non-territorialised networks of capital accumulation. The territorial congruence of economic, political and cultural practices upon which cultural policy and conceptualisations of citizenship, participation and representation have depended has been significantly destabilised in the last two decades. Economic production and distribution, political participation, social integration and identity-formation are now stretched across various networks and spatial scales (Apparadurai 1990; Collins 1990). The multiplication of sites and scales through which symbolic forms are institutionally produced and consumed implies that individuals are not subject to coherent interpellation as national subjects, but are addressed as members of minoritised communities existing at a number of scales and organised through both areal and networked spaces.

The rescaling of economic and political processes relocates the centres of institutionalised decision-making over cultural practices to which transformative political projects need to address themselves. While this might imply a multiplication of possible sites and forms for intervening positively in the government of culture, it is also associated with a widening gap between the institutionalised scope of formal political representation and the diverse grievances to which representative institutions are asked to respond. Rather than continuing to think of the effectivity of cultural policies on the model of regimes of monitorial observation in contained spaces of visibility, it might therefore be useful to shift paradigms, taking the complex articulation of multiple and dispersed spaces characteristic of media technologies like radio and television as models for a distinctively liberal, governmental understanding of the forms of power exercised through the deployment of cultural technologies.

V Governing media publics

Radio and television might be thought of as paradigmatically liberal, governmental technologies. They address a large population that is spread out across an open space, and is characterised by a high level of discretion over action. Rather than an enclosed, territorial conception of power, thinking about media requires a networked conception of social-spatial power, one that works less through realising predictable effects of prescription, and more by providing resources for action whose appropriation is liable to considerable variation in effects (see Murdoch 1998). The spatial and temporal disjunction that defines electronic media means that the configuration of identity and conduct through these mediums involves a greater degree of uncertainty than is characteristic of more formalised, enclosed cultural institutions. If media technologies have a role in cultivating the conditions for citizenship, then this cannot be adequately thought of on the analogy of direct surveillance of individualised subjects in enclosed disciplinary spaces. The multiplicity of institutional locales, and especially their spatial dispersion, that make up the media means that the consumption of the symbolic forms distributed through radio and television is not dependent on the prior inculcation of habits or conduct in cultural institutions such as schools or universities in the way that the expansion of mass-mediated, print-based popular culture historically has been.

There is certainly potential for conceptualising media, or 'teletechnologies' as Derrida has taken to calling them (Derrida and Stiegler 2002), as means for governing the conditions of democratic citizenship. These technologies serve as channels of political communication, but also more broadly as mediums through which the activities of citizens are rendered into potential objects of regulation. However, in so far as the medium of this attempted regulation is popular culture, mediated democratic citizenship tends to flatten the cultural conditions of democratic participation (Ouellette 1999; Simons 2002). The attraction of governing populations through media technologies is therefore haunted by the persistent fear that media publics are essentially ungovernable. Popular media cultures draw on other, less formalised competencies, which are in turn subject to different forms of regulation. Furthermore, the phenomenology of media space-time (being at more than one event-place at once) means that the forms of rule that can be exercised through mediated communication cannot be conceptualised along the lines of traditional cultural pedagogies.

The effects of visibility and surveillance characteristic of electronically mediated forms of communication involve different distributions of power from Foucault's enclosed disciplinary spaces (Thompson 1995: 132–48). The distinctive spatialities and temporalities of media culture introduce a degree of unpredictability not provided for in theorisations of culture that continue to take territorial locales as their models of cultural power. The break between sites of media address and sites of reception of media culture shapes the sorts of power-effects inscribed into these communications networks. As discussed in Chapter 2, while it is possible for public or private organisations to manage what gets produced and circulated, it is not possible to manage the contexts and conduct of cultural consumption tightly. Thus, while it remains possible to think of media as technologies of the self, they should not be thought of in terms of the detailed disciplining of conduct under conditions of direct institutional supervision. The government of conduct through media culture is necessarily a thoroughly mediated, and therefore somewhat uncertain, process. To return to the scope/intensity distinction, the mediazation of culture (ibid.: 46) extends the scope of rule across potentially vast geographical areas and into myriad dimensions of life, but is also distinguished by a very significant diminution of the intensity of rule that can be secured through this extension.

Teletechnologies provide the conditions for forms of social inter- action which are not regulated by the condition of co-presence of sub- jects contained within a field of the gaze, but are instead characterised by the spatial and temporal absence of subjects to one another. They enable various forms of action at a distance not just metaphorically but actually. They provide the conditions of possibility for people to inter- vene and influence events that occur in places that are temporally and spatially distant from the locales of everyday life, not just vicariously, but by acting in their own contexts in new ways and for new ends (Silk 1998; Boltanski 1999). The distinctive forms of rule that define mass media cultural technologies, extending opportunities for shaping con- duct, but with less tight control over the forms of engagement with cultural forms, mean that the forms of political action carried on through such media are less to do with direct mobilisation, and more to do with working on patterns of identification. The media are therefore crucial sites for contested struggles over the conditions for the forma- tion of new subjectivities. Such a politics makes the media into a site for 'a new form of governmentality, concerned with the rules by which groups may claim subject-status' (Patton 1993: 161).

A vital axis of conflict in this sort of politics is the production of knowledge through which audiences are made knowable. The separa- tion of production and reception characteristic of mass media does not imply a complete autonomy for consumption. Media audiences may be spatially dispersed, but they are still defined and constituted by refer- ence to constructs of space, such as home, the car or the office. These sites are themselves the object of various technologies of administration (Berland 1992). There are numerous rationalities by which the disposi- tions of audiences and the spaces of media consumption are managed. In the interstices of the dispersed and fragmented geographies of mass media practices, a range of new fields of knowledge, technologies of representation and modes of expertise proliferates. The dual emphasis upon the knowledge by which the sites of media transmission and of media reception are negotiated, and upon the social production of the material spaces that connect and separate them, underscores the rele- vance of thinking of the governmental rationalities of media in terms of regulatory technologies rather than tightly controlled technologies of discipline. With radio and television, populations are made the objects of strategies of governmental power indirectly, through the deployment of extensive apparatuses, such as statistics and ratings, which allow the recursive monitoring of collective conduct and behaviour. Audiences, as the objects of policy in public and private media institutions, provide a prime example of the different forms of power implied by the distinction between discipline and government. The behaviour represented by the various representations of the audience is not equivalent to the actual behaviour and conduct of individualised subjects. Audiences are the product of selective decisions by different actors that deploy technologies through which they aim to exercise power by being able to authoritatively represent audience preferences, wants and interests (Hartley 1996: 64–5).

The actual detailed disciplining of subjects in space and time is a qualitatively different practice from regulatory technologies of government such as statistics, opinion polls, censuses or audience ratings. As forms of action upon action, these regulatory technologies do not directly induce particular conduct, but are mediums that aim to make something more or less likely. They are 'methods of probability', not mechanisms of enforced normalisation (Deleuze 1988: 71–3). They enable the general contexts of conduct to be regulated, providing repertoires of conduct to dispersed populations, but are not directly analogous to modes of social control through direct supervision within a spatially structured organisation of the gaze. And these practices do not involve the training of subjects or their total immersion in an institutional locale. They address individuals not so much as subjects, but as abstract singularities: a viewer, a voter, a consumer and so on. As technologies for the regulation of conduct outside of structured relations of proximate surveillance, they involve highly mediated and indirect forms of monitoring in which the relationship of the subject of government to norms of conduct is significantly more attenuated. In short, the technologies that render the audience-subject of radio or television capable of being the object of various strategies of government (statistics, numbers, ratings, focus groups) indicate the extent to which there is a constitutive lack of exact fit between the rationalities of public and private media institutions and actual processes of normalisation. The image of disciplinary power is inappropriate to mediated cultural technologies, since they do not depend on direct surveillance and monitoring. The problem of governing spatially extensive networks of communication is not that of maintaining discipline over clearly circumscribed subjects within territorial space. Rather than thinking of the mediazation of culture as merely an extension of tightly controlled modes of conduct carefully managed in enclosed locales, this implies attending to the ways in which diverse and dispersed locations are articulated together through various agents and technologies of regulation.

The distances built into media technologies account for the historically bifurcated approach to governing media audiences, characterised both by an acknowledgement of the high degree of autonomy of dispersed subjects, and by a countervailing imperative to protect audiences, not least from their own worst inclinations. This dual focus has been significantly reordered with the changing organisation of regulatory regimes in the last two decades. On the one hand, the constitutive autonomy of media audiences has been interpreted in terms of consumer sovereignty, to justify the commercialisation, privatisation and liberalisation of media economies. By privileging the sovereign consumer exercising choice based on privately formed tastes and preferences, the populist rhetoric of neo-liberalism justifies rolling back structural regulation in line with free market principles. However, this economic liberalisation has been associated with a revivification of conservative ideological agendas to protect and uplift media subjects, justifying new forms of moral regulation over media systems. Contemporary media policy, mixing economic deregulation with increased concern over cultural and moral standards, has thus become characterised by a political rationality centred on what Toby Miller (1991) has characterised as a split subject, one that is understood to be simultaneously a subject of sovereign autonomy and a subject in need of guidance and oversight. This theme will be explored in more detail in the chapters that follow.

VI Conclusion: recuperating legitimacy

Anglo-American poststructuralism is deeply suspicious of the understanding of communication that is implied by conceptions of self-governing subjects of democratic citizenship. This chapter has traced one authoritative source of this suspicion to Foucault's account of disciplinary power, suggesting that his work is characterised by an abiding ambivalence towards norms of autonomy. A critical appropriation of Foucauldian work on governmentality can assist in understanding the role of media culture in cultivating the conditions for democratic citizenship. In this model, culture is understood as connecting to power through the active, selective and differential development of capacities for self-actualisation. Teletechnologies like radio and television are substantively liberal mediums, inasmuch as they work only on and through the capacity for autonomous action by dispersed social subjects. A

Foucauldian approach to a democratic politics of need is therefore directed towards an analysis of media institutions as providers of symbolic resources through which particular issues are problematised, particular identifications made possible, and particular modes of subjectivity made practicable. After Foucault, citizenship is thought of in terms of repertoires of attributes which are actualised only in relation to various technologies and practices: 'Rights and responsibilities cease to be metaphysical attributes of the person, and appear instead as socially conferred capacities and capabilities: governmental techniques produce the individual *as* citizen. Men and women participate in democracy, one might say, but they do not participate under circumstances chosen by themselves nor in the terms defined by the formal rights of citizenship' (Donald 1992: 135). The idea that the practice of freedom or autonomy depends upon being in a relationship with apparatuses that enable action is important because it is connected to a more circumspect definition of power. In his later work, Foucault (1983: 217–19) argues that power relations, relationships of communication and objective capacities constitute three types of relationship that are inextricably linked but not identical. As a form of relation that is distinct from force, violence or domination, power is thereby defined in a way that readmits the normative value of relations of consensual communication as a means of evaluating political relations (see Johnson 1997).

In fundamental ways, the theme of governmentality indicates a different political imagination to the resistance problematic most often ascribed to Foucault. Governmentality, in linking individual actions and large political institutions, defines power as a structure of actions on actions, which depends upon and maintains a conditional mode of freedom as agency. Power and freedom, in Foucault's later work, are forms of more or less asymmetrical *relations*, in which power and freedom are 'each the condition for the possibility of the other's existence' (Bové 1990: 85). The co-dependence of power and freedom opens up the analysis of the institutional and practical conditions of different forms of citizen action, without appealing to abstract principles of the self, reason or freedom.

Habermas (1988) once found Foucault's ambivalence towards power inexcusable. In his historical archaeologies and genealogies, Foucault analyses power as a positive modality of action operating beyond the scope of formal legitimisation, while implicitly appealing to a critical, normative understanding upon which the shock value of his counter-histories remains dependent (Anderson 1992; Fraser 1989: 17–34). But perhaps this ambivalence is faithful to the very structure of modern democratic power itself. The relationship between power as productive of effects, and power as a sinister presence, is never open to resolution through a watertight theoretical rationalisation, but is always in the process of negotiation. This is a comforting conclusion perhaps, allowing as it does a neat reconciliation between Habermas and Foucault. But this reconciliation is only possible on condition that Habermas' latent theoreticism is resisted, and Foucault's persistent lack of attention to the symbolic indeterminacy of democratic modalities of power is amended. The problem of legitimacy, once understood as passing through the unstable loops of representation, is not open to final theoretical resolution, but nor is it wholly irrelevant to the practical forms of a politics that aspires to be democratic in form as well content. As already noted, in current theoretical disputes, Habermas and Foucault have come to stand for two, much older, opposed models of political power (see Dunn 2000: 49–51). One of these models emphasises domination of some by others and focuses upon mechanisms of coercion (Foucault). The other emphasises forms of co-operative action-in-concert as the means of defining and realising human needs (Habermas). In one model, the failure of power to lead to just outcomes is always anticipated; in the other, this failure is used as a diagnostic device (ibid.). Perhaps the real difference between these two visions is a pragmatic one, a matter of temperament (James 2000: 8). Each points up certain issues, leads to particular sorts of analysis, and therefore has its own uses. The pessimistic view that power is nothing but pure force, and that it can never devolve into legitimate rule, is a useful prophylactic against excessive credulity in the face of the public manifestation of concentrated power. But it can lead to a flattening of significant differences between regimes, and an occlusion of political opportunities. In the last analysis, the theoretical critique of legitimacy is as limited as its formal theoretical rationalisation. Legitimacy is an insistent fiction, and a practical fact: 'the claim to democratic political legitimacy, however muddled or fraudulent it may usually be, is of urgent causal importance in modern politics' (Dunn 1990: 2).

Rather than thinking of the inherent democracy of intersubjective communication as serving as the basis of actual democratic practice, or of democracy as just another form of generically antagonistic power relations masked by an ideology of reciprocity, our attention in the following chapters is therefore turned to the analysis of the practical politics of making claims to democratic legitimacy, and the role these claims play in shaping the outcomes of mediated democratic publicity. Each of the following chapters develops a specific theme from Habermas' account of the cultural dimensions of a postfoundational understanding of radical democracy. Thus, Chapter 5 explores the role of constitutional law in determining the meanings ascribed to democracy when applied to the regulation of new communications technologies. Chapter 6 examines the understandings of social solidarity in a transnational democratic polity emerging in European Union media policy. And Chapter 7 investigates the forms of associational culture being fostered through the restructuring of mass media in a new democracy, using the case of South Africa.

5

The public use of legal reasoning: the First Amendment as communications policy

If the public forum is to be free and open to all, and in continuous session, everyone should be able to make use of it. All citizens should have the means to be informed about political issues. They should be in a position to assess how proposals affect their well being and which policies advance their conception of the public good. Moreover, they should have a fair chance to add alternative proposals to the agenda of political discussion. The liberties protected by the principle of participation lose much of their value whenever those who have greater private means are permitted to use their advantage to control the course of public debate.

John Rawls (1972: 225)

I The Supreme Court between facts and norms

In his procedural reconstruction of democratic legitimacy, Habermas (1996) argues that in constitutional democracies, law is the medium in which the tensions between ideal commitments to democratic rule and popular legitimacy are reconciled with the actualities of political and socio-economic inequality are reconciled. And as discussed in Chapter 1, freedom of expression is a central principle in any functioning democratic polity. This chapter brings together these two themes. In the twentieth century, the First Amendment of the United States Constitution became the symbol of free speech principles, not only in the US, but globally, not least through the medium of American popular culture. 'Congress shall make no law [. . .] abridging the freedom of speech, or of the press' has come to stand for a principled commitment to personal liberty and democratic self-government. However, in practice, the First Amendment is far from being a simple statement of unabridgeable principle. In certain respects, First Amendment jurisprudence, under the final auspices of the Supreme Court, has become an instrument of communications policy-making. The Court serves as a policy-maker primarily through judicial review of the constitutionality of the actions of other players in the policy process, and through statutory interpretation (Dahl 1957). This role should not be overestimated, and the Court's agency is dependent on a very circumscribed set of competencies (see Baum 1998). The Court does not initiate policy, since it cannot take up any issue it wants to for judicial review (Baum 1993). Nor can the Court draw upon the forms of enforcement characteristic of other policy actors: 'Lacking any direct ability to enforce its judgements, the Court must rely on other political actors if it is to act effectively as an institution of government' (Tushnet 1999: 64–5). And the Court only addresses particular policy fields, and does so through a highly particularistic method. As a political actor, the Supreme Court can therefore be characterised as definitively governmental in the sense discussed in Chapter 4. It only acts upon policy arenas at a distance, by shaping the context for actions of other actors, specifically by defining the meaning of constitutional rights: 'The Court is not highly effective in enforcing rights, but it often legitimates efforts to achieve them and thus provides the impetus for people to take legal and political action. Its decisions affect the positions of interest groups and social movements, strengthening some and weakening others' (Baum 1998: 272–3).

Broadly speaking, approaches to the role of the Supreme Court as a political actor tend to be polarised between normative idealism and sceptical realism. In John Rawls' revised account of the foundations of political justice in a constitutional democracy, a premium is placed on the institutionalisation of forms of reasoning that require decisions and judgements to be publicly justified and explained. Public reason is defined as public by virtue of being the reason of the public (presupposing participation); by taking the good of the public as its subject (bracketing particular conceptions of the good); and by being open to view (it is made in public) (Rawls 1993: 213). For Rawls, a Supreme Court is the 'institutional exemplar' of this public reason: it is 'visibly and on its face the creature of that reason and of that reason alone' (ibid.: 235). Judges are expected to justify their decisions by reference to principles, not matters of politics or policy (see Dworkin 1985: 9–32), and thus constitutional law is meant to encourage broader forms of political conduct in which giving reasons is routine.

Rawls' investment of such significance in an independent but structurally unaccountable institution implies that basic questions of democratic procedure should not be open to broad determination by practices of popular participation, but reserved instead for judicial review. The legitimacy of the judicial system, in Rawls' account, depends on its decisions being based upon, and being seen to be based upon, the norms of public reason. The justification for this constitutionalisation of democratic procedure is that such matters should not be made by actors who have substantive interests in particular outcomes. However, it is open to question whether, in practice, the US Supreme Court can be considered to have no substantive interest in cases concerning such basic 'devices of democracy' as the system of free expression (Schauer 1994). The form of judgement through which judicial decision-making is exercised, the written opinions of the Court, should in principle conform to norms of rational argument. But these decisions need also to be communicated to the Court's various publics (Berkson 1978). The appearance of neutrality and objectivity is critical to the legitimacy of the Court, and to the effectiveness of its decisions in certain areas of policy. In maintaining this appearance, the relations between the Court and the news media are pivotal. The press is a linking mechanism that enables the Court to have effects through attracting attention and maintaining a particular reputation that can be used to get things done (Cook 1998: 156–62). Furthermore, as the Court's role as a policy actor has increased, so it has become subject to forms of indirect lobbying mediated by news media (Davis 1994: 146–58). Thus, in important ways, the Court works to shape the media landscape, but it also works through the media. In certain fundamental respects, there is therefore a convergence of interests between the Federal Courts and the news media in the United States, in so far as the dependence of the Court on the press as a conduit to broader publics implies that the news media are themselves an important constituency shaping the Court's decisions in significant areas of constitutional doctrine, and not least that of First Amendment law (Tushnet 1993).

Rawls' vision tends to obscure the extent to which the Supreme Court is a thoroughly political institution in its own right. In contrast to his image of constitutional law as reaching principled decisions and regulating the norms of political conduct, from the perspective of critical legal studies, law is understood as an essentially political instrument for the reproduction of existing relations of power. Critical legal studies understands law as a set of discourses that produce effects by ascribing differential truth-value to different statements, and by distributing subject-positions to actors in legal institutions (Morrow and Puren 1998: 275). The handing down of legal judgements in a public-oriented register is, from this perspective, a means of masking the ideological operations of law as a support for economic and political power. In acknowledging the political nature of law, critical legal studies veers towards throwing out the baby with the bathwater, evacuating any normative significance that adherence to the forms of legal decision-

making in a constitutional framework may have. However, it is not necessary to reject the normative content of law completely, only to recast
it in more modest terms. The loss of independent foundation for judgement implied by critical legal studies' 'indeterminacy thesis' only
heightens the inescapable appeal to contested conceptions of the good
through which legal reasoning works (Cornell 1992: 94). Rather than
being delegitimised as a veneer for power, law is revalued as a set of
practices whose 'importance is now rediscovered as contingent and
institutional rather than necessary and universal' (ibid.: 301). On this
reading, law remains an unavoidable and valuable formative context for
progressive political intervention precisely because of the importance of
this arena in shaping the system of rights (Unger 1983: 667–70).

The regulatory system of US media and communications is distinguished by the assertive role of the Federal Courts, and more broadly of
the discourse of constitutional law, in policy-making. The Supreme
Court is in part a quasi-administrative agency (in turn, the Federal
Communications Commission, the regulatory authority with responsibility for media and telecommunications, is in part a quasi-judicial
body). The significance of the Federal Courts lies in no small part in
determining the very dimensions of the regulatory space of the media
and communications sector – deciding what areas can be legitimately
subject to regulation and which actors can be legitimately ascribed
standing in the regulatory, policy-making and judicial processes
(Hancher and Moran 1998: 153–5).[1] Constitutional law therefore plays
an important part in defining the boundaries between public authority
and private life. Over the last three decades, a progressively more conservative Supreme Court has steadily redefined this boundary to find
that a whole series of activities in the communications field is essentially private, not involving state action, and therefore falling under
expanded First Amendment protection from legislative action.

One of the functions of First Amendment jurisprudence is to determine just which spaces will count as publicly accessible forums for
expression. In US constitutional law, public forums are those spaces
such as public squares, parks and street corners that have traditionally
been considered the archetypal forums for speakers to address a public
audience.[2] Supreme Court decision-making over the last thirty years has

1 See Clark (1985: 39–59) for a discussion of the distinctive role of law in policy and politics in the United States.
2 Public forum doctrine rests on the principle that certain spaces are opened by state
   action for expressive activity by the public, and are accessible to all. Thus, for mediums
   (like broadcasting, cable or the Internet) to be assigned public forum status, the main
   criterion is that the courts find they are constituted by significant government action.

been characterised by a marked reluctance to extend public forum recognition to non-traditional public spaces such as shopping malls or airports. This is indicative of a deference towards private property rights and the rights of the public as consumers not to be offended as they go about their purchasing. This prioritisation of rights of abstract individual autonomy has become a basic theme in media-related cases. The political significance of access to traditional public forums cannot be separated from, and indeed might well be heightened because of, the Court's increasingly assertive role in sustaining the inaccessibility of the media system to broad citizen access (Horwitz 1993: 239). In the process, whole areas of public policy are moved beyond the scrutiny of representative institutions in the name of replacing administrative and bureaucratic decision-making procedures with the populist promise of free markets and technologically induced serialised choice. In effect, a whole variety of ways in which public policy subsidises and constitutes media and communications systems (see Cook 1998: 38–60) is effaced by the increasingly assertive claims of media corporations to be wholly private entities, a position upheld by successive Court decisions.

II Liberal subjects, republican speech

The precise significance of the First Amendment's speech and press clauses for complex policy areas such as broadcasting, cable television or the Internet will depend upon the conception that one holds of the purposes of freedom-of-expression principles. It is common to identify three broad arguments regarding the value of freedom-of-expression. One argument privileges freedom of speech because it is the instrumental means of arriving at the truth. A second, similarly utilitarian argument privileges so-called political speech, as a means of ensuring participatory self-government. A third position sees freedom of speech as a value in itself, as the vehicle of self-realisation and self-fulfilment, in which individual autonomy, defined against state interference, is the most privileged value (see Barendt 1985: 8–23).

One role of First Amendment communications law is the definition of the subjects who are ascribed speech rights. Free speech has come to be understood in legal judgement and in broader public discourse as primarily an attribute of speakers, rather than by reference to the purpose of speech. At the same time, constitutional adjudication has given increasing authority to forms of reasoning based on the authority of expertise and evidentiary findings, side-stepping the commitment to the giving of reasons by reference to normative principles, by appealing instead to constructions of facts. These two features are in fact closely related, since the determination of the characteristics of technologies and of markets plays a central role in resolving a fundamental tension between abstract free speech principles and mediated communications systems. Universal access to mediated communications like radio and television for all speakers is not plausible, leading to the conundrum that media organisations are the bearers of free speech rights as speakers but also serve as forums for other speakers (Fiss 1996a: 14). The fundamental question is whether this tension should be resolved by considering organisations involved in mediated communications (that is, corporations) as natural persons with speech rights, and whether in turn those speech rights are understood to have individual autonomy as their highest objective. In the 1980s and 1990s, the model of free speech that gained increasing ascendancy proposed that the First Amendment is an essentially libertarian doctrine which protects individual autonomy against the always imminent danger of government restriction, and that the free market is the best means of ensuring the realisation of the freedoms protected by the First Amendment. This is related to the increasingly successful assertion of autonomy by communications corporations, modelled on natural persons, a position which necessarily implies the severe restriction of measures to open up access to media systems to a broader array of voices and interests (ibid.: 15). The First Amendment has been expanded to defend a particular set of policy prescriptions that favour deregulation, consumer sovereignty, the commodification of public services, and the definition of the public primarily in terms of consumers (Fiss 1996b: 35).

However, a simple reading of the Court's decisions in ideological terms will hardly suffice. In part, shifts in constitutional doctrine are related to the internal dynamics of constitutional law-making itself. Fundamental divisions over the role of the judiciary in a constitutional democracy have shaped First Amendment decisions (see Lazarus 1998). Media and communications policy provides an opportunity for working out contested models of constitutional interpretation. By constructing technological change as an independent and natural process, Supreme Court Justices can engage in doctrinal debate about the proper modes of interpretation, the application of rules and the appropriate use of analogies (Price and Duffy 1997). Understandings of technological change are closely connected to conceptions of the geographies of different mediums, and in both respects, determinations of legal principle are inextricably related to definitions of the state of factual knowledge.

The relationship between First Amendment law, geography and communications policy can be approached from two directions. First, it involves the political construction of the jurisdictional scales through which communications markets are constituted and regulated. The 1934 Communications Act established the Federal Communications Commission (FCC) as the regulatory authority for US broadcasting and telecommunications. Consistent with the federalist tradition of interstate commerce regulation from which it emerged, the FCC's licensing policies for radio and subsequently television services reflected a strong commitment to 'localism': broadcast stations were licensed as local stations, limited to broadcasting within defined localities, and in principle bearing certain public interest responsibilities to local communities. In practice, the economics of broadcasting dictated that few local stations could afford to produce adequate local programming, stimulating the consolidation of national networks providing programming for locally owned broadcast stations (Le Duc 1987: 13). This leads on to the second dimension of the geographies of First Amendment media regulation. Conceptualisations of the physical characteristics of media, embodied in such administrative and legal concepts as scarcity, invasiveness and the distinction between wireline and wireless communications, all contain evaluative understandings of the spatialities that differentiate mediums. In fundamental ways, these imaginary geographies of media and communications help define the boundaries between the forms of action that will and will not be ascribed the status of protected speech.

It is important to underscore that First Amendment decision-making is inherently normative, in the sense that is concerned with prescribing the limits of legitimate behaviour (Fish 1994; Post 1998). The jurisprudence of free speech involves the drawing of boundaries – between categories of speakers, between different media, and above all, between speech and non-speech (Fiss 1996a: 123). Speech is a functional term referring to a more or less broad but necessarily limited range of activities that are considered worthy of protection by reference to some specified communicative purpose (Schauer 1982: 91). The most significant boundary is between speech and conduct, the latter being defined as any activity that is not primarily expressive of ideas. This is an inherently unstable, unpredictable delimitation: flag burning is understood as expressive conduct, therefore as protected speech; burning a military draft card is not, and nor is begging (see Mitchell 1997; Horwitz 1993). The significance of this distinction for media policy is that it rests on a specific philosophy of communication, according to which it is possible to separate the meaning of an expression from the medium of an expression. This is enshrined in the principle of content-neutrality, which holds that government can legitimately regulate speech activities as long as it does not do so on the basis of or to the detriment of any particular substantive content of messages. Content-neutrality rests on the idea that comprehensive doctrines of the good life can and should be bracketed, and only universal norms of right derived from reasonable procedures be allowed to guide state action. In the area of media and communications law, this boundary between the good and the right is expressed in the position that the First Amendment protects 'the abstract fact of communication', irrespective of the value of particular positions (Post 1995: 1249).

Content-neutrality has come in for a wide array of criticisms. A broad variety of political perspectives invokes the higher good of political speech as the proper standard of First Amendment law. From a communitarian, civic republican perspective, content-neutrality enshrines the ascendancy of a deracinated, abstract liberal understanding of the unencumbered self, thus enabling the substitution of self-expression for self-government (Sandel 1996). A conservative original-intent reading of the First Amendment applies a very limited understanding of what constitutes legitimate political speech to justify extensive state censorship of art, literature or television (Bork 1971). Both radical feminists and critical race theorists have challenged the presumptions of content-neutrality, calling into question the presumption that speech is only a matter of beliefs. They argue instead that certain forms of speech constitute direct harm, and can therefore be legitimately regulated (MacKinnon 1993; Matsuda et al. 1993).

The idea that the primary purpose of the First Amendment is the protection of political speech for the purpose of popular self-government is most closely associated with the First Amendment absolutism of Alexander Meiklejohn, for whom the negative words of the clause represented a positive affirmation of popular sovereignty: 'The freedom that the First Amendment protects is not, then, an absence of regulation. It is the presence of self-government' (1961: 252). This interpretation accords considerable scope to state actions that promote certain sorts of speech: 'the First Amendment does not protect a "freedom to speak". It protects the freedom of those activities of thought and communication by which we "govern". It is concerned, not with a private right, but with a public power, a governmental responsibility' (ibid.: 255). Meiklejohn reads the First Amendment as protecting speech that is used in the service of 'governing the nation'. His approach found considerable practical endorsement in the decisions of the liberal Warren Court of the 1950s and 1960s. The civic republican philosophy of free speech as an instrument of popular self-government has recently been revived by writers such as Owen Fiss (1996b) and Cass Sunstein (1995a), who have developed left-liberal critiques of the increasingly corporate friendly libertarian interpretation of the First Amendment as protecting the speech rights of autonomous individual speakers.

The collectivist tradition linking Meiklejohn to Fiss and Sunstein reconciles liberalism and civic republicanism by allowing individual autonomy an instrumental function in rational public debate, but only by implicitly limiting the scope of democratic self-determination to deliberation over a pre-selected range of substantive issues carried on according to pre-established conventions of civility.[3] This effectively disallows the legitimacy of forms of expression that challenge the boundaries and norms of what counts as public discourse (Post 1993). The First Amendment can be understood to affirm the importance of public discourse for a collective purpose, but only by protecting the legitimacy of counterdiscourses that are critical of public norms of reason, deliberation and civility, and which might therefore undermine collective consensus (Post 1990: 642–3). The value of free expression can be located within a triangular relationship between norms of civility without which deliberation is not possible, the instrumental imperatives of organisations to make decisions, and the freedom of critical discourse to problematise both these other dimensions (Post 1995: 685). This implies that 'the boundaries of public discourse cannot be fixed in a neutral fashion' (ibid.: 683), but only according to a conditional stabilisation openly justified in relation to a particular, contestable conception of the good.

The application of content-neutrality implies drawing distinctions between message and means of transmission, content and form. There are two axes on which this line drawing takes place. First, the limits are drawn with reference to the content of speech. First Amendment case law distinguishes a hierarchy of speech values (obscenity, false advertising and fighting words are not accorded protection; commercial speech and indecent speech are accorded some protection; the highest level of scrutiny is reserved for political speech). Second, boundary drawing distinguishes between different modes of dissemination characteristic of particular media (see Post 1990: 667–79). Since the 1940s, the Supreme Court has applied First Amendment principles differently to different communications mediums, so that there is a tradition of treating each as medium as a law unto itself. In practice, the two modes of delimiting the boundaries of protected speech – by reference to content, or by

3   If this first move is reminiscent of Habermas' resolution of liberalism and communi-
     tarianism (1994a), then the second restriction is lifted in his application of the weak
     public/strong public distinction discussed in Chapter 3.

reference to the medium of transmission – are combined in different ways case by case. The technically public qualities of different mediums are difficult to distinguish clearly from the substantively public purposes imputed to them. First Amendment jurisprudence has tended to view technologies that are ascribed the status of being inherently public through their very means of transmission with great suspicion. The uncertain scope and destination of address characteristic of certain media (the paradigm is broadcasting) has consistently been considered a problem, not least because it runs up against the contradictory political and cultural implications that follow from privileging free speech rights as rights of individual autonomy.

The status of broadcasting exemplifies a fundamental feature of First Amendment methodology with respect to mediated communications. US constitutional law is in large part a common law tradition, in which decisions are made not simply by reference to constitutional text or legislative history, but by drawing analogies between new and existing fields (Sunstein 1996: 80–1). Analogical reasoning is crucial to the development of First Amendment law in previously uncharted areas, and especially in media and communications law. In particular, analogical reasoning is central to the iterative process of constructing precedents (Cornell 1992: 146–7). The practical role of analogical reasoning is related to the underdetermined nature of legal decision-making in any particular case, and is in turn related to the unanticipated consequences of particular decisions. Once made, a specific analogy can be reinscribed to justify new findings of substance or principle. Constitutional law is, then, a field of strong performativity, in which the deployment of words, narrative, analogies and other rhetorical devices is bolstered by institutionalised patterns of enforcement, rule following and inducement (Butler 1997). With this in mind, the rest of this chapter tracks the history of analogical reasoning in First Amendment communications law. This will illustrate the way that, in judging the qualities of different mediums of transmission, First Amendment jurisprudence functions as a realm for defining what counts as substantively public or private by reference to particular understandings of the sites and spaces into and through which communication reaches.

III The peculiar characteristics of broadcasting

The US tradition of public policy and media law has relatively weak grounds for positive action by government to maintain various public interest objectives (Barendt 1993). The First Amendment in particular has often been interpreted as embodying a presumption against state action. It is common to distinguish three models of First Amendment law: a print-based model, in which First Amendment protections are most strict; a broadcasting model, in which they are more restricted; and the common carrier model (common carriers are not traditionally considered to be speakers at all), in which conduit and message are considered to be separate. These distinctions are derived from constitutional case law and the administrative rules of public agencies. The 1934 Communications Act distinguished between broadcasters and common carriers (telephone companies), both regulated by a federal agency, the FCC (see McChesney 1993). From the 1940s, the legitimacy of communications regulation was premised on two related doctrines. First, a narrowly technical understanding of the mismatch between the potential number of available frequencies and the number of broadcasters was enshrined in the spectrum scarcity rationale for regulation.[4] Second, an implicit impact rationale rested on the apparently unprecedented ability of the public medium of radio to invade the domestic sanctuary of the home.

Considerations of the constitutionality of broadcasting regulation have rested on a taken-for-granted narrative that establishes the factual basis for federal regulation. In this narrative, unregulated broadcasting descended into chaos in the 1920s, and order was established by setting up federal regulation from 1927 (Streeter 1996: 74–5). Broadcasters were constitutionally recognised as fiduciaries – in return for a grant of an exclusive broadcasting frequency, they were expected to meet certain public interest obligations in terms of programming. The narrative of order imposed upon chaos, and of broadcasters as public trustees, presented commercial broadcasting as the only rational system of organising mass communications. Basing the constitutional rationale for regulation on the factual basis imputed to the technical characteristics of broadcasting technology means that there is a built-in tendency for the expansion of technologies, or the emergence of new ones, to trigger deregulatory policy measures (Hoffman-Riem 1996: 52; Le Duc 1987: 170–4).

The principle of public trusteeship in broadcasting was enshrined in the so-called Fairness Doctrine, an administrative guideline (it was never actually passed into legislation by Congress) according to which

---

4   Since the objectives of the FCC's frequency allocation policies were to have a large
    number of privately owned local stations, scarcity is as much an administrative product
    as it is a technical fact.

broadcasters should provide coverage of contrasting viewpoints on issues of public importance. The Fairness Doctrine was central to the politics of media regulation from the 1940s through to the 1980s, and still retains symbolic power in contemporary debates (Aufderheide 2000: 173–84). It enshrined a particular understanding of the primary subjects of freedom-of-expression principles in contexts of mass-mediated communications. It presupposed that free speech principles could only be given substance in the context of broadcasting 'by giving precedence to the right of the American public to be informed on all sides of public questions'.[5] The Fairness Doctrine therefore expressed a broader understanding in policy, regulation and constitutional law, according to which the speech rights of audiences and the interests of broadcasters did not naturally coincide.

The question of who the rightful agents of the public interest are in a system of mediated mass communication became an explicit focus of political mobilisation in the 1960s, with the emergence of a broadcast reform movement (Horwitz 1989: 247–52). In 1966, community groups were granted standing as legitimate representatives of the public interest in FCC licence renewal hearings, a decision that further stimulated citizen access activism (Horwitz 1996). The decision fundamentally redefined the terrain of interest group representation in communications policy and law: 'The conception of the regulatory agency as itself the *embodiment* of the public interest gave way to a conception of the regulatory agency as a political, quasi-legislative forum wherein competing interests would vie to define the public interest' (Horwitz 1989: 201). In 1971 the FCC established procedures for community ascertainment of licence renewal. These required licensees to ascertain the relevant issues of concern to their local communities. In principle at least, the production of knowledge was made the condition for facilitating broader public participation in processes of licence renewal, and so making broadcasters more responsive to communities in meeting their fiduciary responsibilities to local communities. The entry point for activists and organisations into the policy process therefore depended upon the localism embedded in the FCC's frequency allocation and licensing rules, with campaigners challenging broadcasters on the grounds that they did not cater adequately for the interests of local communities. Thus, 'the structure of the regulatory system in part structured the pattern of reformist activism' (ibid.: 358), not least in terms of the spatial scale of mobilisation and organisation. The

---

5 'Report on editorializing by broadcast licensees', *FCC Reports*, Volume 13, 1257 (1949).

localised orientation of campaigns inhibited the development of effective lobbying and organisation capacity at a national scale. While the FCC was opened up to pluralist interest group representation, it was business interests in broadcasting, as well as the increasingly assertive cable television industry, that in the long term proved most effective in organising at national level, and therefore in influencing national legislative and regulatory agendas.

The high point for the broadcast reform movement was the Supreme Court's *Red Lion* decision in 1969 upholding the constitutionality of the FCC's Fairness Doctrine.[6] In this case, the Fairness Doctrine was challenged on the grounds that the requirement to air diverse opinions represented an unconstitutional content-based regulation. The *Red Lion* judgement upheld the scarcity rationale, arguing that broadcasting was characterised not just by technical spectrum scarcity, but also by allocational scarcity. The *Red Lion* majority proposed that the system of broadcasting depended on a form of state action conferring a preferred position on private entities. The Court upheld the principle of treating different media according to different rules, and restated the principle that it was the rights of the public that took precedence over the asserted rights of licensees:

> It is the rights of the viewers and listeners, not the right of the broadcasters, which is paramount [. . .] It is the right of the public to receive suitable access to social, political, aesthetic, moral, and other ideas and experiences which is crucial here. That right may not constitutionally be abridged either by Congress or by the FCC.[7]

Red Lion did not confer a constitutional right of reply or access, it merely held that such rules were not presumptively unconstitutional. As the 1970s progressed, the tide of legal reasoning and regulatory policy began to turn decisively against expansive interpretations of the public interest championed by citizen access campaigns. The shift towards a strong presumption in favour of broadcasters' speech rights and against the applicability and enforceability of access principles dovetailed with an increasingly influential intellectual critique of the principles underlying FCC public interest regulation of communications media. This ascendant position held that since all economic goods are scarce, broadcasting is not distinguished on this count from other sectors, so

6   *Red Lion Broadcasting v. FCC*, 395 US 367 (1969).
7   Ibid.

licences should be allocated by the price mechanism, and granted as property rights, just like other scarce goods. This argument was first advanced in the 1950s (Coase 1959). But by the 1980s, with the ascendancy of the law-and-economics movement, what was once a maverick position had become orthodoxy in mainstream legal and economic analysis of communications in the US academy and legal establishment (see Fowler and Brenner 1982). From this perspective, administrative decision-making is costly and inefficient, and should be replaced by a system in which speech rights and property rights are formally equated. The public interest standard is considered to be dangerously ill defined, allowing unfettered regulatory discretion. When put into practice, this position has the effect of transferring greater and greater areas of public policy out of the arena of formal public scrutiny, substituting for them the populist promise of free markets and technologically induced serialised choice.

As the Supreme Court has become more politically conservative and business activism more effective, and intellectual paradigm shifts have assaulted the philosophical assumptions underwriting *Red Lion*, the ways in which media organisations are categorised for constitutional purposes have been transformed. *Red Lion* described broadcasters as licensees, proxies and fiduciaries, to underscore the concept of broadcasters as public trustees whose autonomy was less protected than that of print media (Bollinger 1991: 72). Access campaigns gained legitimacy in relation to broadcasting by distinguishing this medium from print on the grounds that it was really a conduit. The politics of First Amendment categorisation is now strongly shaped by the efforts of media and communications corporations to have their activities defined on the model of print, and more generally to have the print model of free speech established as the norm of a converged First Amendment media jurisprudence. The pattern of judgement since *Red Lion* has steadily reoriented the discourse of free speech, so that first broadcasters, then other media organisations, are increasingly interpellated in terms of a vocabulary of editorial rights.

The argument that broadcasters should be treated primarily in terms of private journalism, implying that protection of First Amendment rights should override fiduciary responsibilities, was first established by the Supreme Court in 1973.[8] In 1974, the Court rejected the argument that citizen access to media outlets in the form of a right of reply should be extended to the print media.[9] The Supreme Court has increasingly

---

8   *Columbia Broadcasting System v. Democratic National Committee*, 412 US 94 (1973).
9   *Miami Herald Publishing Company v. Tornillo*, 418 US 241 (1974).

upheld the position that the essence of freedom of expression in mediated communications inheres in principles of journalistic discretion and editorial autonomy.[10] Defining broadcasters as speakers severely limits the scope for measures to extend public interest standards of accountability and access to broadcasting, since enforcing rights of access would in principle amount to forced speech, which is not allowed by First Amendment law. In defining broadcasting in terms of editorial autonomy, the Court introduced a broad definition of what constituted editorial action as 'the selection and choice of material' for transmission. This definition contains the potential for other types of communications entities (cable operators, telephone companies) to lay claim to the status of speakers with protected speech rights.

In the mid-1970s, the Supreme Court extended protected speech status to commercial speech.[11] The extension of First Amendment protection to commercial speech was initially justified on the grounds that it was not the identity of the speaker that was the key issue, but whether the form of expression at issue was protected speech or not. No other precedent existed to extend speech rights to corporate entities other than the principle that the First Amendment was primarily concerned to inform public debate, and thus commercial and corporate speech was recognised on the grounds of the public's right to receive information.[12] The most famous and still most controversial corporate speech case is *Buckley v. Valeo*, the Supreme Court judgement on campaign finance that found that 'money is speech'.[13] This judgement erased the constitutive role of the courts, the legislature and the FCC in constituting the system of mediated public communications as one in which public speech depended on the expenditure of money. In *Buckley*, the majority decision effectively renounced *Red Lion*: 'the concept that government may restrict the speech of some elements of our society in order to enhance the relative voice of others is wholly foreign to the First Amendment'.[14] This implies a definition of speakers' rights as absolute and inviolable, and assumes this guarantee of autonomy is sufficient to meet the broader public purposes of freedom-of-expression principles.

The uneven path to assigning protected speech rights to corporations has moved from the conditional extension of First Amendment

10   *FCC v. League of Women Voters of California*, 486 US 364 (1984).
11   *Bigelow v. Virginia*, 421 US 809 (1975); *Virgina State Board of Pharmacy v. Virgina Citizens Consumer Council*, 425 US 748 (1976).
12   *First National Bank of Boston v. Bellotti*, 435 US 765 (1978).
13   *Buckley v. Valeo*, 424 US 1 (1976).
14   Ibid.

protection to commercial speech (to ensure that the interests of the public in receiving commercial information were served), to the ascription of full subject status to corporations, with full rights of self-expression and not to be compelled to speak. In the 1980s, the Court upheld the right of corporations not to have to associate with the views of others without their consent.[15] Thus, the right not to have words put into one's mouth, which is derived from notions of freedom of conscience, was extended to corporations, imbuing non-human entities with the qualities of self-expression, will and conscience usually reserved for natural persons. The discursive construction of corporations as legal persons, or actants, with speech rights has had wider significance for media and communications law.[16] Importantly, media and communications corporations have not gained First Amendment protection by relying on the direct analogy with the press (see Schauer 1998b), but by reference to a more abstract analogy of editorial autonomy. Since the commercial speech cases of the 1970s maintained that the identity of the speaker was not decisive in determining whether First Amendment rights were at stake, this principle meant that any entity exercising discretion over what was communicated through its channels of transmission could be understood on the analogy of editorial selection.

These changes in constitutional doctrine dovetailed with an internal regulatory dynamic within the FCC to shift the parameters of First Amendment interpretation towards an emphasis on the speech rights of corporate actors, understood on the analogy of natural persons with liberal rights to individual autonomy. Judicial decisions widening standing in the 1960s transferred the burden of meeting public interest standards to broadcasters and regulators. The success of the broadcast reform movement in intervening in the administrative oversight of broadcasting stimulated a deregulatory dynamic from the FCC that was initially driven as much by lack of institutional capacity as by ideological shifts (Horwitz 1989: 261). Requirements on broadcasters to maintain records of programming were scaled back, culminating in the 1980s with the replacement of community ascertainment of licence renewal with so-called postcard renewal, in which renewal was almost guaranteed and subject to little public scrutiny. If the deregulatory logic of the FCC was initially an internal, administrative one, by the 1980s, the FCC had become a leading promoter of free market understandings of media

---

15 *Pacific Gas and Electric Co. v. Public Utilities Commission of California*, 475 US 1 (1986); see also *Consolidated Edison Co. Of New York v. Public Service Commission of New York*, 447 US 530 (1980).

16 See Greimas (1990: 102–38) on the discursive construction of legal actants.

and communications sectors. Rule changes effectively transformed the public interest into a synonym for idealised consumer choice. Principles of media pluralism in the market-place of ideas were reduced to a narrow model of quantitative diversity of the number of media services available (Napoli 1999). The constitutional principle of content-neutrality supports this purely numerical understanding. It presumptively invalidates considerations of pluralism in terms of the content of viewpoints disseminated through the media.[17]

The quantitative interpretation of diversity proved fatal for the traditional rationale for public interest broadcasting regulation, which was based on narrowly technical understandings of scarcity. In the mid-1980s, at the prompting of lower Federal Courts, and in response to further moves by public interest groups to oblige effective enforcement, the FCC unilaterally abandoned the Fairness Doctrine that the Supreme Court had found constitutional in 1969.[18] The FCC's rule change in this case redefined the factual basis for understanding the nature of broadcasting markets. It argued that the Fairness Doctrine no longer served the public interest because, first, information markets were now characterised by abundance rather than scarcity, and, second, it claimed that there was evidence that the rules on editorialising had a chilling effect, inhibiting broadcasters from airing controversial issues in the first place. The FCC constructed the *Red Lion* judgement as turning wholly on the empirical issue of scarcity, which it in turn defined in purely numerical terms.[19] *Red Lion*'s argument about allocational scarcity, that demand for access to the airwaves (by citizens as speakers) outstripped supply, was rejected on the grounds that the number and types of information sources available to consumers (as viewers and listeners) had vastly expanded since the 1960s. The FCC invoked the Supreme Court's post-*Red Lion* emphasis on the editorial autonomy of broadcasters to argue that the Fairness Doctrine was an unnecessary and unwanted imposition on journalistic discretion.

17   The Supreme Court has found that certain measures to promote specific sorts of programming are constitutional; for example, in the case of rules for ensuring minority ownership of broadcast licences, and in the case of cable television must-carry regulations. While these decisions indicate a lingering acknowledgement that communications markets will not necessarily produce plural media content if left to themselves, they also confirm a deeper assumption that diversity of ownership is a sufficient guarantee of viewpoint pluralism.

18   'Fairness Doctrine report', *FCC Reports, 2nd Series, Volume 102*, 143–253 (1986).

19   'Memorandum opinion and order on the Fairness Doctrine', *FCC Record, Volume 2*, 17, 5048–9 (1987).

The FCC's elimination of fairness rules connected an interpretation of the facts to an argument for redefining the standard of constitutional review relevant to assessing the constitutionality of the regulation of electronic media. It argued that functional similarities between mediums should be the basis of First Amendment judgement, not supposed physical differences between mediums.[20] The peculiar characteristics of broadcasting no longer applied, and therefore the print model should be applied to broadcasting and other media that were defined as having an editorialising function.[21] This in turn involved a rejection of the balancing approach to the rights of different parties used in *Red Lion*. The FCC redefined the constitutional understanding of the relationships between the speech rights of different actors in contexts of mediated communications, arguing that the rights of communications organisations and the public were consistent rather than contradictory, and best served by ensuring the operation of a competitive market for audiences.[22] This resolution works only by redefining the public primarily as a collection of individualised consumers.

The elimination of the Fairness Doctrine is indicative of the changing dimensions of the discursive space in which the subjects and purposes of First Amendment rights are defined. While relying primarily on an interpretation of empirical facts, the FCC also drew upon and codified the shift already staked out by the Supreme Court since the 1970s, which accorded rights of editorial autonomy to corporate actors. This relationship between normatively grounded disputes about the bearers of rights and empirically grounded disputes about the facts is constitutive of the distinctive role of legal reasoning in US communications law (Streeter 1996: 128–32). The expansion of standing to include citizens' groups in the 1960s was associated with a shift in the weight accorded to certain forms of knowledge. In turn, the assignment of speakers' rights to corporations since the 1970s has been associated with the embedding of new narratives of fact and new forms of legal interpretation and academic legal and economic expertise. The broad trend over the last three decades has been for increasingly contentious questions of constitutional interpretation in the fields of media and communications to be resolved by displacement, with the questions being rewritten as matters of the factual record. This trend has only been exacerbated by the proliferation of new communications technologies.

20 Ibid., 5056.
21 Ibid., 5053.
22 Ibid., 5057.

IV Cable television and the
constitutional problem of
new technology

In First Amendment law, cable television is the paradigmatic new technology (Horwitz 1991). Community Antenna Television (CATV) first developed in the 1940s as a means of distributing broadcast signals to localities proximate to the service areas of local licensees unable to pick up broadcast reception (Brown 1981: 79–86). From the 1960s, with the introduction of the microwave relay of signals, and then in the 1970s of satellite technology, cable shifted decisively to providing television services from remote areas, a shift that was associated with a concentration of ownership within the cable industry. The initial diffusion of CATV occurred outside of the FCC's jurisdiction. In the late 1950s, the FCC found that it had no jurisdiction over cable as a common carrier, because cable services were not merely conduits for the messages of others; but nor did it have jurisdiction over cable as broadcasting, since these services were transmitted by wire not radio waves.[23] Cable television combined features of both common carriers and broadcasters, but in a way that slipped between the clear categorical distinctions that governed FCC rule-making.

Cable television therefore initially developed through a diffuse pattern of localised municipal and state regulation. Since cable systems required the use of public rights of way (streets, sidewalks, telegraph poles), local franchising agreements were awarded to cable companies as local monopolies in return for the reservation of some channels for government information, education and public access use. It is in this context of local regulation that the notion that cable television constituted a natural monopoly emerged. As cable developed from a supplementary service to providing original programming, broadcasters mobilised successfully to get the FCC to reverse its earlier position on cable. When cable television began to deploy microwave relay technology, the FCC asserted regulatory jurisdiction over cable on the grounds that it now fell within the purview of the regulation of wireless services.[24] Subsequently, however, the FCC argued that it was the detrimental impact of cable television on the viability of broadcasting (and by extension the FCC's own administrative function), rooted in principles

---

23   'Frontier Broadcasting Co. et al. v. J. E. Collier and Carl O. Krummel, Laramie Community TV Co. et al.', *FCC Reports, Volume 24*, 251–6 (1958); 'First report and order: CATV and TV repeater services', *FCC Reports, Volume 26*, 403–59 (1959).
24   'Re-Carter Mountain Transmission Corp.', *FCC Reports, Volume 32*, 459–86 (1969).

of localism, which justified its assertion of jurisdiction over cable (Le Duc 1969). The regulatory requirement for cable operators to carry local broadcast signals on their networks (so-called must-carry rules)[25] depended on treating cable as ancillary to broadcasting. The Supreme Court upheld this derivative justification of cable regulation on the grounds that it was essential to the FCC's statutory responsibility to maintain a localised, 'free' broadcasting system.[26] In the early 1970s, the FCC developed its first extensive regulatory rules for cable television. These formalised existing requirements that cable operators carry local broadcast signals, required provision of access channels, and limited cross-ownership.[27]

The history of constitutional regulation of cable television has continued the convention of deciding the status of speech and speakers by reference to a categorical calculation of the nature of the medium of transmission. At different times, both regulators and the courts have applied the analogies of broadcasting, common carrier and press to cable television. The difficulty of settling on a single analogical rule for cable television has in turn meant that, at times, must-carry rules and public access obligations have been found unconstitutional, and at others constitutional (Smith 1997; Le Duc 1988). In the 1980s, cable operators secured formal recognition as First Amendment speakers. The Supreme Court sided with the argument that, by virtue of original programming and the exercise of editorial discretion over which stations and programmes to include in their packages, cable companies were clearly involved in speech activity that fell within the First Amendment's field of reference. In 1984, Congress eliminated the regulation of cable rates, while maintaining the local monopoly privileges of cable operators by retaining local franchising and restricting telephone companies from providing video services. As cable rates spiralled upwards in the late 1980s and early 1990s, Congress backtracked, and in 1992, passed the Cable Television Consumer Protection and Competition Act. This reintroduced the must-carry rules that Federal Courts had previously found to lack statutory basis.

Cable operators challenged the constitutionality of the must-carry provisions of the 1992 Act on First Amendment grounds. The Supreme

25 'First report and order: micro-wave served CATV', *FCC Reports, Volume 38*, 683–759 (1965); 'Second report and order: CATV', *FCC Reports, 2nd Series, Volume 2*, 725–820 (1966).

26 *United States v. Southwestern Cable Co.*, 392 US 157 (1968); *United States v. Midwest Video*, 406 US 649 (1972).

27 'Cable television report and order', *FCC Reports, 2nd Series, Volume 36*, 143–325 (1972).

Court's two judgements on this issue (so-called *Turner I* and *Turner II*)[28] are central to establishing the parameters of First Amendment policy-making in the era of deregulated, converged, digitalised communication (see Sunstein 1995b). The case turned on the question of whether local television broadcasting was threatened by cable television's market strength. In *Turner I*, the Court found that must-carry rules were content-neutral, arguing that the value of diverse and local programming they protected distinguished between speakers on the grounds of means of transmission, not on the grounds of content. A justifiable government interest in protecting free television was threatened by the gate-keeping discretion of cable companies to keep broadcast signals off their systems. The constitutionality of the must-carry rules was therefore premised on the characterisation of cable as having a bottleneck power over the question of which media entered subscribers' homes. This finding invalidated the analogy with newspapers, on the grounds that cable operators exercised far greater control over access. The cable bottleneck is not merely a technological fact, but a composite figure which combines judgements regarding the technical features of different mediums, understandings of the economic dynamics of cable and broadcasting markets, and idealised assumptions about the value of 'local' and 'free' television. And its significance extends beyond 'old' media like television, since the question of bottlenecks and gate-keeping have become central to the constitutional regulation of Internet communications as well.

The outcomes of First Amendment cases depend not only on ideological positions on a liberal-conservative continuum, but on more complex divisions over issues of constitutional interpretation, doctrine and judicial activism. As already suggested, media and communications cases are divisive because the construction of such cases in terms of technological change provides the opportunity for Justices to try out attempts at doctrinal redefinition. New technology cases are also significant because of the extent to which they depend on specific understandings of empirical evidence. In such cases, findings about the empirical facts of technology 'are often determinate of constitutionality' (Schauer 1998a: 2312). *Turner I* dealt only with the standard of constitutional scrutiny relevant to cable. It deferred judgement on the factual basis of whether eliminating must-carry would negatively impact on broadcasting the case back to lower courts. In *Turner II*, the Court found that government regulation was legitimate in pursuit of

---

28   *Turner Broadcasting System Inc. v. FCC*, 512 US 622 (1994); *Turner Broadcasting System Inc. v. FCC*, 520 US 180 (1997).

media diversity, but did so specifically on the grounds of substantial evidentiary findings. *Turner I* and *Turner II* therefore illustrate the shifting balance between knowledge, expertise and constitutional interpretation in the constitutionalisation of US communications policy over the last three decades. In certain fundamental respects, technology cases like these exemplify a trend towards the delegalisation of constitutional law (Schauer and Wise 2000), in so far as the role of non-legal knowledge displaces explicit recourse to contestable, normative interpretations. This has ambivalent implications. On the one hand, the increasing importance of evidence in legal and administrative procedures governing communications policy provides access points for specific sorts of participation by certain actors (Shields 1995). However, the evidentiary turn in constitutional interpretation displaces open arguments over the meaning and purpose of rights and the public interest with apparently value-free arguments over the empirical record.

Deregulation of the communications industry in the 1990s allowed greater competition in local radio and television markets, liberalised market entry rules, and lifted restrictions on cross-media ownership between telephone companies and cable companies. The deregulatory legislative agenda connects with constitutional policy-making in contradictory ways. While in the 1970s and 1980s, the cable industry proved highly successful in rolling back certain sorts of regulatory restrictions by asserting First Amendment rights, the very success of this strategy opened up the cable sector to new forms of constitutional oversight. As speakers, exercising an editorial function, rather than mere common carriers, cable companies have been subjected to successive attempts by Congress, state legislatures, municipalities and the FCC to regulate programming on obscenity and indecency grounds. The 1992 Act removed cable operators' immunity from liability for obscenity and indecency, and thus opened up a new phase of First Amendment policy-making that has implications not only for broadcasting and cable, but also for the treatment of Internet communications and of digital technology. The legal and administrative construction of new communications technologies has increasingly been shaped by a split regulatory regime of market liberalisation combined with neo-paternalist cultural regulation.

V *Changing channels: from scarcity to impact*

Since the 1970s, the scarcity rationale has been supplanted by a stronger application of an impact rationale that further supports the ascendancy of a particular understanding of individual autonomy as the model of free speech rights. The impact rationale depends in no small part on representations of the vulnerable child. The most assertive and effective grassroots mobilisations in US media politics since the 1970s have been public interest organisations such as Action for Children's Television, campaigning for children's media rights (Montgomery 1989). These organisations have been highly effective in mobilising locally and nationally in the courts and in shaping legislation (P. O'Neill 2000). Children are oddly liminal figures in the ascendant regulatory paradigm of consumer sovereignty and abstract individual autonomy. They are constructed as subjects of choice in the market-place, without being ascribed the status of moral subjects in their own right. This has important implications for the way the relationship between media and citizenship is conceptualised. All viewers can easily be characterised in the same terms as those ascribed to children, a feature of discourses of media regulation that John Hartley (1999: 218–19) dubs paedocracy, or government by children. The figuration of the vulnerable child, as a passive subject in need of protection and guidance, has become increasingly important to the definition of the public meanings of communications technologies in the US.

The impulses behind communications policy, both economic and cultural, have traditionally focused upon regulating the space of the home. The home is the site of intersection for public virtues and private moralities (Silverstone 1999: 94). The status of broadcasting in particular has been crucial to the extension of an individual autonomy interpretation of the First Amendment, on the grounds that broadcast radio and television is an excessively public medium that transgresses the boundaries between the inside and the outside of the home. The notion that mass communication is invasive has been a concern since the 1930s, and has been one basis for justifying regulation. Television in particular has been understood as 'a guest in the American home', although a rather capricious one, having a corrosive impact on parents' primary responsibility for children's education, but also being assigned a special responsibility in assisting them in that duty.[29] Given this historical construction of broadcasting as an ambivalent technology of public morality, obscenity and indecency law has become crucial to defining the public purposes of this and other media.

Definitions of obscenity and indecency in constitutional law are overdetermined by the characteristics ascribed to different communications

---

29 'Report on broadcast of violent, indecent, and obscene material', *FCC Reports, 2nd series, Volume 51*, 423 (1975).

mediums. Obscenity and indecency law conventionally focuses upon two spatial dimensions of communication: where such materials should be available; and the mediums of their transmission. While various forms of zoning restriction deal with the first issue, it is the mobility, or the communicability, of obscene and indecent material that is most problematic for communications law. The Supreme Court's first consideration of the constitutionality of obscenity legislation in the 1950s established the principle of contemporary community standards, according to which what counted as obscene and indecent material was best determined by reference to the conventions of particular communities of interpretation.[30] Subsequently, the Court found that government could not infringe the right of individuals to possess obscene material in the privacy of their own homes. This underscored the focus of obscenity law upon the transmission of materials.[31] This judgement relied on a model of respecting individual autonomy, but it implies in principle that government can legitimately regulate certain media to ensure that people are not compelled to listen or to view materials they deem offensive. In 1973, in *Miller v. California*,[32] the Court rejected the existence of a single national standard of what constituted obscenity on the grounds that this implied a levelling down process, whereby the standards of the least tolerant community would predominate over those of more liberal ones. The idea of a national standard was considered abstract, in contrast to the concrete scale of individual states. *Miller* established the principle that it was legitimate to prohibit 'the dissemination or exhibition of obscene material when the mode of dissemination carries with it a significant danger of offending the sensibilities of unwilling recipients or of exposure to juveniles'.[33] Protecting minors is here elided with the inviolable right of adults not to be exposed to uninitiated communications. Publicness is thereby defined negatively, as an excessive feature of communications mediums that infringes on rights to attentional privacy, which are in turn conflated with an ill-defined interest in protecting minors from harm.

The pivotal case in the application of obscenity and indecency law to the redefinition of the publicness of media in terms of an impact rationale is *FCC v. Pacifica*.[34] In this case, the FCC argued that broadcasting

---

30   *Roth v. US*, 354 US 476 (1957).
31   *Stanley v. Georgia*, 394 US 557 (1969).
32   *Miller v. California*, 413 US 15 (1973).
33   Ibid.
34   *FCC v. Pacifica Foundation*, 438 US 726 (1978).

was 'uniquely pervasive presence in the lives of all Americans' and was, moreover, 'uniquely available to children'. These twin justifications rely on representing the broadcast audience as captive and passive. In constitutional law, the captive audience theme balances the exposure of audiences to diverse opinions that is the essence of the positive liberties underlying free speech principles, with a negative right not to be compelled to listen to or view materials deemed offensive. The definition of different audiences as captive or not depends on the characterisation of the spaces and mediums of speech. These calculations in turn determine whether particular spaces (public transport systems, streets, the home) are defined as spaces of public communication or not. The crucial issue is the extent to which an audience is deemed to be able to avert its eyes. In First Amendment law, finding speech offensive is not enough to suppress it (it is in fact grounds for according it protection). In *Pacifica*, the Court found that regulating indecent speech that in the abstract might be considered worthy of protection depended in practice on the contexts in which speech occurs. In its judgement, the Court confirmed the differential categorisation of mediums for First Amendment purposes, but revised the grounds for upholding the less protected status of broadcasting. Accepting the FCC's position, broadcast regulation was justified on the grounds of its invasive qualities with respect to the sanctity of the familial home. *Pacifica* redefined broadcasting for constitutional purposes according to its ascribed characteristics of intrusiveness, audience passivity, and the spatial indivisibility of children from adults.

In situations of mediated communications, public and private spaces can be distinguished by reference to different forms of interaction: 'Public spaces are characterised by a relative openness to initiation of communication by others, and private spaces are characterised by a relative closedness to initiation of communication' (Samarajiva and Shields 1997: 541–2). With respect to this distinction, the drift of administrative rule-making and of constitutional case law since the 1970s has been to privilege the imputed privacy rights of autonomous subjects to be protected from uninitiated communication in particular spaces. The idea that broadcasting can intrude into the home without warning is paradigmatic in this respect. When placed in the broader context of commercial speech cases, *Pacifica* is part of a fundamental move away from defining media audiences as a public of citizens, towards a discursive regime governed by a split representation of the public as active choice-makers in the market-place of commodified preferences, but also as potentially susceptible to both offence and harm, and therefore in need of protection.

Considerations of the applicability of *Pacifica* to other mediums have further embedded the individual-autonomy interpretation of First Amendment principles in communications law. In the case of telephone 'dial-a-porn' services, the Court found that telephone and broadcasting were distinct on the same grounds applied in the *Pacifica* ruling: 'In contrast to public displays, unsolicited mailing and other means of expression which the recipient has no meaningful opportunity to avoid, the dial-it medium requires the listener to take affirmative steps to receive the communication. There is no "captive audience" problem here; callers will generally not be unwilling listeners'.[35] In this characterisation, a strong presumption in favour of First Amendment protection is applied to one medium (telephone services) on the grounds that it is used for the purpose of private communication intentionally initiated by the participants, but not extended to another precisely because of its exorbitant publicness. The common carrier status of telephone companies rested on a conceptual separation of content from conduit, which had meant that carriers have not been assigned editorial control over content. This is the basis for the non-discriminatory, universal access principles implied by traditional notions of common carriage. However, the dial-a-porn case acknowledged that carriers did have some discretion over the messages they transmit. Once established, this principle of editorial selection has been used by telephone companies to assert First Amendment rights successfully in order to challenge cross-media ownership regulations (Ross 1998). But the First Amendment challenge to structural regulation has a double edge to it. It opens the possibility of communications corporations being found liable for message content on obscenity and indecency grounds.

Cable television has been central to the practical working out of the pattern of First Amendment application to interactive media technologies. The 1992 cable legislation had imposed must-carry, leased access and public access obligations on operators. Cable operators were given responsibility for regulating indecent programming on these access services. While these provisions were opposed by cable companies on the grounds of forced speech, public interest groups challenged them on the grounds that they gave cable operators effective editorial discretion over the speech communicated over access channels. The resulting constitutional case[36] illustrates the degree of instability concerning the application of rules in a context of rapid technological change. The Supreme Court split into six separate opinions on whether

---

35   *Sable Communications v. FCC*, 492 US 115 (1989).

36   *Denver Area Educational Telecommunications Consortium v. FCC*, 518 US 727 (1996).

communications law required hard and fast rules for the application of analogies, and if so, just which analogies should be used. From one perspective, case-by-case application of analogies is advantageous precisely because it allows particularistic judgements to be made rather than the application of rigid rules. Other Justices argued that clear rules were required. The Court's conservative triumvirate (Justices Rehnquist, Scalia and Thomas) argued that speakers' rights (the cable companies') are primary, and all other rights (those of programmers and viewers) are derivative of these. This position draws a strong analogy between speech rights and property rights. From a third perspective, the cable access question raised anew the issue of whether public forum doctrine should be extended to include electronic media.[37]

In the 1960s and 1970s, arguments for the extension of public forum doctrine had been part of progressive campaigns for extending citizen access to a wider array of communicative spaces (Kalven 1965). The argument works by analogy, but on functional grounds rather than on the basis of physical characteristics of different media, arguing that the most significant forms of public expression now took place in electronically mediated forums like radio and television. The willingness of the Court at least to entertain the public forum argument in the 1990s reflects a broader resurgence of interest in the applicability of the doctrine as a means to challenge the prioritisation of private property rights in communications policy and law. This revival is just part of a search for new standards of rule-making and analogical reasoning in a context in which previously stabilised categorisations have been disrupted. The applicability of public forum doctrine requires a finding that cable television (through local franchising) or broadcasting (through licensing) involves state action. The current trend is towards prioritising the editorial autonomy of communications companies over claims for broadening public access. The Court's general approach has been to limit public forum status to traditional arenas such as streets and parks.

Recent First Amendment case law is therefore characterised by contested interpretative approaches oscillating between the flexible and categorical application of analogies. At the same time, the focus of analogising has been redirected away from the imputed physical characteristics of mediums alone, to a more complex focus on the different interests at stake in communications law, including the protection of children, the promotion of diversity and the protection of free television (Sunstein 1996: 63). Increasing division on the Supreme Court and

---

37   See also *Arkansas Educational Television Commission v. Forbes*, 523 US 666 (1998).

doctrinal uncertainty over the course of communications law have been the context in which the First Amendment implications of new interactive media such as the Internet have begun to be addressed. In 1996, Congress passed the Telecommunications Act, which effectively supplanted the 1934 Communications Act as the guiding legislation for communications and media policy.[38] But the Act was not deregulatory in a simple sense. It exemplified split regulatory impulses, combining market liberalisation with stronger cultural regulation. The 1996 Act included as an addendum the Communications Decency Act (CDA). This imposed liability on communications companies for the transmission of indecent and obscene materials over any 'telecommunications device'.

The immediate political context of the CDA was a broader public debate about the extent of pornographic material available on the Internet. The ensuing constitutional challenge to the CDA bought together an alliance of non-profit civil liberties organisations such as the American Civil Liberties Union (ACLU) and the Media Access Project, journalist and artist groups, with media and communications industry interest groups. The case turned in part on the empirical question of the amount of offensive material on the web, but also on the empirical determination of the nature of the Internet and World Wide Web as mediums. The obscenity provision of the CDA was presumptively constitutional; it was the indecency clause that raised the First Amendment issue of balancing adults' speech rights with the legitimate interest in protecting children. The CDA applied the analogy of children and radio broadcasting used in the *Pacifica* case to children and computers, characterising the Internet as invasive and accessible to children. Lower court decisions found that the broadcasting analogy did not apply to the Internet, on the grounds that the user controls which sites are accessed. The Internet was constructed as a distinctively interactive medium, in contrast to the active–passive division that shapes understandings of broadcast communication. This interactivity raised the question of what constituted contemporary community standards in the case of the Internet – the community of origin or the community of final reception? (See Hadley and Samarajiva 1997.) In the emerging jurisprudence of cyberspace, definitions of the geographies of communications remain crucial. Cyberspace is contrasted to the apparently tangible presence of old mediums like bookstores, the mails and broadcasting. In fact, the difficulty of clearly delineating proximate from

38   See McChesney (1999) for a discussion of the politics, or lack of it, behind this
      legislation.

virtual communities in applying community standards criteria has characterised media law since the development of radio in the 1920s and 1930s. The most recent round of constitutional judgements on new media highlights the extent to which the regulation of media turns on the interpretation of the liminal position of communications technologies (public and private, individual and social, national and international). Mediated communications are routinely represented as parasitical, as intruding upon a properly integral context, but also as providing crucial support to the sustenance of those activities they potentially undermine.

The issues of which analogy to apply to Internet communications, and of what the relevant community was, were taken up by the Supreme Court in its judgement on the CDA in *Reno v. ACLU*.[39] The Court's finding that the CDA violated the First Amendment embedded in legal discourse a particular interpretation of the technical qualities of new communications media. The Internet was found not to be characterised by spectrum scarcity (the *Red Lion* analogy) and not to be pervasive or invasive, because users do not just stumble across content (the *Pacifica* analogy) and the communicator was not able to select an audience (the dial-a-porn analogy). In refusing to apply existing analogies to the Internet, including that of the press, the Court maintained the convention of basing judgements on categorical understandings of the techno-spatial characteristics of different mediums. The Internet was characterised as an essentially boundless medium, situated in no particular geographical location. In *Reno v. ACLU*, the Court found that in cyberspace, the sender of messages could neither determine the identity of the receiver nor control the geographical distribution of materials. In this and other Federal Court decisions, the Internet is constructed essentially as a conduit, and therefore there is no publisher liability for the speech of third parties. Application of the community standards principle to Internet communications would imply that the least tolerant community would judge the content of messages. Courts have found that, 'under current technology', content providers cannot prevent material from entering any geographical location.

The trend in recent Federal Court judgements is to present Internet communication as geographically unconstrained in the distribution of symbolic materials, a construction that rests on comparison with the bricks-and-mortar outlets and the mail system that have previously served as the models for obscenity and indecency law. This interpretation of the Internet as an immaterial, mediumless medium provides a

---

39   *Reno v. ACLU*, 51 US 844 (1997).

significant boost to those arguments that hold that cyberspace is essentially ungovernable. The dominant rhetoric of cyberspace law presents a stark opposition between regulation or no regulation, when in fact the relevant question is what sort of regulation will shape the interactive media landscape (and not least under what conditions of accountability and public scrutiny). Decisions about the development of new media technologies are not made in cyberspace, they are made in the same institutional and political fields as before. As Lessig (1996: 1408–9) notes, in this respect the relevance of the CDA and subsequent legislation,[40] even if found unconstitutional after the fact, is to induce self-regulation by encouraging the development and application of technologies of zoning and control. Legislation is just one part of a strategic game, involving private business, public interest campaigners and the courts, to induce changes to Internet architecture that meet concerns over accessibility to minors. The substitution of alterations to the code of interactive media for administrative and regulatory oversight displaces contested public judgements regarding the scope of public communication into apparently neutral technologies, effectively secreting a set of normative decisions about privacy and individualism into the design of technology (Lessig 2000).

The drift of constitutional law over the last three decades, by installing a particular paradigm of the autonomous subjects of free speech rights, has fuelled a trend towards finding technological fixes as the best means of regulating the mediated home-place, on the grounds that technology expands the capacity of parents to choose. To a considerable extent, the 'harmful to minors' standard has certainly been used as a way of legitimising conservative cultural agendas and as a cover for cultural censorship (Heins 2001). Nevertheless, a critique of this trend that simply rests on the presumption that such measures contravene children's own rights of individual autonomy begs all the difficult normative questions, which are not to do with a simple choice between autonomy and control. After all, as already indicated in this chapter, the shift to an impact rationale for cultural regulation relies on the invocation of, rather than the denial of, principles of individual

---

40 In 1998, Congress passed the Child Online Protection Act (COPA), meant to address the problem of excessive breadth that had scuppered the CDA. The constitutional issues raised by the legislation centred upon the questions of whether the application of the community standards principle was relevant to the World Wide Web specifically. The constitutional challenge to COPA has reaffirmed the tradition of treating mediums as laws unto themselves, and has confirmed the legal inscription of Internet technologies as immaterial mediums (*Ashcroft v. ACLU*, no. 00–1293, 13 May 2002).

autonomy. The real effect of such discursive shifts is to elide the paradoxical and inherently normative relationship between the *attainment* of autonomy and the *ascription* of autonomy (Post 1993: 672–3), presenting autonomy as a naturalised but implicitly gendered norm of masterful conduct of oneself and others, rooted in a particular image of normalised familial relations. It is this elision that carries the heaviest costs for democratic values, since it puts beyond question the scope and reference of principles such as autonomy, self-government or the public interest, whose democratic value lies in large part in being kept open to challenge and redefinition.

VI Conclusion: privatising free speech

The last three decades have seen the rise of a First Amendment jurisprudence that is presumptively hostile to various forms of state action, and increasingly sympathetic to the defence of private property rights. The willingness of the Federal Courts to entertain First Amendment challenges to public interest regulation of communications 'introduces litigation uncertainty into the legislative process by allowing opponents of new programs to argue credibly that the proposed programs might be held unconstitutional' (Tushnet 1999: 75). Thus, corporations have been able to deploy the governmental effect of constitutional law, reshaping the norms of policy-making by introducing the prospect of constitutional challenge on First Amendment grounds into communications policy formulation. The routine invocation of the First Amendment is, however, the outcome of a longer, more complex process. The emergence of a free market reading of the First Amendment in communications law is the outcome of the combination of administrative shifts, intellectual arguments, and political mobilisation by public interest groups and business organisations. The Federal Courts facilitated enhanced citizen access to the regulatory process, and have in turn helped to shape the lines of strategy adopted by corporations seeking to circumvent pressure for greater public access and accountability. It is important to emphasise that this facilitating role is underdetermined. Constitutional legal reasoning is characterised by 'incompletely theorised agreements on particular outcomes' (Sunstein 1996: x). The broader significance of particular cases depends on the retroactive construction of judgements as precedents. The reiterative authority of particular decisions is, as a consequence, shaped by the politics of legislation, knowledge and litigation that determines which cases make their way through the federal judicial system. The role of constitutional law is quite specific in this broader play of forces, involving as it does the assignment of meaning to key terms of legal discourse, such as public interest, competition and free speech. The ascription of constitutional rights to particular actors shapes broader arenas of public policy, establishing the norms of what is open to regulation. The effects of constitutional decisions, in inducing change to legislation or inviting further litigation (see Baum and Hausegger 1999), tend to be highly mediated by the capacity of other political actors to mobilise resources.

The guiding focus of First Amendment media and communications jurisprudence with respect to definitions of public space has moved away from the issues of citizen access that dominated in the 1960s and 1970s, to issues of the protection of minors. The nature of analogical reasoning has shifted away from questions of the extent to which mediums can be characterised as scarce, towards the extent to which different mediums can be characterised as invasive. In both respects, it is broadcasting that represents the baseline of judgement. In the mid-twentieth century, it was with reference to broadcasting that an expansive, access-based interpretation of the public significance of mediated communications was developed. However imperfect in practice, this represented a bulwark against highly individualist interpretations of free speech principles as a protection of speakers' rights, which, when applied to mediated mass communications, translated into a defence of private property rights in the means of public communication. The consistent pattern of constitutional law since the 1970s has been for communications corporations to challenge the extension of these principles to new media (cable being the paradigm) by claiming First Amendment rights as speakers. In this way, First Amendment jurisprudence has come to be central to the definition of the meanings of public communication.

The embedding of the imaginary geographies of communications mediums in law plays a pivotal role in determining the subjects of policy processes and the subjects of mediated speech. This process includes definitions of the jurisdictional scale at which communications can be regulated, as in the persistence of localism in FCC broadcasting regulation, the bifurcated jurisdiction (federal and local) over cable television, and the problematic definition of the relevant scale at which community standards of decency and offence are operative. It also involves, much more pervasively, understandings of the sites and spaces of communication. Representations of the home have been central to the inscription of media into constitutional law since the 1930s. Whereas previous approaches had balanced a sense of the home as simultaneously a private space of family life and a component of an extended public realm, increasingly the home has come to be constructed as a resolutely private communicational space. In turn, this is related to an increasing focus upon the supposedly inherent technological characteristics of mediums with respect to the extent to which they facilitate individual initiation of communication. The discourse of technologically induced choice has a populist ring to it, not least when it is attached to the argument that new technologies reduce the reliance of users and audiences on intermediaries. However, the dual legal construction of communications companies as speakers, and of the public as individual consumers, erases the essentially mediated character of communication. It thereby occludes the problematics of representation, justification and accountability, by embedding the market and technology as value-neutral mediums for the expression of the common will. Of course, the design of markets and technologies embed their own norms of conduct. But the elevation of these 'steering media' as devices for unmediated expression closes off the public contestation of the validity and legitimacy of those norms.

In the latest round of constitutional rule-making, stimulated by the proliferation of on-line interactive media, the Federal Courts have maintained the principle of distinguishing new technologies on the basis of categorical distinctions between mediums. The predominant criterion of analogical similarity and difference is now the judgement of the extent to which mediums require affirmative steps by users to access material (cable, telephone and Internet do; broadcasting and the mails do not).[41] This means that questions of obscenity and indecency have come to take on a particular significance in defining the publicness of different media. First Amendment obscenity and indecency law posits a model of subjectivity in terms of the exercise of individual autonomy in initiating or refusing communication. This is combined with a representation of the home as the privileged site for the exercise of individual autonomy, and by extension, the imputed rights of attentional privacy trump public availability and exposure to different viewpoints in defining the new communications media.

The general tenor of First Amendment case law has been, therefore, towards privatising free speech. This does not refer simply to upholding legislation that promotes the economic liberalisation of communications markets. The Supreme Court has certainly tended to defer to legislative authority in this field, while being much more assertive in reversing legislation aimed at cultural regulation of communications. This pattern does not necessarily involve a strong contradiction. The

41   *US v. Playboy Entertainment Group*, 509 US 823 (2000).

recurrent tendency is to define government action that respects current distributions of economic power as neutral and as a form of state inaction, and those which attempt to adjust those distributions as partisan and constituting state action (Sunstein 1995a: 28–34). This erases the ways in which markets, corporate entities, contract and property rights are all forms of private activity that are constituted by the public action of law and regulation. It is connected to the elevation of the principle of editorial autonomy as embodying the essence of free speech issues in media and communications cases. Likewise, in obscenity and indecency cases, the courts increasingly privilege concepts of personal autonomy, an understanding that dovetails nicely with the broader ascendancy of individual consumer sovereignty as the figure for understanding the public interest in economic regulation of communications. The treatments of both structural regulation and the regulation of obscene and indecent material therefore converges in sustaining the central image of the consumer exercising choice as the primary subject of free speech rights. This is indicative of a more fundamental privatisation of the First Amendment, and by extension of the discursive dimensions of public space. Previous justifications for communications regulation (scarcity, state action) posited the active citizen-subject engaging in public debate as their model. The rise of impact rationales for regulation rests on the individualised split subject of neo-liberalism, simultaneously empowered of choice but vulnerable to harm. And this implies a strong definition of free expression in terms of the protection of private speech, rather than in terms of maintaining a public realm of openness to other perspectives.

6

Deficits of communication: practising democracy in European Union media policy

The initial impetus to integration in the direction of a postnational society is not provided by the substrate of a supposed 'European people' but by the communicative network of a European-wide political public sphere embedded in a shared political culture.
Jürgen Habermas (1998: 153)

I The ends of European identity

Habermas (2001: 89) has recently suggested that the European Union (EU) might serve as the 'the initial form of a postnational democracy'. He argues that any European-wide democracy cannot be presumed to depend upon on the norm of a pre-political cultural unity (Habermas 1998: 106–61). Any future European political culture must be premised not on thick cultural ties between citizens, but on more abstract identifications with a system of political rights (Habermas 2001: 18–19). At the heart of public and academic debates about the trajectory of European integration is the question of whether strong models of cultural solidarity between members of a community can or should be translated upwards from the nation-state to a continental scale, or whether any putative model of European citizenship would depend upon the development of more abstract, less exclusivist conceptions of the relationships between citizenship and solidaristic identities (Preuss 1998). These issues are connected to broader conceptual questions concerning the difference that scale makes to the forms of participation and representation in an emergent European polity (Schmitter 1999; Siedentop 2000). To a considerable extent, there already is a European polity, or better still, a plurality of polities, made up of networks of policy knowledge, social movement mobilisation and interest group representation. It is worth emphasising the network qualities of this polity, since this allows a better grasp of the combination of functional and territorial modes of representation that is characteristic of EU policy-making (Jachtenfuchs et al. 1998). In a spatially complex polity such as the EU, citizenship practice is necessarily mediated, with rights of participation and consultation assigned to collective actors.

This chapter examines these themes through the example of the changing rationalities of EU-level media policy initiatives. One reason for using media policy as an entry point for understanding these broader issues is because of the importance given to practices of communication in understandings of the practical problem of transforming a nascent European *polity* into a functioning European *demos*. Elite understandings tend to equate European democracy with the efficient communication of information to a distanced, dispersed citizenry. In this understanding, media and communications take on a double significance, as mediums for shaping patterns of identification amongst culturally diverse populations, and as channels for ensuring effective political communication. EU audio-visual policies have therefore come to serve as an arena for working out contested models of the means and objectives of European integration, and in particular for competing understandings of the relationships between cultural identity, media and citizenship.

During the 1970s and 1980s, a raft of *de facto* cultural policies emerged from different directorates of the European Commission, the administrative agency of the EU that is responsible for initiating policy proposals. In the 1980s, concern over the EU's so-called democratic deficit led to culture being identified as an instrument for enhancing the legitimacy of the elite-driven European project. This is the context for the early development of audio-visual policy as a means of creating a European cultural space, centred on the *Television Without Frontiers* initiative. Its objective was the creation of a single market for broadcasting by harmonising regulatory standards across member states. It combined elements of external protectionism with elements of internal market liberalisation. The *Television Without Frontiers* directive of 1989[1] was the culmination of a decade-long policy debate centred on the problematic of media and European identity. Its broader context was the development of a worsening trade deficit between European economies and the United States in the audio-visual sector. EU initiatives in the 1980s and into the early 1990s appropriated the vocabulary of cultural imperialism to present American media culture as weakening common European identities, whilst presenting the European media

1   'Council Directive 89/552/EEC of 3 October 1989 on the coordination of certain provisions laid down by Law, Regulation or Administrative Action in Member States concerning the pursuit of television broadcasting activities', *Official Journal of the European Communities L 298*, 17.10.89, 23–30.

sector as potentially uniting European citizens around a shared set of symbols (Miller 1996). The media sector was therefore ascribed a dual economic and cultural value, in which measures to create a single market in audio-visual goods and services dovetailed with the objective of drawing together disparate national cultures.

Television Without Frontiers, and in turn the negotiations for a cultural exemption to the liberalisation of trade in services during the Uruguay GATT round in the early 1990s, have become the paradigm for the critical analysis of EU media policy. The dominant focus of these critiques has been upon the essentialist and exclusionary conceptions of European identity invoked in policy initiatives (Morley and Robins 1995; Schlesinger 1993; Shore 1993). These critiques tend to take at face value the assumption that policy initiatives have the primary objective of shaping the identities of ordinary people around a shared set of symbols of European unity. From this perspective, critical attention is focused on the bounded, static and exclusionary definitions of European identity (Morley 1998; Shore 1996). The most telling criticism of the focus of EU media policy upon issues of identity is Schlesinger's (1997) argument that it misunderstands the nature of political solidarity, which is based less on symbolic identification than upon active participation in practically meaningful political and civil processes. If Schlesinger's point carries weight, then it also implies that the critical analysis of EU initiatives in the field of culture and media needs to adjust its terms of reference. An identity-based cultural theory tends only to reiterate the problematic of identity it takes as its object of analysis. Rather than simply unpacking the discursive exclusions of constructions of European identity, it is more fruitful to analyse what policies actually set out to achieve practically by way of changing patterns of conduct. Cultural policies, broadly conceived, are increasingly characterised not by simple models of shaping identity through symbols, but by the objective of reshaping affiliations by encouraging forms of practical participation. A social developmental model of cultural policy, one long supported by the separate Council of Europe, has grown in influence in the EU. This model sees cultural activities as a medium for sustaining social cohesion and fostering civic bonds (Beale 1999).

In fundamental respects, EU media policies have moved decisively away from symbolic conceptions of identity and culture. The 1990s saw the development of an agenda of market liberalisation, commercialisation and privatisation in EU communications and information policy. This was associated with and encouraged the restructuring of European media systems. The explicit objective of EU initiatives has been to encourage the development of large, vertically and horizontally integrated media and communications corporations, which will be able to benefit from economies of scale to provide European-sourced programming and to compete in global markets. The cultural objectives of EU media policy have shifted away from a focus on unified identity, towards the protection and promotion of the cultural diversity that has come to be seen as the distinctive characteristic of European culture. Properly functioning markets, able to respond to consumer demand, are understood to be the best means of ensuring that this diversity is sustained. Diversity has been inscribed in policy as a function of consumer demand, not as the outcome of active citizen participation in political processes (Schlesinger and Doyle 1995).

This new paradigm has emerged at the same time as an explicit agenda for promoting European citizenship has taken on enhanced significance in EU policy-making. The meaning of citizenship, and its relationships to media cultures, have therefore become increasingly contested in the decade since culture was legally recognised in the 1992 Treaty on European Union as an object of EU regulatory action. At the same time, the enhanced role of the European Parliament (EP) and other subsidiary institutions of the EU (in particular, the new Committee for the Regions (COR)) has meant that the political opportunity structures through which this legal recognition of culture has been practically implemented has given enhanced impetus to actors whose objective is a more assertive EU role in cultural policy. The grafting of an 'ethic of participation' onto elite-driven policy initiatives has changed the patterns of consultation and representation through which EU cultural policies, including audio-visual policy, have developed (Bellamy and Warleigh 1998). The shaping of EU initiatives for media and culture around a discourse of citizenship, when connected to institutional changes in opportunities for the participation of a broader range of policy actors, has provided a foothold for different actors to challenge and contest dominant conceptions of citizenship, media and democracy.

Since 1992, the Commission has been concerned to find examples of best practice that in principle reconcile the different imperatives of culture and economy, moving from arguments over the so-called cultural exception towards a position that holds that cultural and economic imperatives are complementary. Copyright harmonisation and audio-visual policy are held up as examples of policy where the economic logic of market integration and harmonisation facilitates the promotion of cultural diversity by guaranteeing the effective expression of individualised consumer preferences. The saliency of this approach has been contested by other actors within the EU institutional apparatus, and by other actors engaging with the EU policy-making process. Increasingly, the invocation of citizenship objectives has been a means of contesting the strongly economistic model of cultural policy promoted from the Commission in particular. At the same time, audio-visual policy has been resituated within broader agendas for developing 'the information society'. And it has been assigned a role in helping to achieve multiple objectives related to coherence, enhancing employment and addressing the democratic deficit.

II A tale of two deficits

The place of cultural and media policy in the broader politics of creating an 'Ever Closer Union' in Europe can be characterised in terms of two related deficits of communication. First, as already suggested, a key imperative underwriting the development of policy in the audio-visual area has been the persistent and growing deficit in the trade of audio-visual commodities between the US and Europe. The trade deficit is constructed as having both economic and cultural implications for integration. The media and communications sectors were recognised in the 1990s as contributing significantly to economic growth and job creation. At the same time, a residual trace of the discourse of cultural imperialism implies that the audio-visual trade deficit is detrimental to the well being of European cultures. This connects to the second deficit to which media and communications policy is addressed, the much-debated democratic deficit suffered by the EU.[2] This policy field is shaped by a conviction that media practices and communications technologies can be deployed to make up for the shortfalls of the democratic deficit. The idea that the democratic deficit is a case of communication failure is reflected in the changing terms of recent policy initiatives (Meyer 1999), as well as in more specific agendas for improving the political communication strategies of the Commission in particular (Ward 2001). In particular, the position of public service broadcasting in EU audio-visual policy has become highly contested precisely

---

2   Bellamy and Castiglione (2000) argue that the EU suffers from not one, but three, overlapping forms of democratic deficit: one of *accountability*, referring to the lack of effective influence by citizens on EU decision-making; one of *sovereignty*, referring to a lack of a clear apportionment of administrative responsibility between the different scales of political jurisdiction with the EU; and one of *legitimacy*, referring to the lack of public debate in and popular legitimacy of the EU.

because both EU institutions and national policy elites have identified this sector as crucial to communicating effectively with citizens.

EU media and communications policy indicates that citizenship practice in the emergent European polity is highly mediated. One of the features of this field is the extent to which abstract commitments to citizenship participation are giving practical expression through a variegated politics of knowledge. This derives from the distinctive nature of the EU as a form of state. Until very recently, the institutions of the EU have had little significant role in either redistribution or financial stabilisation, the two main functions of the modern nation-state. The EU has therefore been characterised as a regulatory state (Majone 1996). The primary instrument of EU action is the production of regulations, especially the harmonisation of national laws and standards. It operates 'not by administering anything directly, but rather by aligning the diverse powers of existing national, professional, private and public organisations' (Barry 2001: 73). The EU acts by trying to modify the contexts of action of other actors, such as institutions, companies, parties and individual citizens. Knowledge and expertise are the key resources mobilised by a regulatory state and by those actors engaging with its institutions. This understanding informs the dominant interpretation of EU policy-making as inherently technocratic, dominated by the deployment of expertise in exclusive policy networks. The dominance of technocratic decision-making is indicative of the attempt to depoliticise political conflicts. However, if knowledge is the key to the ways in which EU policy-making operates and has effects, then in turn knowledge is likely to be the key to the forms of political conflict that emerge when technocratic depoliticisation fails. Regulatory policy-making provides particular opportunities for participation, in processes of judicial review or administrative consultation, for example. The growing importance of evidence and knowledge in policy-making opens up further access points for new forms of mediated participation.

There is a methodological point worth making here, one that picks up on issues discussed in Chapter 4. Governmentality studies is particularly appropriate to an analysis of EU institutions, not least because of the attention it pays to the politics of knowledge in shaping the fields of action of different social actors. However, there is a tendency in much of the work in this paradigm to focus on the internal rationales of institutions and organisations as if these were autotelic. As a form of policy analysis specifically, governmentality studies underplays 'the extent to which policy failure arises from active mobilisation against particular policies, legitimised as a citizenship right. It also limits an understanding of one of the more important political trends of the last two decades: popular opposition to forms of public expertise seen as distant and unaccountable' (Flew 1997: 100). EU policy-making exemplifies both of these points. One of the unforeseen consequences of the top-down agenda of European citizenship has been to provide a discursive resource for the mobilisation of opposition to particular policy initiatives in the name of citizenship. Equally, such mobilisation has problematised the highly select forms of participation characteristic of expert policy networks. So, while culture has been increasingly governmentalised as an object of EU-level policy initiatives, this process generates unanticipated effects, facilitating new pressures for broader participation in decision-making procedures (Barnett 2001b).

EU audio-visual policy has tended to be highly technocratic, with participation restricted to representation by business organisations. But the legitimacy problems associated with technocratic decision-making procedures in the EU have stimulated the emergence of new forms of consultation, participation and representation since the beginning of the 1990s (Raedelli 1999). The development of a contested politics of media pluralism is one example of this. The emergence of media pluralism as a policy issue has been associated with the broadening of participation to include trade unions, public interest groups, arts and culture organisations. This broadening of participation has been mediated by the changing opportunity structures of EU policy-making, not least through the enhanced role of the EP, as well as the COR and Economic and Social Committee (ESC), in EU decision-making. These interests have used these EU institutions to promote an alternative agenda for media pluralism on the grounds that this will facilitate the enhanced accountability of both EU and national policy actors to a wider range of citizen actors.

If the centrality of knowledge to the operations of the EU is one medium of new forms of mobilisation and participation characteristic of an emergent Euro-polity, then the complex spatial scales of EU action add another dimension to the differentiated and unpredictable nature of policy-making within a regulatory state. EU policy-making involves a variety of both functionally and geographically defined actors in decision-making (Marks 1993). Neither EU institutions nor member-state governments are able to control policy and regulatory agendas completely. This is in large part a problem of inadequate administrative and knowledge capacity. For policy-making to proceed, and for policy decisions to be effective, EU agencies have to establish alliances with policy experts and interest groups operating at national, subnational, and transnational levels:

Public policy-making within the EU and the member-states is more fragmented and decentralised than is often supposed, involving a wide range of actors. In consequence, both state-centred perspectives and supranational accounts prove inadequate. Neither member-states nor Brussels can control the policy agenda. EU organisations lack the capacity to push a European view, with the Commission having to vie with other EU bodies whilst being split into numerous competing directorates and surrounded by a variety of specialist committees. Within this set-up, purely national interests also prove hard to push, partly because the complexity of the issues often makes it unclear where these lie, and partly because they have to compete for a voice with policy experts, regions and transnational interest groups.

> (Bellamy 1999: 201)

The differentiation of EU policy-making into a set of distinctive styles means that European citizenship is fragmented (Wiener 1997), in the sense that different policy fields assign rights of participation, consultation and expertise in different ways and to different actors. The rest of this chapter tracks the ways in which the evolution in the 1990s of a contested agenda for European-wide media policy and regulation reflects the ways in which the changing institutional context of EU policy formulation has generated new political possibilities, and how these have led to the formation of new patterns of influence between EU and non-EU actors.

III Harmonisation, pluralism and the politics of scale

The main emphasis of EU media policy through the 1980s and into the early 1990s was on establishing a single, European audio-visual market. The sector was given an enhanced role in boosting economic growth, driving industrial restructuring and promoting job creation. There has been a built-in tendency in EU initiatives towards the encouragement of media concentration and cross-media mergers (see McQuail and Siune 1998). The understanding of media economics embedded in Commission initiatives since the early 1990s holds that the creation of a large, EU-wide market for audio-visual goods and services requires and in turn further stimulates large, horizontally and vertically integrated media and communications companies. These large companies will be able to take advantages of economies of scale,

the argument goes, and overcome the persistent problems of fragmented distribution and underinvestment that beset the European
media sector. This predisposition towards the concentration of ownership is based on the Commission's assessment of the weaknesses of the
audio-visual sector, according to which the European media sector suffers from four weaknesses: it was fragmented into national markets,
due to different rules and regulatory systems, and because of embedded patterns of cultural taste and consumption; the production sector
was dominated by small entities; it was characterised by low levels of
cross-border circulation and distribution; and the sector did not attract
sufficient investment. These four weaknesses in turn inform the twin
objectives of EU audio-visual policy: developing an effective single
market, building on the *Television Without Frontiers* directives; and
improving competitiveness in the sector in order to stimulate a strong
production sector to match increased demand stimulated by the proliferation of channels. This second emphasis is the theme of a number of
related policy areas divided between different Commission directorates,
including policy on media ownership, technological convergence and
the information society.

The model of media ownership and control developed by the Commission has, however, been subject to greater contestation since the
early 1990s, with the development of a more coherent agenda for the
protection and promotion of media pluralism. There are strong paternalist traditions in European media policy and regulation, which have
informed EU approaches since the 1980s. The emphasis on protecting
European cultures translated into the dominant emphasis upon tariffs
and subsidies as the key policy instruments of EU audio-visual policy
developed in the 1980s. While this paternalist paradigm has persisted,
the 1990s saw a decisive reordering of the terms through which the subjects of public media culture were interpellated into media policy discourses. The rise of an agenda of market liberalisation has been
associated with a new understanding of the public interest objectives
served by policy and regulatory measures. The protectionist cultural
and economic model pursued through the 1980s and into the early 1990s
has been supplanted by a model in which the market has been constructed as the medium for reconciling the aims of economic integration
and the promotion of cultural diversity.

The liberalisation of media policy at the EU level has gone hand in
hand with the ascendancy of the vocabulary of consumer sovereignty as
the main reference point for media debates (Pauwels 1999). This marks
the emergence of a split system of media regulation in the EU, turning
on the contradictory figure of the sovereign consumer. On the one hand,

the coupling of free market principles with a faith in technologies is the means of ensuring the responsiveness of media production and distribution sectors to the diverse tastes of European consumers. On the other hand, there is an emphasis upon ensuring that consumers are protected from the possible harms of unfettered markets. There are two dimensions to this, one economic and one cultural. First, consumer protection implies an enhanced role for competition law as an instrument for guarding against unfair competitive practices. Second, it has involved developing measures for targeted content regulation, particularly in terms of regulating against harmful media content directed at children. Both of these areas of consumer protection have become important entry points for public interest group lobbying, but they both situate questions of media citizenship squarely within a field in which subjects are understood primarily as consumers in a market-place. The politics of consumer protection, competition law and the protection of minors is, then, a means of redefining the dimensions of the paradigm of media liberalisation, not of challenging its fundamental presuppositions. This paradigm can be characterised as neo-*liberal* precisely because it privileges a particular model of individualised preferences (for commodities, or parties, or cultural tastes) as the essence of democratic decision-making. It installs an abstracted model of individual autonomy as the reference point for democratic choice. This displacement of participation in practices of deliberation over the formation of needs and preferences (that is, of politics) is distinctive of economic-liberal theories of democracy (Sunstein 1992).

The assumed reconciliation of economic liberalisation with the socio-cultural and political roles of media through the creation of free markets in audio-visual goods and services was first signalled in the Commission's 1992 green paper on media pluralism, a response to lobbying on the issue from the EP and other agencies.[3] The green paper treated media concentration primarily as an issue concerning single market objectives, requiring consideration of technical issues of access to networks and problems of market failure. From this perspective, there was no contradiction between internal market and competition objectives on the one hand, and cultural and political pluralism in media on the other hand. Media concentration was conceptualised as a problem of market inefficiency, properly dealt with by competition law. The green paper characteristically aimed to depoliticise contentious policy issues by recourse to technocratic forms of regulation.

3   Commissions of the European Communities (1992), *Pluralism and Media Concentration in the Internal Market*.

In this respect, it failed. It stimulated extensive mobilisation against the paradigm it proposed, mobilisation that was facilitated by new consultative procedures introduced in the Maastricht Treaty. Both the EP and the ESC served as mediums for the expression of alternative positions by interest groups at the national and regional levels. Commercial interest groups were broadly supportive of the market orientation favoured by the Commission, while public service broadcasters, trade unions and journalist organisations tended to press for greater acknowledgement of the distinctive cultural and political significance of issues of media concentration and pluralism (Iosifides 1999; Kaitatzi-Whitlock 1996). In the alternative perspective, which has been most strongly developed by the EP in partnership with national and subnational actors, media concentration is more than a merely economic problem, and media pluralism is more than a matter of numerically diverse media outlets. It is interpreted instead in terms of the plurality of representations, viewpoints and information sources available to citizens.

The green paper on media pluralism stimulated a significant degree of political contestation over the direction of EU-level media policy that had not previously characterised this field. One way of understanding this break out of conflict is in terms of a basic opposition between economic and cultural-civic models of media, between consumerism and citizenship. Alternatively, rather than simply accepting the good/bad dualism implicit in this frame, this conflict can be interpreted in terms of different substantive moral conceptions of public life. The economistic model of citizenship focuses upon diversity as best delivered through markets and consumer choice. In contrast, the mobilisation against market liberalisation proposes a different model, one which emphasises cultural diversity and pluralism as the attributes of coherent territorially embedded national, regional and local communities. This depends on a more communitarian model of citizenship, one which emphasises national and minority cultural rights (Moreira 2000). The division between these two discourses cuts across EU institutions, with certain directorates of the Commission being strongly deregulatory in their approach to media and communications, while others are more amenable to the positions of the EP in reining in the excesses of the technologically deterministic agenda of economic liberalisation.

Invoking a civic-cultural approach to media against the predominant economism of the Commission is a way of trying to establish the importance of certain scales of jurisdiction. Culture is an important term in contested definitions of how the principle of subsidiarity should be applied to media and communications policy.[4] It is routine for culture and subsidiarity to be coupled together against the economistic thrust of harmonisation measures. The extent to which the culture/economy split is an element in the politics of scale in the EU is underscored by the fact that it is the EP, ESC and COR that have been most assertive in pushing a civic-cultural reading of media policy against the Commission. The influence of these institutions has been enhanced by changed decision-making procedures post-Maastricht. Each serves as a important medium for the articulation of interests embedded at national and regional scales for which the promotion of linguistic and cultural diversity and political pluralism are connected to arguments for decentralised forms of policy-making and regulation. The conflict between harmonisation and subsidiarity in media policy, framed through an oppositional staging of economy and culture, is therefore best thought of in terms of a disputed politics of jurisdictional scale.

The contentious politics of media regulation that emerged during the consultation process surrounding the 1992 green paper was in large part supplanted by a fundamental shift in EU media and communications from 1994 onwards. Audio-visual policy has been placed in the context of an ambitious programme for the information society, referring to the application of digital technologies to media, telecommunications and the development of new interactive mediums. The rise of the information society agenda has contributed further to the explicit politicisation of media and communications policy, generating a set of conflicts concerning the significance of convergence for national regulatory systems, for public service broadcasting, and for the relevance of public interest objectives in media policy.

IV Contesting convergence and regulating deregulation

The discourse of convergence has become a new arena for contested positions on the future of media regulation in the EU. Understood as the process whereby digitalisation enables previously separate computing, broadcasting and telecommunications applications to be delivered through the same technological medium, convergence has become

---

4   Subsidiarity refers to the principle whereby the EU takes action only when the proposed action cannot be taken by member states by reason of scale or effects of action. It implies establishing effective representative democratic decision-making at a variety of spatial scales (MacCormick 1997).

embedded in EU discourse as the inevitable teleology of technological change. What remains open to debate is whether technological convergence implies market convergence. This would imply the loosening of media ownership regulations, enabling the horizontal and vertical integration of media sectors, and the formation of large companies able to exploit economies of scale and synergies. One position holds that the conventional distinctions between broadcasting, where content regulation has been legitimate, and telecommunications, understood as a common carrier, are increasingly anachronistic. The implication is that the norms of telecommunications should be applied to broadcasting, and the latter treated as an element of industrial and competition policy. A more proactive model defends the legitimacy of positive regulation in pursuit of cultural diversity and viewpoint pluralism.

The dominant trend in Commission discourse has been towards the relaxation of national regulations on cross-media ownership between sectors and concentration of ownership within and between them. The ascendancy of a deregulatory agenda reflects the more effective lobbying of the telecommunications industry at EU level compared to nationally embedded public service broadcasters (Hills and Michalis 1999). This impulse towards liberalisation has been given further impetus by the 1996 Telecommunications Act in the US, which has stimulated a wave of mergers in the communications sectors. Just as in the 1980s, EU policy throughout the 1990s was reactive with respect to US policy and market developments. However, whereas in the 1980s the strong presumption of policy had been towards protectionism, in the 1990s the EU approach shifted to explicit emulation of US media and communications industries. Thus, EU policy has been premised on empirical understandings of the structural conditions for the international competitive success of US media corporations, according to which the size of the US domestic market enables large, integrated companies to amortise production costs at home, thereby enabling them to compete more effectively in international audio-visual markets. This analysis informs the dual objectives of EU policies, the creation of a single market in audio-visual services, and the consolidation of media companies with European-wide production and distribution capacities. And it holds that the main objective of EU regulation should be to help overcome the impediments to technological and market convergence. Ownership regulations restricting corporate consolidation, and the tradition of sectoral regulation of broadcasting and telecommunications, are both singled out as the main barriers to further development of an internationally competitive EU communications sector. Both are also closely associated with what is considered as the anachronistic persistence of national regulatory systems. Thus, the reordering of the instruments and objectives of media regulation is closely tied to the geographical rescaling of regulatory responsibilities.

The dominant trend in EU media and communications policy through the 1990s was towards the application to both broadcasting and new media of a model of market liberalisation first developed in the telecommunications sector. The driving force behind this move was the information society initiatives developed by the Commission Directorate with responsibility for information and technology policy. The stimulus behind media policy debates in the mid-1990s was the 1994 Bangemann Report.[5] The Report argued that for Europe to realise the potential of new technologies and to develop an information society, national regulation of communications had to be replaced by EU-wide market liberalisation. It was framed in relation to two broader discourses. First, it placed media and communications policy in the context of the heightened importance in EU policy of economic growth and employment, arguing that these both depended on the ability to exploit information and communications industries fully to drive economic transformation. Second, the Report deployed a determinist interpretation of the inevitable convergence of communications to argue that national regulation was obsolescent. It also argued that existing forms of sectoral regulation should be replaced because they substitute administrative measures for consumer demand, and introduce inefficiencies into market operations. Competition policy was presented as the sole legitimate form of regulation, ensuring fair competition and non-discriminatory access to digital communications networks. The discourse of convergence presents the combination of interactive technology, free markets and large companies able to exploit economies of scale as the best guarantee of cultural diversity, because this complex is understood as the means of ensuring that the media production sector is responsive to consumer demand. The ideal of consumer sovereignty realised through technologies and markets rests on an individualisation of cultural diversity (Schlesinger 1997). The discourse of convergence secretes a particular understanding of democracy into media and communications policy, in which the combination of free markets and interactive technologies is meant to facilitate the exercise of choice by individual consumers. Participation is thereby reduced to market decisions between serialised consumption options.

---

5   Bangemann High Level Group on the Information Society (1994), *Europe and the Global Information Society: Recommendations to the European Council*, 26 May. Brussels.

The shift in the terms of policy discourse marked by the Bangemann Report was given further impetus by the Commission's 1997 green paper on convergence.[6] This argued that the audio-visual sector was a key area for job growth in the coming decade. The realisation of this potential depended on structural changes to the media and communications industry that would ensure growth, enabling the European industry to compete effectively with US programming as distribution outlets expanded. The publication of the green paper was just the start of a consultation process that developed into a two-year review of EU communications policy, in which different directorates of the Commission developed alliances with other EU agencies and interest groups. The dominant theme of the consultation and review process was the meaning of media pluralism. The outcome was a significant shift away from the puritanical liberalisation paradigm that the discourse of convergence had initially been mobilised to promote.

The initial consultation process on the green paper was dominated by industry players, including European and non-European communications corporations; by national governments; and by national regulatory authorities. In addition, national and European-wide journalist federations, trade unions, public interest groups and viewers' and listeners' organisations contributed to the process. While this formal consultation took place, wider moves to redefine the direction of EU media policy culminated in the European Audiovisual Conference in 1998. This provided an important focus for the mobilisation against the liberalisation agenda contained in the convergence green paper, bringing together representatives from member states, the EP, the ESC, and various interest groups concerned both to maintain stronger public interest objectives and to protect the legitimacy of national regulation. Given the extent to which the discourse of convergence rested on the argument that national regulatory systems were an impediment to liberalisation, the contestation of this model involved a defence of the continuing legitimacy of national policy and regulation, and especially of public service broadcasting. Member-state governments have resisted the ceding of complete control over media policy to the EU level, because of the importance of this sector, both economically and as a channel of political communication. National regulators had an in-built institutional interest in maintaining a role for national-level policy, since this was their very *raison d'être*. And a broad-based network of cultural

6   Commissions of the European Communities (1997), *The Convergence of Telecommunications, Media and Information Technology Sectors, and the Implications for Regulation: Towards an Information Society Approach*. COM(97)623 Final, Brussels.

activists, journalists, media and trade unions mobilised in defence of the interests of their broader constituencies. This was a European-wide mobilisation of expertise, interests and representative bodies, involving both national and European actors, to protect nationally embedded organisational and institutional interests. The Audiovisual Conference established a review of audio-visual policy. The resulting report laid out an alternative model of the objectives of audio-visual policy, based on the argument that the media had distinctive social, cultural and political roles in sustaining the democratic values of free expression, linguistic and cultural diversity, and social cohesion.[7]

The outcome of the Commission's public consultation on the convergence green paper indicated a move away from the purist market-liberal position, and made a stronger case for the continuing legitimacy of public interest regulation in communications policy.[8] The consultation report presented a revised defence of the categorical distinctions upon which the public interest regulation of audio-visual sectors has traditionally depended. It argued that the case for regulatory convergence had failed to distinguish between technologies and content. This in turn was seen as a symptom of more general failure to acknowledge the distinctive public interest objectives served by audio-visual media, as distinct from telecommunications services. These lay in the promotion of democracy, freedom of expression and education.[9] The strong emphasis of the public consultation report was, therefore, on reasserting the distinctive qualities of broadcasting. It counterposed two understandings of public interest: a minimalist telecommunications model that emphasised universal access; and a more proactive broadcasting model which emphasised positive measures to promote democracy, monitor content and sustain cultural diversity. From this perspective, reconciling economic and cultural imperatives depended upon further developing positive measures to promote investment in European audio-visual content, the new path to both creating jobs and increasing the range of content available to European audiences.

7 *The Digital Age: European Audiovisual Policy*, Report from the High Level Group on Audiovisual Policy, 26.10.98, Brussels.

8 Commissions of the European Communities (1999), *The Convergence of Telecommunications, Media and Information Technology Sectors, and the Implications for Regulation: Results of the Public Consultation on the Green Paper*. COM(99)108 Final, Brussels.

9 C. Tongue (1998), *Opinion on the European Commission's Green Paper on The Convergence of Telecommunications, Media and Information Technology Sectors, and the Implications for Regulation*. Brussels: European Parliament.

The investment-oriented interpretation of media pluralism was related to concerted moves at the end of the 1990s and into the new century to defend the position of public service broadcasting in the overall European media ecology. Public service broadcasting has a seemingly precarious position within the liberalising thrust of EU industrial and competition policy. It has become common for private media and communications corporations to argue that government funding for public broadcasters (through license fees or subsidies) represents a form of unfair competition that contravenes EU rules. The counterposition developed by public service broadcasters, public interest groups and some trade unions is that public service broadcasting is a basic feature of a distinctive European model of media and communications policy, in which the values of diversity and pluralism are positively promoted through the regulation of a mixed broadcasting system. It is argued that the tradition of balancing state and market is one important element of shared European identity, which enables in turn the balancing of economic, socio-economic and political roles of the media. From this perspective, a viable public service broadcasting system is important for the maintenance of pluralism not only in the abstract, but more specifically because public service broadcasters tend to be the main investors in original European-sourced content. Thus, the defence of public service broadcasting rests not on politico-cultural grounds alone, but on a particular interpretation of the economics of investment in European audio-visual production as well.

The consultation over the convergence green paper and the parallel review of audio-visual policy signalled a move away from the narrowly technocratic, liberalising agenda of the information society paradigm promoted by the Bangemann Report, towards a more activist model of the role of regulation in promoting economic and cultural objectives. As already suggested, the recurring motif in EU audio-visual policy is the opposition between economy and culture, associated with the imperative of finding neat resolutions to the apparent contradictions between these two principles. And this is best understood as a means of negotiating the complex scalar politics of EU decision-making in this sector. While the information society paradigm collapses economic and cultural imperatives in an argument for the harmonisation of regulation across the EU, the counterposition has tended to retain an emphasis upon the distinctiveness of culture and economy in order to defend a more strongly federalist perspective on EU decision-making, which combines local/regional, national and EU scales of jurisdiction. The 1999 communications review is an example of this impulse towards differentiation and reconciliation in EU policy discourse. It argued that the audio-visual sector mattered for two related reasons. First, this sector had the potential to create large numbers of highly skilled jobs.[10] Second, this sector is understood to have an important role to play in social, cultural and educational affairs, shaping the availability of information and the ways in which identities and values are constructed.[11] The investment-based, productionist position, while distinct from the technocratic market liberalism of the information society paradigm, is still located this side of a decisive break from an older tradition of protectionist cultural policy that characterised earlier EU initiatives, in which EU action was premised on an irreconcilable opposition between economy and culture in the audio-visual sector. It represents a revised economic liberal perspective, in which the role of state regulation at national and supranational levels includes proactive measures to encourage private sector investment in audio-visual production and distribution.

The approach to regulation that emerged from the consultation process after 1997 also reaffirmed the separation of regulation of transmission infrastructures from regulation of content: 'services providing audio-visual content should be regulated according to their nature and not according to their means of delivery'.[12] The retention of different regulatory approaches is, however, no longer premised on sectoral categorisations. The new model supposes that harmonised competition rules are adequate to regulate the supply side of media sectors, ensuring fair access to networks. However, cultural regulation (in the interests of diversity, protection of minors, free speech and so on) is understood to require a less harmonised approach that allows greater discretion to national regulatory regimes. This division between supply-side concerns and cultural regulation reflects ongoing conflicts over the jurisdictional scales at which regulation of media and communications will be embedded, and marks the reluctance of member states to cede authority to the EU over broadcasting in particular, and over cultural regulation more generally.

The point of contact for the economic and cultural elements of audio-visual policy objectives is the reiterated spectre of US dominance of European media markets. The continuing concern over the impact of US media culture and the persistent problem of a trade deficit of billions of dollars in this sector are now read in terms of the blocked

---

10   Commissions of the European Communities (1999), *Principles and Guidelines for the Community's Audiovisual Policy in the Digital Age*. COM(99)657 Final, Brussels, p. 6.
11   Ibid., p. 7.
12   Ibid., p. 2.

choices of EU citizens. The economic significance of the trade deficit is connected to an understanding of its cultural implications that emphasises the need for active intervention to promote investment in European content.[13] There are two important emphases that set the new approach apart from older models of the cultural exception. First, European culture is understood as characteristically diverse. The objective of policy aims less to create a single shared identity, more to protect and promote Europe's apparently defining cultural and linguistic diversity. Second, the main policy objective that emerges from this interpretation of the cultural implications of EU–US audio-visual trade is not for protectionist measures, but for the development of positive policy instruments that will attract investment into the production of European content and improve the efficiency of European distribution networks. Accordingly, the guiding emphasis of EU media and communications policy in the wake of the contested debate over convergence is a strong argument for treating the audio-visual sector as an exemplary cultural industry:

> The audio-visual industry is not an industry like any other and does not simply produce goods to be sold on the market like other goods. It is in fact a cultural industry *par excellence*. It has a major influence on what citizens know, believe and feel and plays a crucial role in the transmission, development and even construction of cultural identities. This is true above all with regard to children.[14]

The policy discourse of cultural industries enables the audio-visual sector to be distinguished on cultural grounds in ways that restrict the undifferentiated application of a telecommunications model in this field, while providing the justification and defining the instruments of positive regulatory intervention in the sector.

By the end of the 1990s, the terms of EU media policy debates had therefore been fundamentally reordered when compared to the dominant themes and understandings that underwrote arguments about cultural exception in the early 1990s. However, this did not mean the unchallenged ascendancy of the deregulatory, pro-market position announced in the Bangemann Report. The dimensions of media and communications policy have become keenly contested between different actors within and around the opportunity structures opened up by post-Maastricht policy-making procedures. In particular, the proposed

13   Ibid., p. 7.
14   Ibid., p. 8.

harmonisation of sectors around a deregulatory agenda has been successfully supplemented by a position that holds that technological developments do not eliminate the need for positive regulation in the public interest. None the less, the public interest is now defined in ways that acknowledge the ascendancy of free market principles across the audio-visual sector. Thus, proactive public interest regulation is now premised on the protection of diversity threatened by market concentration, the protection of minors menaced by proliferating and unregulated media platforms, and the protection of consumers from the ill effects of market failure.

V Communicative efficiency and the future of public service broadcasting

The deregulatory emphasis of EU media and communications policy actually involves the harmonisation of regulatory regimes at a supranational scale, as well as a shift in the norms of regulation from public interest standards to measures to ensure competition and market access (Collins 2002). The marketisation of communications infrastructures is facilitated by the actions of the EU, in concert with member states and other state and non-state agencies. EU policy in media and communications has become a site in which different rationales for regulation are contested. The outcome of the convergence debates in the mid- and late 1990s was a regulatory paradigm that reasserted categorical distinctions as the basis for differentiated regulatory regimes. But the shared terrain of these debates is the assumption that the objectives of media and communications policy are, in principle, best served by market principles responding to consumer demand.

There is now a broad consensus across the different directorates of the Commission with a share of responsibility for media and communications policy that there is a teleology of declining regulation built into technological change. Policy discourse now turns on a narrative of old and new media, in which free-to-air broadcasting is supplanted by pay-TV, pay-for-view and video on demand, and in turn by broadband interactivity. This technological shift is presented as a steady enhancement of user control and choice, necessitating a concomitant reduction in regulation. The opposition of twentieth-century analogue to twenty-first century digital, of scarcity to abundance, is associated with a narrative of growing consumer control over media. The supposedly high social impact of broadcasting is conflated with the low level of user control and interactivity, and contrasted to the higher user control and full interactivity of narrowcasting. The discursive assignment of a set of cultural characteristics (degrees of publicness, choice, impact) to technology erases the practices of mediation which continue to shape the cultural forms characteristic of digital and interactive mediums, so underwriting the installation of the individual consuming subject as the figure of democratic communication. In this model, regulation is not necessarily reduced, but redefined around new objectives. There is an enhanced emphasis upon regulating to prevent market failure, and a much stronger orientation towards inducing self-regulation of media institutions. Four principles are now invoked to justify continuing light-touch content regulation: freedom of expression and pluralism; cultural and linguistic diversity; the protection of minors; and consumer protection. These four objectives indicate the residualisation of public interest within the overall logic of neo-liberal communications policy. They reflect also the characteristic splitting of the subject of neo-liberal media regulation. On the one hand, in shaping media policy around the figure of the sovereign consumer, investing confidence in technologically induced choice and interactivity, regulation must ensure that consumer choice is translated into effective demand that induces changes in supply. However, at the same time, measures for the protection of the vulnerable viewer and listener connect up with the goals of consumer protection and pluralism to focus regulation upon the contexts of choice and discretion by privatised media subjects. Consumer protection, pluralism and diversity all depend, it is presumed, primarily upon ensuring low access barriers that will enable the flourishing of narrowcasting and niche marketing, so that diverse tastes and viewpoints will be met by competition for audiences and subscribers.

EU communications and media policy is therefore not simply deregulatory. It has redefined the objectives, instruments and subjects of regulation around a model in which cultural, political and economic imperatives are reconciled through the shared understanding of benign market forces. One area in which media regulation has been expanded is in policy on the protection of minors in broadcasting and new media (Mitchell 1998). Initiatives on children's media rights are indicative of the distinctive form of polity emerging around cultural and media issues in Europe. It takes the form of a European-wide networks of organisations and campaign groups, sharing issue-specific interests and addressing particular actors in member states and the EU. In this case, there is a fundamental tension in this field between the general emphasis of EU policy on the free flow of media services, and the development of effective supranational regulations to meet objectives of protecting minors. This was a key concern driving the mobilisation against the market liberalisation proposed by the convergence green paper. EU agendas for children's media rights retain a strongly protectionist, paternalist emphasis on protecting children. The contradictions between cultural protection and market liberalisation have been reconciled by a policy focus upon developing both self-regulation by corporations and technologically facilitated parental control measures. In this field, as in others, the role of the EU has been one of co-ordination rather than enforcement, establishing guidelines and norms that provide the context for further policy debates at both EU and national levels. At the same time, the concerns over the protection of minors have been one theme through which national-scale jurisdiction over cultural regulation has been reaffirmed.[15] This is another example of how the representation of the figure of the vulnerable child is deployed to argue for a general relevance of public interest standards, invoking a series of associations between children, family life, socialisation and orderly public life.

The heightened importance of children's media rights in EU debates connects up to the question of the future of public service broadcasting. The crisis of public service media across Europe was in part facilitated by EU measures to open up communications markets, and in turn has been sustained by the invocation of harmonised competition law by commercial media corporations to question the legitimacy of state support for public broadcasters. Public service broadcasting is at the centre of the contentious politics of EU media and communications policy in the early twenty-first century. The purely economic treatment of this sector favoured by private commercial interests is stymied by the shared interest of national political elites and EU institutions in maintaining effective channels of political communication with their constituencies. The maintenance of public service broadcasting has therefore become a key objective of member states, but has also been recognised at EU level as having an important role in contributing to social cohesion and integration objectives (Libertus 2000). The renewed importance ascribed to public service broadcasting still rests on an instrumental conception of media and a narrowly communicative conception of democracy and legitimacy. Democracy is understood in EU communications and media policy in two related ways: as a means of choice-making best secured by a combination of technology and properly functioning markets; and as the communication of information to citizens through channels of

15 'Council recommendation on the development of the competitiveness of the European audiovisual and information services industry by promoting national frameworks aimed at achieving a comparable and effective level of protection of minors and human dignity', *Official Journal of the European Communities L 270*, 7.10.98, 48–51.

public media. On this interpretation, democracy is easily reduced to a function of more efficient communication between elites and citizens.

The new approach to regulation developed in the wake of the convergence green paper is based on a functional distinction between carriage over infrastructure (which is reserved for economic regulation) and content (which allows for assertive public interest regulation). This approach thus assumes that it is possible to separate meaning and medium. As discussed in Chapter 5, there is in fact a tendency for the significance of content to be overdetermined by the representation of the specific medium of transmission in question. This is likewise implied by the definition of 'communication to the public' deployed in EU law as the principle of distinguishing broadcasting from other services, such as telephone, e-mail, and so on. This definition deduces the substantively public significance of communications mediums from the technically public nature of the transmission platform (that is, from one to the many). Public service broadcasting is thereby defined as a public good, accessible to all citizens, not merely as a non-commercial addition providing programming only for minority audiences.[16] The definition of public service broadcasting as a public good, serving cultural, social and democratic objectives that are best achieved by maintaining national public broadcasting systems, runs up against the imperatives of harmonised competition rules. This contradiction was at the heart of the initiative to enshrine the principle of public service broadcasting in EU law in the mid-1990s. The revision of the EU Treaty in 1997 included a protocol explicitly acknowledging the legitimate role of public service broadcasting in European media systems. It establishes the legitimacy of public funding for public service broadcasting by member states, but only 'insofar as such funding does not affect trading conditions and competition in the Community to an extent which would be contrary to the common interest'.[17] The broader context for this measure was the threat from commercial media corporations to use EU competition law to challenge public subsidies as a form of unfair competition. Public service broadcasters across Europe have increasingly cross-subsidised public service programming with commercial ventures, as well as competing for advertising revenue.

The 1997 initiative on public service broadcasting enshrines in EU law the guiding principle of EU media policy discourse, according to which

16 'Council resolution concerning public service broadcasting', *Official Journal of the European Communities* C 30.2.99, p. 1.
17 'Protocol on the system of public broadcasting in the member states', Protocol Annexed to the *Treaty Establishing the European Community*, 1997, Brussels.

audio-visual Europe is characterised by a dual system of strong public service and dynamic private sector. The contentious politics of public service broadcasting funding is not just a matter of culture versus economics. It is about contested understandings of the actors and scales at which media systems should be governed. The protocol balanced the objectives of public service broadcasting defined at the national scale by member states and the 'general community interests' of competition law and harmonisation measures invoked by commercial media. But the protection of public service broadcasting is far from a wholly defensive move. There is a more assertive position according to which public service broadcasters are understood to be crucial loss leaders in the promotion of a European audio-visual content industry, on the grounds that they invest significantly more in European-sourced programming than do commercial broadcasters and the EU itself (Levy 1999: 152). None the less, the enhanced legitimacy of public service broadcasting rests on a redefinition of its funding basis that simply reiterates a fundamental contradiction. The legitimacy of public funding is based on a public service remit, but this has been redefined in terms of investment in original programming, an objective which is driving the further commercialisation of public service broadcasting through cross-subsidisation and international marketing.

Having once been relatively marginal to EU policy debates, broadcasting has become increasingly important as an object of contentious politics, as the agenda of information and technology policy has gained in importance in achieving growth and employment objectives. This enhanced significance derives from both the economic and political problematics of integration. One lesson of the *Television Without Frontiers* initiatives is that without effective measures to support European content production, the drive to create a single market in audio-visual services will worsen the existing imbalance in audio-visual trade. This theme connects to both cultural and economic concerns in the EU, and has led to the identification of public service broadcasters as having a leading role to play in promoting investment in a European content industry, the vibrancy of which is understood to be crucial to harnessing the benefits of the information revolution culturally and economically. This economic defence of public service broadcasting connects to a more specifically political imperative, from both member states and EU institutions, to maintain effective channels of political communication and information. In both respects, policy has been shaped by a concern to establish the conditions for more efficient communication. On the one hand, the liberalisation of markets is understood as the best means of ensuring that consumer preferences are communicated through effective price signalling. On the other hand, the democratic deficit is understood in terms of communication failure, requiring more effective communication of information from the EU and member states to citizens. Therefore, as issues of legitimacy have increased in importance in shaping EU-level policy initiatives in media and communications, this has been associated with the heightened significance of broadcasting, understood as a medium of political communication and as crucial to the development of a diverse European content production sector.

VI Conclusion: participation in Europe's virtual democracy

In the 1990s, the harmonisation of liberalised media and communication regulation across the EU was interrupted by the assertion of subsidiarity by a combination of member states and public interest groups. In general, this is an area in which member states have been reluctant to delegate authority to EU. In the specific case of audio-visual policy, this is because of the importance of broadcasting as a medium of political communication, and because of sensitivity to charges that integration will eliminate distinctive linguistic, cultural, regional identities. Technocratic policy-making in cultural and media sectors generates conflict, and the knowledge-based regulatory state activity of the EU opens up new opportunities for participation by collective actors concerned to apply subsidiarity principles against harmonisation of media and communications regulation (Harcourt and Raedelli 1999). This mobilisation against harmonisation is not a national versus supra-national conflict, but takes place at the European scale itself, and is mediated by EU institutions themselves. The emergence of networks of political action, lobbying and advocacy, which are closely tied to the circulation of knowledge, is indicative of the crystallisation of a number of distinct but overlapping European-wide public spheres, made up of networks of communication in which various actors contribute to and hold both state and non-state actors accountable to norms of public deliberation, participation and accountability. European-wide publics might take the form of distinctive social movement mobilisations, but also, and more commonly in the area of media and communications, of the development of Europeanised epistemic communities engaging with policy formulation. Such networked forms of mobilisation are distinguished by the combination and recombination of territorial and functional alliances, depending upon the styles of policy characteristic of different policy fields.

The outcome of the distinctively networked politics of scale in the EU is that the redefinition of regulation has been ambiguous, with partial harmonisation in the area of infrastructure regulation offset by the retention of content regulation at the level of member states. The significance of media and communications cannot be understood solely in terms of competing understandings of European identity. The idea that EU cultural policy is directed by the aim of creating a single shared cultural identity is at odds with the actualities of policy developments in the 1990s. There is a heightened focus upon the role of media and cultural practices in facilitating greater participation by citizens in European projects. Policy in this sector combines concerns over cultural representations of Europeaness, with economic concerns over growth and employment, and political objectives of legitimacy. The characteristic dynamic of EU policy initiatives is to discursively reconcile these different cultural, economic and political rationales. Increasingly this has been done by reference to a discourse of market liberalisation supported by effective consumer protection and competition regulation. The development of audio-visual policy is best understood in relation to institutional responses to the multi-dimensional interpretation of the EU's democratic deficit, so that media and communications industries are seen as providing jobs (thereby helping to bolster social cohesion), as means of political communication, and as mediums for the expression of cultural diversity that is often understood to be threatened by the imperatives of harmonisation and integration. In the case of audio-visual policy, the assertion of cultural diversity has been the basis for a divided resolution of the problem of the jurisdictional scale at which regulation will be ordered. The division between treating broadcasting as a medium of pluralism and diversity and the creation of a single audio-visual market therefore maps onto a scalar division between the imperatives of harmonisation and the application of subsidiarity principles.

This chapter has shown that the evolution of media and communications policy reflects changes in the forms of political mobilisation and interest group representation within the EU more generally, indicating the tentative emergence of an ethic of participation mediated by non-governmental organisations (NGOs), trade unions, business interest groups and advisory groups. In the process, a purely economistic approach to media and communications policy has been complicated by the fact that this field in particular has considerable potential significance in enhancing the legitimacy of the EU as a whole. If communication is understood to be the key to addressing the democratic deficit, then this idea has been understood according to a rather anaemic conception of the nature of democratic legitimacy, in terms of communicating the objectives of integration effectively. This approach indicates that the EU's deficit of democratic legitimacy is a narrowly conceived as a procedural issue. It therefore dodges understandings of democracy based on broader, plural modes of participation, but it also evades the possibility that even were EU agendas better communicated, European citizens might retain substantive positions at odds with the institutional and economic objectives of elite-led integration. While the emphasis on improved communications does support efforts to enhance participation in decision-making and also in broader European practices, it defines democracy narrowly, in terms of being consulted on the implementation of policies whose actual objectives are taken for granted. In the final analysis, the trajectory of media and communications policy in the EU therefore reveals a public philosophy of democracy as managed participation. In contrast to this anaemic vision, the future legitimacy of necessarily mediated citizenship-participation in EU policy-making is likely to depend upon the extent to which networks of experts, interest groups and NGOs are able to facilitate genuinely multi-dimensional communication between political institutions and citizens.

7

Media, development and democratisation: mediated citizenship in South Africa

Democracy has to be seen as creating a set of opportunities, and the use of these opportunities calls for an analysis of a different kind, dealing with the practice of democratic and political rights.

Amartya Sen (1999: 154)

I Democratising media

Chapter 3 discussed how Habermas' procedural account of the subject-less streams of public communication presupposes that the vitality of a democratic public sphere depends on a pluralistic associational culture. This chapter pursues this theme by discussing the politics of media policy in South Africa during the transition from apartheid to formal democracy in the 1990s. The South African case-study illustrates three linked dimensions of the relationship between media, democracy and the public sphere. First, it indicates that the sorts of political opportunities opened up by media and communications technologies are shaped by a politics that goes on around media regulation. Second, it illustrates the ways in which media systems facilitate different forms of political action by popular movements. Third, the South African experience illustrates that the public, democratic significance of media and communications practices has as much to do with changing everyday cultural values as it does with more obvious forms of political action. In this respect, it also reveals the extent to which media publics increasingly articulate cultural norms that are no longer contained within national regulatory spaces.

Historically, South African broadcasting has been dominated by the South African Broadcasting Corporation (SABC). Broadcasting was an integral element of apartheid policies (Tomaselli et al. 1989). Radio consisted of separate-language stations, broadcasting for separate audiences, in discrete territorial units. The National Party (NP) government delayed the introduction of television until the mid-1970s, out of the fear that it had the potential to create unifying identifications across ethnic and racial divisions (Nixon 1994). With the introduction of television in the mid-1970s, infrastructure and programming sharply differentiated between channels on the basis of race.[1] Given both its dependent relationship with organised Afrikaner nationalism and the apartheid state on the one hand, and its financial dependence on advertising revenues on the other, the history of the SABC has hardly accorded with the principles of Reithian public service broadcasting that, in principle, it was supposed to embody.[2] Broadcasting in South Africa has not therefore served as a common space of public communication. It has been used to reproduce notions of separate and distinct populations, with their own separate cultures, living in particular geographical spaces. The current technological infrastructure of broadcasting still largely reflects apartheid-era policies of differential investment in infrastructure and services. Media audiences in South Africa are highly fragmented in terms of unequal access to material resources, and in terms of different cultural tastes, interests and capacities. And radio, rather than television, is the universally accessible cultural medium in South Africa.

In post-apartheid South Africa, mass communications have been assigned a number of objectives, summed up in the triptych of diversity, democracy and development.[3] These objectives include representing the nation to itself, supporting reconciliation amongst historically divided and antagonistic social groups; acting as a channel of political communication, enabling citizen participation and enhancing legitimacy; and being a driver of economic development. The democratisation of the post-apartheid state has coincided with and further encouraged the liberalisation of media and communications sectors. Corporate unbundling and black economic empowerment initiatives have transformed the ownership of broadcasting, print media, publishing and

1   The main private television company in South Africa is M-Net, began in 1985, and now providing a variety of encoded terrestrial and satellite subscription services in South Africa and throughout the continent. The late 1970s and early 1980s also saw the establishment of broadcasting services in the nominally independent homeland states of Transkei, Bophuthatswana, Venda and Ciskei, services which were either incorporated into the SABC or privatised in the 1990s. In 1998, a new free-to-air terrestrial television service was licensed, e-TV.

2   John Reith, the founding figure of the British Broadcasting Corporation, personally advised the so-called fusion government on the formation of the SABC on a visit to South Africa in 1934.

3   Independent Broadcasting Authority, *Triple Inquiry Report on the Protection and Viability of Public Service Broadcasting Services, Cross Media Control of Broadcasting Services, and Local Television Content and South African Music*, August 1995, Johannesburg: IBA.

telecommunications. New radio and television services have been set up. The SABC has been restructured as an independent public service broadcaster. However, a vibrant alternative press closely associated with the political mobilisation against apartheid has suffered severe decline. New technologies, such as satellite television, the Internet, mobile telephony and digital media, have all rapidly established a foothold in South African communications markets. All of these processes have gone hand in hand with a rescaling of South African media economies and media cultures. Inward foreign investment in South African media and communications industries has been matched by a continental drift of South African capital into African media and communications markets (Barnett 1999d). In this conjuncture, a key issue of political conflict has been over the form and purpose of regulatory institutions. The development of new regulatory authorities following both the transition to a constitutional democracy and the liberalisation of markets represents a significant reordering of political opportunity structures. Policy forums, consultative procedures, the development of constitutional case law, and the emergence of mechanisms of open government have all opened up new spaces for participation, representation and contestation in policy-making. New procedures and discourses have therefore reshaped the politics of representation in and around the mass media. At the same time, the monitoring and evaluation of transformation have heightened the significance of certain sorts of knowledge and expertise, and the liberalisation of media has increased the significance ascribed to markets as mediums of cultural representation.

II *The politics of independent regulation*

In the period between the unbanning of political organisations in 1990 and the inclusive, non-racial democratic elections of 1994, the main impetus for the reform of state broadcasting into a pluralistic, independent system came from civil society groups aligned with the Mass Democratic Movement (Louw 1993). A loose affiliation of left-liberal independent civil society organisations challenged the attempt by the apartheid government to effectively privatise broadcasting prior to a formally negotiated political settlement between the NP and the African National Congress (ANC). The ANC's Media Charter reflected the ascendancy of a pluralist position first developed by these civil society organisations over a more centralist, statist position. It recognised the right to receive and disseminate information as a basic requirement of democratic participation, and made a commitment to establishing an independent public service broadcaster regulated by an independent body.[4] The same perspective informed the vision of participatory democracy and decision-making in the Reconstruction and Development Programme (RDP) that formed the basis of the ANC's 1994 election campaign.[5]

Broadcasting reform has been overseen by a newly created independent regulator, the Independent Broadcasting Authority (IBA). This was the product of a fragile and contingent consensus established in the early 1990s on the need to ensure that broadcasting be made independent of direct government and political interference both before and after elections. The first task of the new regulator following the 1994 elections was to hold a broad-ranging public inquiry into the future of public broadcasting, cross-media ownership and local content quotas, which became known as the Triple Inquiry. In many ways, the recommendations of the IBA's Triple Inquiry Report epitomised the principles of what has been called regulated pluralism (see Thompson 1995: 240–1). It contained a strong emphasis upon regulating the market for broadcasting services in the interest of viable competition and diversity, by limiting cross-media ownership and encouraging ownership of broadcasting services by historically disadvantaged groups. It was informed by a strong presumption that a pluralist, independent broadcasting system required both the deconcentration of South Africa's highly oligopolistic media industry and the separation of media from the state. However, in fundamental respects, the IBA lacked the structural strength within the broader policy process to enforce this vision (Horwitz 2001: 174–7). With the support of the ANC in Parliament, the SABC (and other established broadcasters, such as the private subscription station M-Net) was able to circumvent the Triple Inquiry process and proceed with its own transformation projects (Barnett 1999c).

The reform of broadcasting has been just one element of a broader shift in the rationalities of cultural regulation, a shift was which under way before 1994, but which have been given added impetus (and legitimacy) since then. Given South Africa's history of state control and censorship of film, radio and television, literature and print media, there has been a strong impulse to shift the administration of cultural practices from direct state provision to forms of market provision, with

4   'The Media Charter of the African National Congress', *Media Development* (1996), 2, 41.
5   African National Congress (1994), *The Reconstruction and Development Programme: A Policy Framework*, Johannesburg.

the state's role redefined as ensuring effective regulation of markets. The IBA's oversight of broadcasting transformation is one example of this process, opening up the sector to competition while pursuing public interest standards in its licensing decisions. Within both policy-making and broadcasting institutions in South Africa, understandings of democracy have been tied closely to the rhetoric of nation-building. The role of the mass media in this process has been seen primarily in symbolic terms, as disseminating appropriate representations of national togetherness that adequately reflect South Africa's cultural diversity. Given the history of broadcasting being monopolised by the SABC, and of oligopolistic print media, the democratisation of the mass media in South Africa in the 1990s was easily assumed to be guaranteed by increasing competition and expanding choice. In turn, diversity has been understood to be best achieved by broadening the social base of media ownership (Tomaselli 1997).

The progress of broadcasting reform since 1994 needs also to be placed in the wider context of the evolving political and economic agenda of the ANC in government. With the end of apartheid, there has been a realignment between capital, the new political regime and organised labour. There also has been a movement away from the original RDP blueprint, which premised economic growth and development upon reconstruction and redistribution. In 1996 a new economic policy framework document, *Growth, Employment and Redistribution* (GEAR), was adopted by the national government. This prioritised fiscal prudence, and implied a clear commitment to reducing state involvement in the economy in order to reduce public expenditure (see Bond 1999). This reorientation of macro-economic policy provides the context for two much discussed processes of economic transformation: black economic empowerment and the privatisation of state-owned assets. Both of these processes have been rapidly advanced in the print and electronic media sectors. The process of black economic empowerment through the extension of equity shareholding has been facilitated by corporate unbundling, driven by the imperative for white-owned corporations to reposition themselves politically and redeploy capital in response to domestic and international political transformations. In the media sector, the IBA's regulatory framework for both radio and television liberalisation obliged white-owned capital to forge partnerships with black empowerment consortia. The IBA therefore oversaw the successful diversification of radio and television in terms of both ownership and programming, facilitating the entry of previously marginalised groups into structures of ownership of privatised and newly licensed radio stations and the new commercial television station, e-TV.

Since 1998, the public broadcaster has also been restructured as a state-owned public corporation, as a prelude to possible partial privatisation. The commercialisation and corporatisation of the SABC have gone on at the same time as policy-making has become increasing bureaucratised. The influence of independent civil society organisations with connections to broader popular movements has declined since the high point of the Triple Inquiry in 1994–5, being supplanted by stakeholder organisations representing particular interests within the communications industry. The civic and cultural imperatives that predominated in 1994 and 1995 have been subsumed by an agenda of economic development premised on the internationalisation of the media and communications industries. In this context, the importance of policies promoting investment in local content in music and programming has been enhanced. Diversity has been redefined to connect matters of cultural representation to investment in local media production. This shift answers both to domestic policy concerns and to the objectives of export-oriented industrial policies. This reconciliation is best expressed in the SABC's adoption of the ubiquitous discourse of the 'African Renaissance', an all-encompassing brand that simultaneously fits objectives of nation-building and the positioning of the SABC as Africa's premier broadcaster.

The legislative corporatisation of the SABC in 1998 confirmed the relocation of broadcasting policy within the overall context of economic policies aimed at boosting the international competitiveness of domestic industries, and implied a more limited role for regulatory agencies and the further expansion and commercialisation of radio and television services. In 2000, after much delay, the IBA was formally integrated into the telecommunications regulator, forming a single Independent Communications Authority of South Africa (ICASA). The newly merged regulator is more narrowly concerned with spectrum regulation, licensing and market access, in contrast to the broad policy-making remit originally ascribed to the IBA. The national interest in media and communications has therefore been clearly redefined in terms of economic development and growth. This shift in emphasis in broadcasting policy needs to be seen in the context of telecommunications restructuring. Telecommunications dwarfs broadcasting as an economic sector, and is an integral element of the ANC's programme of infrastructure development. The significance of subordinating broadcasting to this broader agenda is indicated by the fact that telecommunications reform, which has been driven by the economic considerations of international competitiveness, has been undertaken in an increasingly centralised, statist fashion which circumvents previous processes of consultation and participation (Horwitz 1997). The rapid advance of both corporate unbundling and privatisation in the media industries pinpoints a central ambivalence over the practical meaning of the independence of broadcasting organisations and regulators in the changing South African broadcasting environment. Primarily, independence has referred to independence from direct state interference, but in practice this has involved a much greater role for private capital and market mechanisms in the broadcasting sector than before. Given the highly uneven patterns of ownership and access to capital, the critical challenge remains how to square independence from government while ensuring that broadcasting remains independent of the influence which follows from the unbridled market power of established interests.

In South Africa in the mid-1990s, the politics of independent regulation saw significant successes for progressive organisations in establishing procedures for accountability, transparency and public participation in communications policy. This success has been pivotal to the pluralisation of post-apartheid media cultures. But the ongoing internationalisation of the South African government's media and communications policy has seen the degree of participation and accountability curtailed by a prioritisation of investment-led regulatory principles. In turn, however, there is an emerging network of Southern African media advocacy sharing information and expertise, and engaging in multiple policy contexts (Barnett 2002).

III New media, new politics

While there has undoubtedly been a great deal of structural change in the South African media and communications sectors in the 1990s, there is very little agreement amongst politicians, academics and policy-makers about the meaning of it all. Changes to media ownership, regulation and staffing over the last decade can be read as marking unprecedented progress (Berger 1999), or just as easily interpreted as cosmetic, reflecting a superficial racial substitution that masks growing socio-economic inequality (Boloka and Krabill 2000). In public debates, the extent to which the post-apartheid media are considered adequately transformed depends on whether their role is seen in terms of sustaining the legitimacy of a still fragile democracy, or in terms of critically scrutinising the activities of the state (and business) to an extent previously made impossible by authoritarian restrictions.

To assess the significance of media restructuring, it is useful to ask what difference this process has made to the ways in which power is exercised, to the ways in which politics is done in post-apartheid South Africa (see Berger 2000). This requires directing attention not just at media institutions and policies, but at broader patterns of political mobilisation. The attenuation of previous forms of popular participation in South Africa since 1994 needs to be understood in the wider context of the fundamental transformation of the institutions of state policy-making into bodies that are broadly representative to an extent previously unknown in South Africa (Seekings 1996). The conditions for access to policy forums have been altered, with oppositional strategies towards the state being superseded by more corporatist forms of engagement. Democratisation has been shaped by a tension between the consolidation of the bureaucratic representative practices of liberal democratic institutions on the one hand, and the continuing significance of long-established traditions of mass participation and popular democracy on the other.

However, the common picture of public disengagement from politics might be overstated (see Klandermans et al. 2001). In fact, the transition to formal democracy has involved a restructuring of political opportunities. New policy areas have been opened up to extensive consultation. The new Constitution opens up possibilities for a politics of competing rights-claims both in public discourse and through the courts. And the discourse of delivery and transformation, combined with the establishment of new tiers of government at provincial and metropolitan levels, opens up new opportunities for the scrutiny and holding to account of politicians and state agencies. One would expect to see the emergence of new forms of mobilisation associated with the new structures and discourses of the postapartheid political landscape, characterised by new forms of protest and campaigning, and new forms of identification within and between historically divided social groups.

One of the ways in which political opportunity structures in South Africa have been significantly reordered is the opening up to a broader range of actors of opportunities to organise, mobilise and campaign through media and communications networks. This raises the question of what sorts of new opportunities for political action the evolution of post-apartheid media systems has opened up, and how these potential opportunities have been realised in practice by movements in civil society. To assess the relationships between media restructuring and patterns of political engagement in civil society, it is fruitful to consider the changing news coverage of contentious politics since 1994. William Gamson (2001) has argued that the relationship between media coverage and citizenship engagement can be assessed with respect to the degree to which grassroots activism and protest is represented as a legitimate and effective activity, and in ways that connect up everyday experiences with broad public issues. However, in a context such as South Africa, media coverage is significant not because of its hypothetical role in the mass mobilisation of citizens. Western-based models of the cultural and political significance of mass media, with their focus upon media-induced mass mobilisation or on identity-formation processes, presume social formations with very high densities of media. This assumption does not translate to the South African context (Berger 2002). As a form of political communication, print and electronic media are primarily important in targeting specific social groups and key political institutions (Jacobs 1999). The South African context therefore suggests that media-oriented activism needs to be thought of not so much in terms of a simple media-to-citizen circuit of mobilisation, but rather as a way of attracting media attention as a means by which collective actors attempt to act on the contexts of each other's activities.

Even if the potential of media coverage as a medium of democratic engagement and opposition is acknowledged in principle, it remains the case that the ability of movements to secure media attention is often severely constrained. Following Gamson and Wolfsfeld (1993), media/movement interactions can be understood by assessing the ratio of the *value* to *need* in the interactions between these two sets of actors. Value refers to how much one party's resources are required by the other (for example, how much the media require movements as sources will determine the value of movements to media). Need refers to how far one party requires access to the resources held by the other (for example, how far movements need media attention will depend on the nature of contentious issues, strategy and so on). Normally speaking, this ratio might be expected to favour media over movements, since the latter tend to need the resources of the media (access to the public) much more than the news media need movements as sources. In the specific conditions of political transformation in South Africa, however, the ratio of value to need has moved in a more favourable direction for movements, increasing the value of movements to media organisations at the same time as new political opportunities mean that movements' need for media coverage has been heightened by the transition to representative democratic governance.

This relationship between need and value is crucial to understanding the extent to which the dynamics of media commercialisation in the South Africa in the 1990s might be interpreted as having had a democratising impact on news agendas. A variety of actors is involved in producing news, and there is a high degree of dependence by journalists on information and knowledge produced by public relations companies, corporations, government ministers, social movements, NGOs and so on (Schlesinger 1990). Furthermore, these same actors engage in the strategic, dramaturgical production of newsworthy events (McAdam 1996). News is therefore constructed out of the complex mediation of knowledge, meanings and performances produced and distributed by a variety of actors with different interests. Social movements, parties, governments, interest groups and media institutions themselves can all be understood as signifying agents involved 'in the struggle over how issues will be framed and understood by different groups' (Halcli 2000: 472). From this perspective, the distribution of power between different signifying agents in South Africa has certainly been altered by the process of media restructuring. New political actors (ordinary people, community organisations, NGOs) have gained in credibility as valued and legitimate news sources. New technologies have transformed the speed, frequency and range of distribution that political actors can attain in accessing news organisations. And these same technologies have enabled new forms of communication between activists at an international scale that have significantly altered the strategies adopted locally. To assess the significance of these sorts of changes, it is useful to consider one example of local political activism that is symptomatic of the new forms of political action emerging in the postapartheid period, the case of environmental activism in the city of Durban.[6]

Environmental issues have been effectively redefined in South Africa during the 1990s from green conservationism to brown social justice issues. This process reflects in large part the determined efforts of environmental NGOs to reframe the news discourse around the social impacts of issues such as air and water pollution, waste disposal and unrestricted industrial development. A nationwide environmental movement has emerged in the last decade, but the driving force behind this network has been a set of organisations and groups located in and around Durban and Pietermaritzburg, in Kwa-Zulu Natal province. In particular, the politics of air pollution in the South Durban industrial basin has become a *cause célèbre* in this broader movement (see Wiley et al. 2002). South Durban is the country's second largest industrial cluster, and hence the impact of local campaigns by poor, non-white communities has taken on broader national significance, impacting on policy agendas and galvanising a national environmental activist network. The politics of the environment in South Durban turns on a fundamental clash of discourses. On the one hand, there is a forty-year history of local

---

6   The following section draws on ongoing research on media, movements and democratisation, funded by the Leverhulme Trust.

knowledge of health problems, hazardous leaks and school evacuations, caused by unregulated development of petrochemical and related industries. On the other hand, there is tradition of state and corporate secrecy, combined with the deployment of scientific expertise to delegitimise community claims. Since 1994, the objective of organised activism has been to force industries to inform local communities of potential health risks and of hazardous emissions and leaks when they occur, rather than maintain a culture of denial. And activists have also been concerned that the future development of the South Durban area, which is a key locus of export-oriented national economic growth strategy, should not be stitched up behind closed doors by industry and government, but opened up to participation, consultation and scrutiny from local communities.

An important resource that local activists have set out to mobilise has been media attention. Prior to the mid-1990s, news coverage of local communities' grievances in metropolitan news media was minimal or non-existent. Since 1995, there has been an almost exponential increase in news stories about environmental pollution, much of it garnering national media attention (Svendsen 2001). This is a reflection of changing definitions of newsworthiness, changing patterns of sourcing, and the adoption of highly effective media-oriented strategies by activists. Environmental campaigning organisations in and around Durban self-consciously understand themselves to be pursuing a 'politics of shame', attracting and maintaining media attention in order to exert pressure on private corporations and government agencies. Media attention is a relatively low-cost resource, and post-1994 media restructuring has opened up new potential opportunities for gaining and maintaining such attention. The organisational and economic restructuring of print and broadcast media means that the value of community-based social movements to news organisations has been significantly enhanced. In the newspaper sector, there has been a determined effort to reposition papers, in order to maintain and extend readerships in the face of increasing competition for revenue from other media. The commercialisation of the newspaper industry has engendered a shift in the objectives of news-making towards people-oriented stories reflecting the changes in the new South Africa. These shifts in the norms and practices of routine news-making have also been at work in the broadcast media. In particular, it is the new commercial radio stations (metropolitan and provincial) and television services that have pioneered human-interest news stories and storytelling modes of news presentation, and that have been most receptive to the media-oriented strategies of environmental activists.

Changes in revenue streams, the targeting of new audiences, increased

competition, changing source strategies, and the introduction of innovative news formats all mean that the sorts of information, knowledge
and social networks that grassroots organisations can in principle
mobilise have taken on enhanced value for news organisations. However, successfully cashing in this value depends upon the capacity of
communities for mobilisation, organisation and self-representation in
particular ways. More specifically, the South Durban example also illustrates that an awareness of the dramaturgical dimensions of protest is a
crucial means of attracting significant media attention. If media are a
low-cost resource for relatively poor communities, then it is still the case
that successful mobilisation of media attention requires the adoption of
protest strategies that have the appropriate value to news organisations.
There are various dimensions to this productive framing of news by
activists and movements. For example, the key moment in the consolidation of South Durban environmentalist mobilisation was a visit in
April 1995 by President Nelson Mandela to one of the two oil refineries
in the basin, which have been the main targets of campaigns over air
pollution. Local activists mobilised community protest, successfully
generating news attention for a previously invisible issue, and stimulating the first moves towards effective state and corporate action in
response to community grievances. This initial protest established the
narrative frame of subsequent news coverage, contrasting the promises of the 'new' democratic South Africa embodied in the person of
Mandela with the continuities from the inequitable 'old' South Africa,
exemplified by unaccountable multinational corporations protected by
state secrecy laws.

The further development of a sustained campaign against industrial
pollution since 1995 has involved internal processes of local mobilisation and organisational consolidation. The increase in news coverage of
air pollution issues in South Durban has been primarily facilitated by
the emergence of a single organisational voice (the South Durban
Community Environmental Alliance, or SDCEA) able to represent credibly the concerns of diverse communities and constituencies. This has
depended upon local activists being able to perform their broader legitimacy, as well as being able to stage valuable news events. Organisations
must be seen to be legitimately representative and accountable to the
communities they claim to act for if they are to achieve the status of
news sources. Attracting media coverage is therefore a fundamental
need for this form of activism. It serves multiple objectives, as a means
of validating the activities of activists back to a support base, and of
validating activities to actual and potential funders. But in the South
Durban context, attracting media attention is primarily a means of

establishing public legitimacy, which in turn is an important stepping-stone to establishing standing in the eyes of government and business. In both respects it is worth underlining that for this form of activism, the utilisation of new communications technologies is not an alternative to coverage in mainstream print and broadcast media – it is a means of achieving this broader objective (see Downing 2000).

In the South Durban case, environmental activists have displayed a well-developed understanding of the diverse forms of communication through which to mobilise support locally as a means of mobilising media coverage city-wide, and by extension upwards to provincial and national scales. For example, SDCEA and *groundWork*, an NGO with strong roots in the area, organise a Toxic Tour of the South Durban basin. This is a guided excursion for journalists, academics and other activists, which visits the main *sites* and *sights* of pollution, uncontrolled industrial development, hazardous chemical storage, habitat destruction and much else. It is a means of literally staging the problems and issues facing local communities to mobilise support, resources and attention from outside actors. This is just one example of a creative communications strategy that combines old fashioned face-to-face communication and mass meetings with new communications tactics, including networked Internet communications, e-mailed press releases and performative forms of protest, to publicise the problems of environmental pollution in South Durban.

A major challenge for this sort of media-oriented activism is, however the maintenance of media attention once this initial work is done. This task has required the adoption of innovative campaigning strategies. New communications technologies like the Internet mean that locally embedded movements can maintain routine connections with broad networks of support, thereby accessing various resources, including technical assistance and discursive framing strategies. An example of this was the organisation in 2000 by South Durban activist organisations of a Bucket Brigade campaign, an idea borrowed from US environmental justice movements. The Bucket Brigade monitoring system is, at one level, a simple strategy for empowering local communities in the politics of knowledge surrounding environmental issues, by providing them with a basic capacity to monitor industrial pollution. However, in this case, this educational and empowering initiative was explicitly launched as a media event. The launch of the Bucket Brigade was made into a rolling news story, organised as a national event, starting in Durban but moving on to pollution blackspots in other provinces, with the aim of publicising the inadequacy of both government and corporate monitoring of industrial pollution. The campaign attracted coverage in major metropolitan and national newspapers, and national broadcast news. And the ongoing programme of community-based monitoring provides the capacity to maintain regular media attention through the publications of reports and findings.

A primary objective of South Durban environmental campaigning has been the mobilisation of mainstream media attention as a means of acting upon powerful institutional actors, such as the national government and multinational corporations. In this respect at least, the campaigners have actually been highly successful.[7] The value of these actors to news organisations has increased through a combination of shifts in news agendas, journalist practice and commercialisation, and at the same time, environmental activists have been particularly effective at adopting a repertoire of campaigning and protest strategies that is well suited to the changed criteria of newsworthiness. The case of the media coverage of air pollution in South Durban therefore seems to fit nicely with Gamson's evaluative schema referred to above. There has been an increase in the amount of coverage of community activism and protest, and this coverage provides a clear linkage between everyday experiences and major public policy issues. The ascription of effective agency to citizen mobilisation has become a standard feature of the news frame of environmental reporting on South Durban. Government and corporate initiatives to tighten up emission control, to set up consultative forums, or to fund further research are now routinely contextualised in news coverage as being responses to the sustained mobilisation of local communities. Environmental issues have become a feature of business journalism as well, indicating that the potential social impacts of industrial and urban growth have become issues that business investment decision-making can no longer ignore. And corporations have adopted more professionalised public relations and communications strategies in response to the successful mobilisation of media attention on past practices (Barnett forthcoming).

Having local communities represented as effective agents of policy change in news coverage, or forcing environmental issues onto the agenda of business journalism, does not fit a heroic image of large-scale political transformation. But the emergence of a politics of environ-

7   The high point of the South Durban environmental activism in terms of media coverage came in September 2000, with a week-long series of investigative news stories in Durban's leading daily paper, the *Mercury*. This series of stories, entitled 'Poison in our air', provided unprecedented print and broadcast coverage of local community concerns in the mainstream media, not just at the metropolitan level, but nationally as well. The journalist who authored the pieces, Tony Carnie, was awarded the 2001 CNN African Journalist of the Year Award for Health and Medical Reporting.

mental justice, mediated in no small part by the adoption of a successful media-oriented strategy of mobilisation, is indicative of a fundamental shift in *how* power is exercised and contested in the South African context. Not the least significant effect of media transformation might therefore be an incremental cultural democratisation of news agendas, reflected in the adoption of styles of reporting and modes of address that connect up the norms of everyday life with the conventions of public debate. This is related to the tentative emergence of a culture of democratic publicity amongst government agencies, private corporations and media organisations. This example of modest success illustrates that the capacity of mainstream news media to pursue a critical watchdog role (that is, the vibrancy of the public sphere) crucially depends on the capacities of non-media actors to collect, monitor and distribute knowledge and information (that is, on a vibrant civil society). This point cuts to the heart of policy initiatives to encourage media pluralism. The national government has established a Media Development and Diversity Agency (MDDA) to subsidise a more plural media system, and particularly to encourage a media presence for marginalised social groups. However, on its own, this initiative does not guarantee the development of more diverse media outlets. The recurring problem of such projects in the past has been the lack of capacity amongst community organisations and interest groups able to take up opportunities. This has, for example, been the case with the community radio sector, which has grown rapidly since 1994, but which is also characterised by a high level of failure amongst licensees. The key to sustainable media pluralism lies not in initiatives for media assistance alone, but in the broader politics of programmes to consolidate and promote an autonomous associational culture in post-apartheid South Africa. Initiatives such as the MDDA tend to be informed by an instrumental model of democracy as more efficient communication between government and citizens. What the example discussed here indicates is that the central role of media practices in deepening democratisation is to be located in the more complex web of relationships that are cultivating the conditions for the articulation of legitimate opposition to government, business and other powerful actors.

Without idealising news media, it is plausible to suggest that structural changes in the sector have significant implications for the future pattern of democratic culture in South Africa. It was suggested above that South Durban environmental mobilisation was an example of the politics of shame. As discussed in Chapter 2, this notion addresses a fundamental issue in the institutionalisation of democracy, namely the potential for a role of oppositional organisation and discourse (Young

2000: 174–7). Theoretically, the idea of a politics of shame pinpoints the importance of media attention as a crucial lever for bringing pressure to bear on powerful actors. It is not necessary to idealise the democratic potential of media in order to acknowledge the possibility that media attention can be mobilised to act upon the conduct of powerful political and economic actors, especially in a context such as post-apartheid South Africa, where both public and private organisations have publicly committed to the objectives of constitutional government and to discourses of service delivery and institutional transformation. After an initial postelection lull in political mobilisation after 1994, South Africa has witnessed an upsurge of grassroots oppositional activism (Lodge 2001). This is indicative of new forms of issue-based mobilisation that have emerged in the last decade. In addition to the environmental issues already discussed, other examples include national mobilisations around government policy on HIV/AIDS issues, more localised campaigns around housing, infrastructure and service delivery, as well as the role of South African activist organisations in the broader politics of anti-globalisation campaigns (see Bond 2001; Desai 2002). Mainstream media attention has been crucial to these new forms of grassroots activism, for mobilisation and validation purposes, but in particular as a means of exerting pressure on powerful institutional actors.

It is worth noting that the successful adoption of a strategy of media-oriented activism might have significant impacts on the dynamics of movement strategy. Mobilising the relatively low-cost resource of media coverage implies accepting certain constraints, by adopting specific action strategies that accord with the imperatives of newsworthiness. First, this involves developing campaign and protest strategies which have a strong dramaturgical dimension. Second, successful media-oriented political action might also favour the adoption of particular discursive frames. For example, in the case of environmental activism discussed above, a universalising discourse of constitutional rights, when allied to the browning of the environment, provides a means of framing environmental issues as ones that transcend socio-economic divisions, making them more amenable to coverage in news markets that are marked by an imperative to construct cross-community forms of address. Both of these are relevant to the ways that media-oriented activism can also generate a dynamic of organisational change within movements. In the case of environmental campaigning in Durban, the very success of the media-oriented strategy has had a built-in dynamic of transforming movements into more formal, professionalised organisations, as well as partly transforming issue-based campaigns into general human rights organisations.

Returning to the question of the relationship between media transformation and the distribution of social power, the dynamics of environmental activism in South Durban indicates that media restructuring
in the post-apartheid period has had real effects in reshaping how politics is done. It has helped facilitate new forms of political action and the
politicisation of new issues. The restructured South African media landscape has provided significant opportunities for marginalised political
actors both to assert their presence in the public realm and to exert
influence over policy. But if media restructuring can be interpreted as
opening up new opportunities, it should not be forgotten that the capacity to make the most of these is likely to be sharply differentiated spatially, socially and in terms of what issue is at stake. The point worth
repeating, however, is that the political significance of new media technologies, converged communications infrastructures, corporate ownership and market restructuring cannot be deduced in abstraction from
broader patterns of political activity. The democratic potential of
media, old and new, depends on the ability of actors embedded in civil
society to practise well-worn political virtues, by adopting appropriate
repertoires of protest, effectively mobilising resources, and establishing
legitimacy amongst constituencies (Scott and Sharpe 2000). And in this
respect, the place of media in broader patterns of social and cultural
change might be just as important as their more obvious role as a
medium of political communication. It is this issue that is discussed in
the next section.

IV Media, empowerment and cultural democratisation

South Africa comes late to the characteristically modernist project of
deploying culture as a medium for nurturing inclusive national citizenship. It does so at a time when the development of markets in audio-
visual commodities defined not by geographical proximity but by a
congruence of linguistic and cultural traits is encouraging the delinking
of cultural identities from the scale of the nation-state (Sinclair et al.
1996). Processes of economic integration operating at a transnational
scale severely constrain the applicability of old models of national cultural policy as a medium for suturing together national cultures (Shields
and Muppidi 1996; Samarajiva and Shields 1990). At the same time,
however, this process is indicative of the emergence of new forms of
transnational publicness (Ong 1999: 158–61). Transnational media
organisations and markets regulate the circulation of representations of

cultural diversity in important ways, and so in turn they have become an important site for new, transnational struggles for visibility. The rescaling of spaces of cultural normativity means that processes of mediated subject-formation are increasingly articulated around cultural conventions that are not contained within national cultural infrastructures (ibid.). The evolution of South African media cultures illustrates these processes, but it also indicates that this does not imply that national-level public policy is rendered redundant. Rather, in important ways, it indicates the continuing saliency of national-level politics and policy in shaping the dimensions of transnational publics.

South African broadcasting in the 1990s has emerged from a history of division and fragmentation to pursue innovative nation-building media projects that take advantage of the opportunities opened up by processes of media globalisation to realise the principles of active media-citizenship first developed during the struggle against apartheid. In an era of media abundance, paternalist and protectionist models of media policy are increasingly anachronistic (Buckingham 2000). Since even before the first non-racial elections in 1994, the restructured SABC has shown a strong commitment to innovative and broadly conceived educational uses of its radio and television services, for example in the development of voter-education and health 'edutainment' initiatives (Teer-Tomaselli 1995, 1996). These initiatives illustrate the potential of using locally produced mass-media programming in support of an expansive programme of citizenship education. The single most controversial television happening in the post-apartheid period is *Yizo Yizo*, an educational broadcasting initiative. *Yizo Yizo* has been developed at a very particular moment in South African popular culture: 'The continual expansion of the mass media coupled with the removal of the cultural boycotts mean that young South Africans now can receive any amount of media programming form abroad' (Prinsloo 1999: 182). Media activists and educationalists in South Africa have acknowledged the existence of multiple media literacies amongst citizens, children and adults alike (Prinsloo and Criticos 1991). The emphasis of policy has shifted to developing media projects that contribute to the empowerment of learners, rather than assuming an objective of changing consciousness.

Policy in many areas of post-apartheid South Africa is characterised by this will to empower, and this is certainly the case in both education policy and public service broadcasting policy. In this context, *Yizo Yizo* illustrates the creative possibilities of deploying the conventions of global media cultures in progressive ways to open up more dialogic models of media-citizenship, and by extension to shift the terms of public culture. As already noted, radio and television were historically institutionalised as technologies of racial and ethnic separation. The same was true of educational systems. In the case of educational broadcasting, where these two areas directly connect, policy change has been informed by a set of understandings that emerged from oppositional media activism during apartheid, a tradition that emphasised citizen participation in a broad range of media practices. The new paradigm of educational broadcasting elaborated since 1994 emphasises the developmental potential of broadcasting in supporting the transformation of educational practices. The main innovation of the South African model has been to broaden the definition of educational broadcasting beyond the narrow confines of formal educational contexts, and redefine the subjects of educational broadcasting beyond the narrow reference to children in school.

Broadcasting has been identified as having an important role to play in changing public perceptions of the scope and purpose of education, and also as a resource to provide multimedia support to teachers and schools.[8] Using broadcasting to empower citizens rests on the assumption that the subjects of educational broadcasting are not just children, but adults as well. This is mirrored in the broadened conception of education introduced in the fundamental overhaul of South African education signalled in 1997.[9] The adoption of 'learner-centred' approaches in education dovetails with the recommendation that popular programming formats and genres, including documentary, soap operas, talk shows and drama series, should be used as vehicles for educational broadcasting in order to attract large, general audiences. Its aims and objectives are no longer contained within the disciplinary matrix of the school, classroom and teacher–pupil relationship. Educational broadcasting has been relocated within the dispersed, anonymous publics constituted by electronic mass media. Educational broadcasting, rather than being considered as a specific niche of programme schedules, has been redefined as a basic element of general programming and scheduling.[10] The multimedia strategy in support of educational broadcasting is doubly important because patterns of media consumption in South Africa are not uniformly based in the home. There is a significant

8 Department of Education (1996), *Educational Broadcasting Plan: Proposal for a Partnership between the Department of Education and the SABC*, Department of Education, Pretoria.

9 Ministry of Education (1999), *Status Report for the Minister of Education*, Pretoria, June.

10 South African Institute for Distance Education (1998), *A School-Based Educational Broadcasting Service for South Africa*, SAIDE, Johannesburg.

amount of out-of-home television viewing, not least in those township communities that have been the main target of recent educational transformation and are the subject of *Yizo Yizo* (Venter and Van Vuuren 2000). The redefinition of the subjects and spaces of educational broadcasting reflects the acknowledgement of the increasingly complex, dense and commercialised nature of South African media cultures resulting from the proliferation and opening up of media markets during the 1990s.

The explicit deployment of popular media culture as a means of cultivating citizenship therefore rests upon the reconceptualisation of the material and discursive spaces in which education and broadcasting are articulated together. It also involves a revised understanding of the roles and relationships between the actors involved in educational broadcasting projects. The mainstreaming of educational broadcasting in terms of scheduling is associated with a fundamental shift in the style of programming, eschewing traditional top-down didacticism, which tended to provide models of appropriate outcomes. In the new paradigm, programmes model processes of acting, with the objective of empowering people to take charge of everyday decision-making. This is a fundamental shift in the rationality of educational broadcasting. As Chapter 4 showed, when identified as potential instruments for realising cultural policy objectives, radio and television can be understood as archetypal governmental technologies, in so far as their deployment in this role rests on a set of procedures that aim to act on the capacities of other social actors to act. The emphasis on using educational broadcasting as a means of empowering South African citizens is symptomatic of this governmental rationality.

Yizo Yizo is the drama series commissioned by the SABC in collaboration with the national government, with the objective of publicising issues of teaching and learning environments in South African townships. The production of the series proceeded only after extensive qualitative and quantitative research into conditions in South African schools.[11] This research served as the basis for the development of the scripts for *Yizo Yizo*. The series was developed with the primary aim of generating wide public debate about educational issues, and of changing the attitudes and behaviour of students, teachers and principals, and parents. In township vernacular, *tsotsitaal*, used extensively in the series, *Yizo Yizo* means 'this is it', 'the way it is'. The status of *Yizo Yizo*'s claim to realism is central both to the realisation of its educational objectives and to the political controversy it has generated. As a conse-

---

11   SABC Education (1999), *Understanding South African Schools in Crisis*, SABC, Johannesburg.

quence, research knowledge has been crucial in evaluating the success of the series, and in defending it against the criticism that the graphic depiction of sex and violence is a glorification that encourages copycat behaviour.

Yizo Yizo was first aired on the SABC's main channel, SABC1, in February 1999, and ran for thirteen half-hour episodes. The programmes were intended to reveal the depth and complexity of the crisis facing South African schools, to model a process of action to create and sustain a culture of learning and teaching, and to stimulate discussion of key educational issues. The show was broadcast at prime time in the evenings, in order to ensure maximum audience penetration of both children and adults. The series provoked almost instant controversy, but also rapidly established itself as the most watched programme on South African television. *Yizo Yizo* is the only drama series on South African television that shows township life, a topic otherwise reserved for news and documentary series. It focuses upon the lives of the children, teachers and parents of a fictional township school. The series dramatises the impact of socio-economic factors upon children's experiences of formal schooling. The storylines cover highly contentious topics such as violence, sexual harassment and rape, HIV/AIDS and drug abuse. In line with the new education policy agenda, the series has also dramatised the role of teachers and administrators in sustaining or undermining effective learning environments, as well as the role of communities in improving the performance of schools.

In addition to the episodes of *Yizo Yizo* itself, the SABC developed an extensive multimedia strategy that aimed both to foster public debate and to provide resources for students and teachers to engage with the issues raised by the series. This included a full-colour *Yizo Yizo* magazine, targeted at children and young people, combining features on the actors in the series with discussions of the issues addressed there. The SABC's national youth radio station, MetroFM, broadcast a talk-show the day after each week's episode. A further feature of the multimedia profile for *Yizo Yizo* was the release of a hugely popular soundtrack CD. Both this and the *Yizo Yizo* magazine illustrate the explicit use of popular commercial media formats to support the primary objective of stimulating discussion of the topics of the television series, such as violence, sexual harassment and rape, drug abuse, HIV/AIDS and gangsterism. The music soundtrack from *Yizo Yizo* is particularly notable, featuring as it does local *kwaito* music. *Kwaito* is a distinctively South African hybrid form of pop music, mixing elements of imported house, hip-hop and rap with home-grown traditional and pop music styles (Stephens 2000). The use of township dance music in the television series was an integral element of the reality-effect created around the programme, and thus a key element both in building a large youth audience and in realising the objective of stimulating discussion about real-world social and policy issues (Smith 2001: 31–2).

Yizo Yizo certainly succeeded in creating an unprecedented level of public debate, both about the state of education in South Africa and about the public role of television representations of social issues. The SABC's independent evaluation of the first series of *Yizo Yizo*, undertaken in the second half of 1999, found that the series 'was phenomenally successful in its attraction and consolidation of a youth audience. It spoke to this audience in a visually new and exciting way that compelled viewers to watch the series, week after week.'[12] The series sparked criticism that the programmes glamorised violence and gangsterism, presented black communities in a negative light, and used unacceptably graphic representations of sex and bad language. *Yizo Yizo* quickly became the focus of newspaper stories about youth crime and school indiscipline, triggering a public debate over whether or not the series was promoting copycat behaviour by encouraging school violence. The key issue of contention in these controversies is the claim that *Yizo Yizo* 'shows it like it is'. This claim has depended on a combination of innovative aesthetic devices (pop music, fast-paced visuals) and the much publicised research undertaken in township schools by the production team prior to the making of the series. So, in addition to its explicit goal of stimulating debate about educational issues, *Yizo Yizo* has also served as the occasion for a public debate about how relationships between media representations and everyday life should be understood.

Yizo Yizo is premised on the assumption that children as well as adults have the ability to distinguish between representations of reality and reality itself. It exemplifies an attempt to generate a public sphere of mediated deliberation, in which various forms of mass media have been used to distribute symbolic resources with the intention of generating innumerable, dispersed dialogues about issues of broad public concern. *Yizo Yizo* makes use of an amalgam of local and global cultural forms to expand the horizons of normative debate in a cultural context in which discussion of sexual harassment, violent crime, abuse and addiction have been either highly moralised or consigned to silence. As part of this strategy, research knowledge has provided an important element in the public legitimisation of the partnership approach to educational broadcasting, enabling the SABC and Ministry of Education to

12   SABC Education (1999), *An Evaluation of Yizo Yizo*, SABC, Johannesburg, p. 81.

reiterate the aims of the series and to claim a high degree of success in attaining these. Research also provided a means by which the opinions of children themselves entered into public debates that were otherwise monopolised by adults. And finally, the research evaluation was used to inform the production of the second series of *Yizo Yizo*. The primary finding of the SABC's evaluation of the first series was that it had been successful in raising issues, but less so in providing 'practical and action-able solutions'.[13] Many viewers felt that the half-hour format of the first series did not provide adequate time to wrap up and resolve different strands of the storyline. The second series, broadcast in 2001, was therefore informed by a stronger commitment to be clearer in modelling the relationships between actions, consequences and solutions.

Yizo Yizo uses a popular television format to build a large audience, but in leaving the classroom, and making creative use of the aesthetics of popular culture, 'edutainment' programming of this sort relin-quishes a significant degree of control over the communication process of educational broadcasting. This is a feature inherent in any policy aimed at governing the conduct of populations through the distanciated mediums of radio and television broadcasting. Even if the multimedia support strategies are effective, there is an unavoidable trade-off between the broader access to diverse audiences that using popular for-mats allows, and the didactic content in terms of practicable solutions that this sort of programming can deliver. The reality revealed by *Yizo Yizo* is, after all, dependent upon the highly sophisticated manipula-tion of conventional codes of genre and format. The effective use of these conventions to establish the authenticity of the programme intro-duces a degree of distance between medium and message, a space within which discussion proliferates, but also inevitably means that the preferred messages might get lost in transmission.

Yizo Yizo 2 was, like the first series, accused of encouraging copycat violence and promoting anti-social behaviour. These critical attacks on the series depended on an implicit, commonsense model of strong media effects, in which children are constructed as natural innocents who are easily influenced into becoming monsters. The ongoing public controversies about *Yizo Yizo* juxtapose different understandings of the relationships between free expression, democratic participation and cultural integrity in the context of a deeply divided society. The defence made of *Yizo Yizo* by broadcasters, educationalists and government has not rested on appeals to libertarian rights of free speech or artistic

13   Ibid., p. 143.

freedom. Instead they point to an opening up of a participatory culture of discussion and criticism that stands in contrast to the censorious traditions both of the old apartheid order and of certain traditions of left cultural criticism and political analysis. The success of *Yizo Yizo* in opening up the educational crisis in South Africa to broad public debate and interpersonal discussion rested on the acknowledgement of the existence of complex popular cultures in South Africa, and of the existence of youth audiences who have sophisticated cultural literacies. The basic premise of the series is that children are neither passive dupes, copycats nor innocents to be corrupted. They are acknowledged as subjects capable of assessing, evaluating and discussing complex public issues. *Yizo Yizo* uses a variety of mass-media platforms and aspects of contemporary popular culture to cultivate inclusive forms of talking-subjectivity. In so doing, it treats children as citizens, as competent participants in mass-mediated public discourse around issues that directly affect them.

By treating children as competent subjects with highly developed media literacies, South African educational broadcasting initiatives have therefore significantly recast the dimensions of public debate for all citizens. This ascription of competency to children is associated with the emergence of a broader culture of empowerment and dialogue. One lesson of *Yizo Yizo* is that the transnationalisation of media publics opens up the possibility of using multimedia strategies to facilitate dialogical practices of educational broadcasting in which children themselves are ascribed agency as subjects of public discussion. The opening up of national media publics to diverse flows of popular media culture provides national programme-makers with new generic forms for addressing audiences. As an example of this process, *Yizo Yizo* makes visible a range of issues, enabling children, teachers and parents to become informed participants in a public debate around a shared set of reference points. It illustrates the potential for broadcasting to link up the everyday experiences of ordinary people with broader political debates, by facilitating a set of mediated discussions in homes, classrooms and playgrounds, as well as on radio, on television and in newspapers. *Yizo Yizo* is, in short, television that helps make democracy work. In contrast to the example discussed in Chapter 5, it illustrates a more progressive version of a paedocratic rationality of media regulation, in which conceptualisations of children's media competencies have opened up, rather than closed down, the discursive dimensions of mediated public space.

The achievements of *Yizo Yizo* in stimulating public debate are indicative of more subtle shifts in the contours of public culture in post-apartheid South Africa. The popularity of *Yizo Yizo* indicates the potential for commercial popular culture to be deployed as a medium for the democratisation of taste (see Scannell 2001b). It serves as a means through which the previously marginalised cultural tastes of the majority of black South Africans have now been registered by powerful national cultural institutions. At the same time, it is worth underlining the structural limits to this subterranean process of cultural democratisation through commercialised popular media cultures. *Yizo Yizo*'s success depends on the conscious use of aesthetic features of an increasingly internationalised and commercialised popular culture that is developing in South Africa. While the success of the series demonstrates that citizenship and consumerism are not necessarily diametrically opposed principles, it also illustrates the uneven way in which the institutional restructuring of post-apartheid mass media is contributing to the commodification of black youth markets. The use of *kwaito* music as the soundtrack drew upon an emerging commercial culture that is a testament to the impact of international markets for cultural commodities upon South African popular culture. In turn, the series gave a significant boost to the further commercial profitability of this genre, raising the profile of artists and boosting sales. However, while the commodification of local music forms has been promoted by the success of *Yizo Yizo*, the series has consistently failed to attract adequate advertising revenue from commercial sources, despite its record-breaking viewing figures. This raises serious problems for the SABC, which is heavily dependent on commercial advertising revenue, in continuing to finance the series in the future.

Yizo Yizo therefore illustrates the contradictions of producing public service broadcasting with universal social objectives, in a context in which public service broadcasters are increasingly dependent upon advertising revenue for their continued operation, as well as facing more and more competition from other media. And it is important to emphasise that the material and symbolic resources required to participate in the sort of extended, mediated public debate stimulated by *Yizo Yizo* remain unevenly distributed according to race, class and gender. The difficulty in attracting adequate advertising revenue is partly a function of entrenched socio-economic inequalities that indicate the limits of market-led cultural policies. The success of the series in meeting its educational objectives needs therefore to be placed in the wider context of the role of an increasingly commercialised South African media system in the uneven commodification of black youth culture, a process that potentially contributes to the broader segmentation of social groups that will entrench inequalities of access to both media technologies and wider cultural competencies.

V Conclusion: scales of
media citizenship

Post-apartheid media policies have been guided by particular understandings of democracy and development, in which values of participation, nation-building, and cultural diversity are frequently extolled. But
South Africa comes late to the process of inclusive nation-formation, so
that socio-cultural integration is taking place in a context in which communications and cultural policies have become means of negotiating
entry into the global economy. The implications of this internationalisation for national-level processes of democratisation are far from
straightforward. Looking at patterns of representation in policy
processes, it has been associated with the attenuation of broad-based
civic participation. However, looked at more broadly, media restructuring has been associated with the emergence of new forms of political
mobilisation, not in spite of, but in part facilitated by, the situational
effects of media commercialisation in changing the ways in which news
is produced. And in terms of socio-cultural integration, *Yizo Yizo* likewise illustrates the place of media institutions in cultivating the conditions for a diffuse process of cultural democratisation. In an era of
media abundance, in which traditional forms of media regulation have
been rendered problematic by the spatial restructuring of media markets and new technologies, sustaining vibrant media publics requires
less protectionist models of media citizenship. The example of *Yizo
Yizo* suggests that supporting citizenship participation by using locally
produced mass-media programming works best when the multiple and
increasingly globalised cultural literacies of citizens are acknowledged.

These overlapping, contradictory tendencies – towards the bureaucratisation of media policy, towards a mediated culture of democratic
public scrutiny, and towards the democratisation of popular media cultures – are indicative of the fault-lines along which the future politics of
democratisation in South Africa will develop. The meaning of democracy remains hotly contested in the post-apartheid period. For some, it
refers to the electoral legitimacy of a government and the formal recognition of basic rights. For others, it refers to the populist legitimacy
of a liberation movement. In this chapter, I have suggested that democratisation in South Africa needs also to be understood by reference to
the emergence, first, of a culture of legitimate and effective extra-
parliamentary opposition, and, second, of a broadly diffused culture of
tolerance, criticism and openness. In both respects, a rapidly transforming media landscape is an important element in mediating the
development of a democratic culture in what remains a highly unequal,

conflict-ridden and divided society. In this respect, using media policy as an entry point into the process of democratisation is useful, since tracking each of the three tendencies noted above illustrates clearly that the politics of democratisation, both formal and informal, is neither neatly contained within the domestic space of a national polity, nor free-floating in a weightless global space. While the South African example indicates that the national scale remains a privileged container for the effective exercise of citizenship, it also indicates the extent to which the politics of media citizenship involves the articulation of interests embedded at spatial scales that flow through, around and under the national scale.

Conclusion: culture and democracy

This book has explored the grounds for an analysis of democracy understood as a broadly cultural formation of practices and dispositions. The Dewey-like formula of 'culture and democracy' in the title of this book is meant to signal a commitment to a post-foundational, pragmatic analysis of the interface between cultural and political processes. Another name for this sort of approach would be the cultural geography of democracy, as long as this is not read in narrowly disciplinary terms. A cultural geography of democracy would be about tracking the formation of the spaces of autonomy, spaces of sociability and spaces of decision through which democracy as a politics is made and unmade. It involves a reflection on the formation of the spaces in and through which practices of civility, tolerance and criticism can emerge. It is guided by a pragmatic calculation of effects rather than abstract political evaluation. And a cultural geography of democracy also involves reflection on first principles, not in the search for higher foundational truths, but as a contribution to one basic practice of democratic culture – the giving of reasons, inviting responses. A cultural geography of democracy would investigate both the cultivation of spaces of democratic practice and the circulation of democracy, understood as a political form constituted and reconstituted only in and through its differential representation in new contexts. If democracy is an essentially contested concept – the parasitical boundary-case of categorical definition – then it calls for a geographical style of analysis not because geography is the study of the particular manifestations of universal principles, but because democracy thrives through an unrelenting movement of translation.

The way one approaches issues of political critique is in part the reflection of an ethico-political decision. The impulses of critical, progressive academic analysis in the current conjuncture are divided between two positions, distinguished by whether one thinks that the greater danger is being 'suckered by power' or 'denied of hope' (Peters 1999: 224). By temperament, it seems to me that it is the latter danger that is most pressing. For this reason, it is important to keep open a space for reflection on normative principles that is easily closed down by the certainties of radical denunciation. In this respect, a reckoning with liberal political theory is indispensable, and a complete renunciation of the inheritance of liberalism is certainly not a morally serious posture, in the strict Kantian sense that one could not coherently will that others adopt this renunciation as a universal principle of action.

It is with this in mind that I have tried to work around some of the usual ways of discussing so-called poststructuralism. The abiding liberal commitments of what might be better thought of as various types of post-Marxist, post-phenomenological thought are all too often ignored. The result is that an abstracted radicalism stripped of its Marxist rigour can easily embrace deeply illiberal critiques of liberal and social democracies. In choosing to focus upon the political-theoretic dimensions of writers such as Derrida or Foucault, it is important not to fall into the trap of reproducing the 'narcissism of small differences' (Garber 2001: 54–5), an impulse towards over-systematisation that is expressed in the staging of caricatured oppositions with other writers (Habermas and Rawls are the usual fall guys). In this book, I have emphasised the ways in which these and other writers share certain overlapping concerns. In this I am only following a broader convergence between traditions of thought that are not necessarily as far apart as is often supposed (see Critchley 1999; Honneth 1995, 1999). Chief amongst these shared concerns is the question of how to understand in a non-metaphysical way the practical resilience of ideals of the public use of reason.

The strands of theory woven together in this book share an interest in practices of autonomy, obligation and responsibility, understood as the cultural conditions of democracy. The theme of autonomy is vital to understanding the value of practices of mediation and representation in instituting the spectral form of public that this book has argued defines modern understandings of democracy. Parsing the usages of democracy in multiple contexts enables us to pinpoint the central role that ideas about representation play in defining the meaning of democracy. First, democracy supposes the legitimacy of forming organisations that represent the interests of different social groups. At the same time, however, democracy supposes a multiplicity of channels of public debate, ensuring that power is exercised in the open and that claims of

representation can be called to account. In contrast to conceptualisations that privilege images of the assembled people, and which allow for
no legitimate delay, distance or intermediation between those who govern and those who are governed, modern understandings of democracy
(including but not restricted to liberalism) are distinguished by a commitment to the irreducible pluralism of mutable opinions, interests and
identities. This connects to the recurring theme of this book, that of
mediation. It has focused on the question of how to understand the *normative* significance of the irreducible *empirical* fact that democratic
rule depends on various forms of human and non-human intermediary,
whether these take the form of parties, social movements or mediums of
free expression. Democracy is stretched out, in time as well as space,
and this complicates a number of cherished assumptions about politics,
justice and citizenship. By placing the analysis of media and democracy
within a broader analytical framework of the dynamics of mediation,
this book has underscored the point that the practical value of democratic principles inheres in the quality of relations, and not in the
authenticities of identity.

I suggested at the outset that democracy is a boundary-concept
whose application to new contexts raises fundamental questions concerning the relative significance of internally connected elements associated with this term – for example, between equality, participation,
political competition and majority rule. Representation is a recurrent
theme and problem in this essentially contested process of translation,
because ideas and practices of representation serve as figures for the
parasitical grafting of political forms into new contexts. The parasitical
quality of representation, as practice and mechanism, turns out not to
be an external prosthesis added to a pure form. Representation appears
instead as the very medium called forward by the foundational absence
at the heart of sedimented understandings of democracy. As discussed
in detail in Chapter 1, representation can be understood as a movement
of differential spatial and temporal relating, which draws together and
holds apart the imperatives of accountability and delegation, popular
sovereignty and personal autonomy. It is a pragmatic instrument that
allows the institutionalisation of democracy in complex, spatially
extensive, conflict-ridden societies, but at the same time it contains
within it an ethico-political affirmation of open-ended, peaceable
contestation as the very principle of democratic rule.

The normative value of representation in democratic theory is closely
connected to the value of autonomy. And autonomy is the privileged
conceptual entry point for understanding the mutual connections
between contemporary cultural theory and political theory. Cultural

studies starts off from a critique of inherited understandings of the autonomy of cultural artefacts and of aesthetic judgement. Political theory revolves around a set of understandings of the autonomous self of ethical responsibility and political obligation, bound together with others by social contracts or communitarian solidarity. This convergence is, in turn, what enables one to imagine an analysis of the 'arts of government' that moves the concerns of cultural theory closer to those of political theory (Barnett 2001a). Democracy, on this understanding, is itself an artful practice, in so far as it involves the formal and informal cultivation of competencies of judging, reasoning, appreciating, performing and responding. And the spaces in which these competencies are formed and exercised are not bound or contained; they are stretched out and excessive.

Autonomy is an important theme in the analysis of the geographies of public communication precisely because democracy is best understood in terms of the unavoidable problem of political control. Democracy is built around finding practical solutions to various paradoxes, and chief amongst these is the paradox of autonomy – autonomy as a practice formed under the auspices of various forms of institutional power, and autonomy as a resource for the containment, limitation and normalisation of centralised power (Ricouer 1965: 270). The value of autonomy is attained, it is a practical achievement, which is a strange thought perhaps, but this is why Dahl's problem of democratic competence is at the crux of a postfoundational understanding of democracy. The later chapters in this book tracked examples in which particular understandings of autonomy have been embedded in policy and institutional design. They illustrate the contemporary assemblage of the subjects of democratic rights (people, collectivities, corporations) in terms of a distinctively neo-liberal form of autonomy. This is autonomy understood as an abstracted capacity to realise individualised, private desires through the exercise of choice (Rose 1999: 84–5). The conceptualisation of representation and publicity developed in the opening chapters shows that a critique of this model of autonomy in the name of the unquestioned good of community, society or collective interests would miss the point about what is the main problem with neo-liberal discourses of individual autonomy. It is not the value of autonomy as such that is the problem, but the detachment of autonomy from a broader web of relations with publicity, accountability and responsibility. Simply asserting the primacy of public values over private autonomy, the social over individualism, risks reproducing serious harm by curtailing important spaces of liberty carved out by progressive political movements. This is the recurrent problem faced by the civic republican reassertions of legitimate political speech discussed in Chapter 5, as well as by the defences of public service broadcasting that counterpose citizenship to consumerism discussed in both Chapter 3 and Chapter 6. Simple avowals of collective values, by asserting the substantive liberties of the ancients over the abstracted liberties of the unencumbered modern self, too quickly pass over the problem of the inherent relationship between the democratic normativity of public participation and the maintenance of a realm of private life. The indissolubility of this relation is what is at stake in Habermas' analytics of system and lifeworld, as well as in Derrida's somewhat more elusive discussion of disclosure and secrecy, public manifestations and spectral hauntings.

If the value of democratic legitimacy is that it rests on the freely given consent to common binding principles, then this implies that the exercise of public reason necessarily depends on a protected space of private, non-political activity (Benhabib 1992: 111–12). This idea implies an alternative understanding of autonomy, what O'Neill (2002b), following Kant, calls principled autonomy. Principled autonomy is realised through a commitment to the giving of reasons in public. Rethinking autonomy and public reason in non-foundational ways underscores the importance of assessing the characteristics of public spaces of communication: 'reasons are the sorts of things we give and receive, exchange and refuse. If anything is to count as reasoned it must be *accessible to others who are to be the audience for that reasoning*' (ibid.: 91; original emphasis). As I showed in Chapter 1, it is quite plausible to rewrite this revised Kantian position on public reason in terms derived from Derrida's affirmative deconstruction, a point worth repeating if only to emphasise the common concerns shared by traditions of thought that are often presented as being mutually hostile. From this broad perspective, the main problem with contemporary discourses of individual autonomy is that they privilege autonomy in terms of self-expression. When applied to contexts of mediated communications, this ideal implies a fundamental privatisation of communicative action, in the sense of closing down the commitment to giving reasons in a public forum upon which effective responsibility and accountability rest.

Disavowing the relation between autonomy and giving reasons in public that defines the specific form of public will that is characteristic of modern democracy enables the public to be resubstantialised as a single, collective subject. The presence of this public is not therefore registered through open debate, but rather, the public will is reduced to 'argument-free acclamation' (Habermas 1990: 138–9). This disavowal and resubstantialisation is a political gesture that connects illiberal traditions of both the left and the right. The problem with the modes of neo-liberal autonomy tracked through Chapters 5 and 6 is that auton-omy is defined as an essentially autonomous value, detached from and even protected from public participation, from the surprise of the unan-ticipated encounter. This is, in the final analysis, a deeply paternalist conception of autonomy (Habermas 1994b: 112–13), granted by a higher authority, but as a practice whose norms of conduct cannot be claimed as the products of subjects' own participation in debate. Democratic legitimacy is essentially connected to the existence of spaces of autonomy related to spaces of participation and representa-tion (Held 1989b: 185–7). This means that the value of autonomy in democratic theory is derived from the presumption that democracy unavoidably involves centralised decision-making of some sort. Democracy is not the name for a mode of being, it is a practical problem of political control.

Bibliography

Allen, J. (1999), 'Spatial assemblages of power: from domination to empowerment', in
    D. Massey, J. Allen and P. Sarre (eds), *Human Geography Today*, Cambridge:
    Cambridge University Press.
Anderson, A. (1992), 'Cryptonormativism and double gestures: the politics of
    post-structuralism', *Cultural Critique* 21, 63–95.
Appadurai, A. (1990), 'Disjuncture and difference in the global cultural economy', *Public
    Culture* 2:2, 1–24.
Arendt, H. (1958), *The Human Condition*, Chicago: University of Chicago Press.
Aufderheide, P. (2000), *The Daily Planet*, Minneapolis: University of Minnesota Press.
Baker, K. M. (1994), 'A Foucauldian French revolution?', in J. Goldstein (ed.), *Foucault
    and the Writing of History*, Oxford: Blackwell, pp. 187–205.
Barendt, E. (1985), *Freedom of Speech*, Oxford: Oxford University Press.
Barendt, E. (1993), *Broadcasting Law*, Oxford: Oxford University Press.
Barnett, C. (1997), 'Sing along with the common people: politics, postcolonialism and
    other figures', *Environment and Planning: Society and Space* 15, 137–54.
Barnett, C. (1999a), 'Culture, government, and spatiality: re-assessing the Foucault
    effect in cultural-policy studies', *International Journal of Cultural Studies* 2,
    369–97.
Barnett, C. (1999b), 'Deconstructing context: exposing Derrida', *Transactions of the
    Institute of British Geographers* 24, 277–93.
Barnett, C. (1999c), 'The limits of media democratization in South Africa: politics,
    privatization, and regulation', *Media, Culture and Society* 21, 649–71.
Barnett, C. (1999d), 'Uneven liberalisation in Southern Africa: convergence and
    democracy in communications policy', *Javnost* 6, 101–14.
Barnett, C. (2001a), 'Culture, geography and the arts of government', *Environment and
    Planning D: Society and Space* 19, 7–24.
Barnett, C. (2001b), 'Culture, policy and subsidiarity in the European Union', *Political
    Geography* 20, 405–26.
Barnett, C. (2002), 'Media, scale and democratization', in K. Tomaselli and H. Dunn
    (eds), *Media, Democracy and Renewal in Southern Africa*, Denver: International
    Academic Publishers, pp. 41–53.
Barnett, C. (forthcoming), 'Media transformation and new practices of citizenship',
    Transformation.

Barnett, S. (1998), 'New media, old problems: new technology and the political process', *European Journal of Communication* 12, 193–218.

Barry, A. (2001), *Political Machines*, London: Athlone Press.

Barry, A., Osborne, T. and Rose, N. (eds) (1996), *Foucault and Political Reason*, Chicago: University of Chicago Press.

Baum, L. (1993), 'Case selection and decision making in the US Supreme Court', *Law and Society Review* 27, 443–59.

Baum, L. (1998), *The Supreme Court* (6th edition), Washington, DC: Congressional Quarterly Press.

Baum, L. and Hausegger, L. (1999), 'Inviting Congressional action: a study of Supreme Court motivations in statutory interpretation', *American Journal of Political Science* 43, 162–85.

Beale, A. (1999). 'Development and "destatisation" in European cultural policy', *Media Information Australia* 90, 91–105.

Bellamy, R. (1999), *Liberalism and Pluralism*, London: Routledge.

Bellamy, R. (2000), *RethinkingLiberalism*, London: Pinter.

Bellamy, R. and Castiglione, D. (2000), 'The uses of democracy: reflections on the European democratic deficit', in E. O. Eriksen and J. E. Fossum (eds), *Democracy in the European Union*, Routledge, London, pp. 65–84.

Bellamy, R. and Warleigh, A. (1998), 'Ethics of participation: citizenship and the future of the European Union', *Millennium* 27, 447–70.

Benhabib, S. (1992), *Situating the Self*, Cambridge: Polity.

Benhabib, S. (1996), 'Toward a deliberative model of democratic legitimacy', in S. Benhabib (ed.), *Democracy and Difference*, Princeton, NJ: Princeton University Press, pp. 67–94.

Bennett, T. (1989), 'Culture: theory and policy', *Media Information Australia* 53, 9–11.

Bennett, T. (1990), *Outside Literature*, London: Routledge.

Bennett, T. (1992), 'Useful culture', *Cultural Studies* 6, 395–408.

Bennett, T. (1995a), *The Birth of the Museum*, London: Routledge.

Bennett, T. (1995b), 'The multiplication of culture's utility', *Critical Inquiry* 21, 861–89.

Bennett, T. (1998), *Culture*, London: Sage.

Berger, G. (1999), 'Towards an analysis of the South African media and transformation, 1994–1999', *Transformation* 38, 84–116.

Berger, G. (2000), 'Response to Boloka and Krabill', *Transformation* 43, 90–7.

Berger, G. (2002), 'More media for Southern Africa? The place of politics, economics and convergence in developing media density', unpublished paper prepared for the International Research Seminar on Convergence: Technology, Culture and Social Impacts, University of Natal, Durban, May 2002.

Berkson, L. (1978), *The Supreme Court and its Publics*, Lexington, MA: Lexington Books.

Berland, J. (1992), 'Angels dancing: cultural technologies and the production of space', in L. Grossberg, C. Nelson and P. Treichler (eds), *Cultural Studies*, London: Routledge.

Birch, A. H. (1964), *Representative and Responsible Government*, London: Unwin University Books.

Birch, A. H. (1992), *The Concepts and Theories of Modern Democracy*, London: Routledge.

Bobbio, N. (1987), *Which Socialism?*, Minneapolis: University of Minnesota Press.

Bollinger, L. C. (1991), *Images of a Free Press*, Chicago: University of Chicago Press.

Boloka, G. and Krabill, R. (2000), 'Calling the glass half full: a response to Berger', *Transformation* 43, 75–89.

Boltanski, L. (1999), *Distant Suffering*, Cambridge: Cambridge University Press.

Bond, P. (1999), *Elite Transition*, Pietermaritzburg: University of Natal.

Bond, P. (2001), *Against Global Apartheid*, Cape Town: University of Cape Town Press.

Bork, R. (1971), 'Neutral principles and some First Amendment principles', *Indiana Law Journal* 47, 1–35.

Bourdieu, P. (1998), *On Television and Journalism*, London: Pluto Press.

Bové, P. (1990), 'Power and freedom: opposition and the humanities', *October* 53, 78–92.

Bridge, G. (1997), 'Mapping the terrain of time-space compression: power networks in everyday life', *Environment and Planning D: Society and Space* 15, 611–26.

Brown, L. A. (1981), *Innovation Diffusion*, London: Methuen.

Brown, W. (1995), *States of Injury*, Princeton, NJ: Princeton.

Brunn, S. and Leinbach, T. (1991), *Collapsing Space and Time*, London: HarperCollins.

Buckingham, D. (2000), *After the Death of Childhood*, Cambridge: Polity.

Butler, J. (1993), *Bodies that Matter*, London: Routledge.

Butler, J. (1997), *Excitable Speech*, London: Routledge.

Calhoun, C. (1989), 'Tiananmen, television and the public sphere', *Public Culture* 2:1, 54–71.

Calhoun, C. (ed.) (1992), *Habermas and the Public Sphere*, Cambridge, MA: MIT Press.

Calhoun, C. (1993), 'Civil society and the public sphere', *Public Culture* 5, 267–80.

Calhoun, C. (1996), 'Comment on John Keane: the death of the public sphere', in M. B. Andersen (ed.), *Media and Democracy*, Oslo: University of Oslo Press, pp. 243–52.

Calhoun, C. (1997), 'Plurality, promises, and public spaces', in C. Calhoun and J. McGowan (eds), *Hannah Arendt and the Meaning of Politics*, Minneapolis: University of Minnesota Press, pp. 232–59.

Canguilhem, G. (1991), *The Normal and the Pathological*, New York: Zone Books.

Canovan, M. (1983), 'A case of distorted communication: a note on Habermas and Arendt', *Political Theory* 11, 105–16.

Carey, J. (1989), *Culture as Communication*, London: Routledge.

Chang, B. G. (1996), *Deconstructing Communication*, Minneapolis: University of Minnesota Press.

Clark, G. (1985), *Judges and the Cities*, Chicago: University of Chicago Press.

Coase, R. (1959), 'The Federal Communications Commission', *Journal of Law and Economics* 2, 1–40.

Collins, R. (1990), *Culture, Communication and National Identity*, Toronto: University of Toronto Press.

Collins, R. (1993), 'Public service and the market ten years on: reflections on Critical Theory and the debate on broadcasting policy in the UK', *Screen* 34, 243–59.

Collins, R. (1994), 'Trading in culture: the role of language', *Canadian Journal of Communication* 19: 3/4, 377–401.

Collins, R. (2002), *Media and Identity in Contemporary Europe*, Bristol: Intellect Books.

Connolly, W. (1993), *The Terms of Political Discourse* (3rd edition), Oxford: Blackwell.

Connolly, W. (1999), *Why I Am Not a Secularist*, Minneapolis: University of Minnesota Press.

Connolly, W. (2000), 'Speed, concentric cultures, and cosmopolitanism', *Political Theory* 29, 596–618.

Cook, T. (1998), *Governing with the News*, Chicago: University of Chicago Press.

Cornell, D. (1992), *The Philosophy of the Limit*, London: Routledge.

Corner, J. (1998), *Studying Media*, Edinburgh: Edinburgh University Press.

Corner, J. (2000), 'Mediated persona and political culture', *European Journal of Cultural Studies* 3, 386–402.

Cox, K. (1998), 'Spaces of dependence, spaces of engagement and the politics of scale', *Political Geography* 17, 1–23.

Critchley, S. (1992), *The Ethics of Deconstruction*, Oxford: Blackwell.

Critchley, S. (1999), *The Ethics of Deconstruction* (2nd edition), Edinburgh: Edinburgh University Press.

Cruikshank, B. (1999), *The Will to Empower*, Ithaca, NY: Cornell University Press.

Curran, J. (1996), 'Media and democracy: the third route', in M. B. Andersen (ed.), *Media and Democracy*, Oslo: University of Oslo Press, pp. 53–75.

Dahl, R. (1957), 'Decision-making in a democracy: the Supreme Court as a national policy-maker', *Journal of Public Law* 6, 279–95.

Dahl, R. (1969), 'The concept of power', in R. Bell, D. Edwards and R. Harrison Wagner (eds), *Political Power*, New York: Free Press, pp. 79–93.

Dahl, R. (1989), *Democracy and its Critics*, New Haven, CT: Yale University Press.

Dahlgren, P. (1995), *Television and the Public Sphere*, London: Sage.

Dallmayr, F. (1993), *The Other Heidegger*, Ithaca, NY: Cornell University Press.

Davis, R. (1994), *Decisions and Images: The Supreme Court and the Press*, Englewood Cliffs, NJ: Prentice-Hall.

Deleuze, J. (1988), *Foucault*, Minneapolis: University of Minnesota Press.

Deleuze, J. (1992a), 'Postcript on the societies of control', *October* 59, 3–7.

Deleuze, J. (1992b), 'What is a *dispotif*?', in T. Armstrong (trans.), *Michel Foucault: Philosopher*, London: Harvester Wheatsheaf, pp. 159–68.

De Man, P. (1983), *Blindness and Insight*, London: Routledge.

Derrida, J. (1973), *Speech and Phenomena*, Evanston, IL: Northwestern University Press.

Derrida, J. (1976), *Of Grammatology*, Baltimore, MD: Johns Hopkins University Press.

Derrida, J. (1978), *Writing and Difference*, London: Routledge.

Derrida, J. (1981), *Dissemination*, Chicago: University of Chicago Press.

Derrida, J. (1982a), *Margins of Philosophy*, Chicago: University of Chicago Press.

Derrida, J. (1982b), 'Sending: on representation', *Social Research* 49, 295–326.

Derrida, J. (1986), 'Declarations of independence', *New Political Science* 15, 7–16.

Derrida, J. (1987), *The Postcard*, Chicago: University of Chicago Press.

Derrida, J. (1988), *Limited Inc*, Evanston, IL: Northwestern University Press.

Derrida, J. (1992), *The Other Heading*, Bloomington, IN: Indiana University Press.

Derrida, J. (1994), *Specters of Marx*, London: Verso.

Derrida, J. (1997), *The Politics of Friendship*, London: Verso.

Derrida, J. (2002), *Negotiations*, Stanford, CA: Stanford University Press.

Derrida, J. and Stiegler, B. (2002), *Echographies of Television*, Cambridge: Polity.

Desai, A. (2002), *We Are the Poors: Community Struggles in Post-Apartheid South Africa*, New York: Monthly Review.

Dewey, J. (1927), *The Public and its Problems*, Athens, OH: Ohio University Press.

Dewey, J. (1980), *Democracy and Education (John Dewey: Middle Works, Volume 9)*, Carbondale, IL: Southern Illinois University Press.

Dewey, J. (1981), *John Dewey: The Later Works, 1925–1953, Volume 1*, Carbondale, IL: Southern Illinois University Press.

Dewey, J. (1984a), *John Dewey: The Later Works, 1925–1953, Volume 2*, Carbondale, IL: Southern Illinois University Press.

Dewey, J. (1984b), 'Philosophies of freedom', in *John Dewey: Later Works, Volume 3*, Carbondale, IL: Southern Illinois University Press, pp. 92–114.

Dietz, M. (1998), 'Merely combating the phrases of this world: recent democratic theory', *Political Theory* 26, 112–39.

Donald, J. (1992), *Sentimental Education*, London: Verso.

Dostal, R. J. (1994), 'The public and the people: Heidegger's illiberal politics', *Review of Metaphysics* 47, 517–55.

Downing, J. (2000), *Radical Media*, London: Sage.

Driver, F. (1994), 'Bodies in space: Foucault's account of disciplinary power', in C. Jones and R. Porter (eds), *Reassessing Foucault*, London: Routledge, pp. 113–31.

Du Gay, P., Hall S., Janes, L., Mackay, H. and Negus, K. (1997), *Doing Cultural Studies*, London: Sage.

Dunn, J. (1990), *Interpreting Political Responsibility*, Cambridge: Polity.

Dunn, J. (1999), 'Situating democratic political accountability', in A. Przeworski, S. Stokes and M. Manin (eds), *Democracy, Accountability and Representation*, Cambridge: Cambridge University Press, pp. 329–44.

Dunn, J. (2000), *The Cunning of Unreason*, HarperCollins: London.

Dworkin, R. (1985), *A Matter of Principle*, Oxford: Oxford University Press.

Edelman, B. (1979), *Ownership of the Image*, London: Routledge, Kegan, Paul.

Elster, J. (1983), *Sour Grapes*, Cambridge: Cambridge University Press.

Elster, J. (1986), 'The market and the forum: three varieties of political theory', in J. Elster and A. Hylland (eds), *Foundations of Social Choice Theory*, Cambridge: Cambridge University Press, pp. 103–32.

Elster, J. (1998), 'Deliberation and constitution making', in J. Elster (ed.), *Deliberative Democracy*, Cambridge: Cambridge University Press, pp. 97–122.

Felski, R. (1989), *Beyond Feminist Aesthetics*, Cambridge, MA: Harvard University Press.

Ferguson, M. (1990), 'Electronic media and the redefining of time and space', in M. Ferguson (ed.), *Public Communication*, London: Sage, pp. 152–72.

Ferree, M., Gamson, W., Gerhards, J. and Rucht, D. (2002), 'Four models of the public sphere in modern democracies', *Theory and Society* 31, 289–324.

Fish, S. (1994), *There's No Such as Free Speech, and It's a Good Thing, Too*, Oxford: Oxford University Press.

Fishkin, J. (1995), *The Voice of the People*, New Haven, CT: Yale University Press.

Fiss, O. (1996a), *Liberalism Divided*, Boulder, CT: Westview Press.

Fiss, O. (1996b), *The Irony of Free Speech*, Cambridge, MA: Harvard University Press.

Flew, T. (1996), 'Cultural technologies and media studies', *Australian Journal of Communication* 23:3, 39–53.

Flew, T. (1997), 'Citizenship, participation and media policy formation', *Javnost* 4:4, 87–102.

Foucault, M. (1978), *Discipline and Punish*, New York: Pantheon Books.

Foucault, M. (1979), *The History of Sexuality*, London: Allen Lane.

Foucault, M. (1980), *Power/Knowledge*, Brighton: Harvester Wheatsheaf.

Foucault, M. (1981), '*Omnes et Singulatim*: towards a criticism of "Political Reason"', in S. McMurrin (ed.), *The Tanner Lectures on Human Values*, Cambridge: Cambridge University Press, pp. 223–54.

Foucault, M. (1983), 'The subject and power', in H. L. Dreyfus and P. Rabinow (eds), *Michel Foucault* (2nd edition), Chicago: University of Chicago Press, pp. 208–29.

Foucault, M. (1985), *The Use of Pleasure*, New York: Pantheon Books.

Foucault, M. (1986), *The Foucault Reader*, ed. P. Rabinow, New York: Pantheon Books.

Foucault, M. (1991), 'Governmentality', in G. Burchell, C. Gordon and P. Miller (eds), *The Foucault Effect*, London: Harvester Wheatsheaf, pp. 87–104.

Foucault, M. (1993), 'About the beginnings of the hermeneutics of the self', *Political Theory* 21, 198–227.

Foucault, M. (1997), *The Essential Works of Foucault 1954–1984, Volume 1: Ethics*, London: Allen Lane.

Foucault, M. (2000), *The Essential Works of Foucault 1954–1984, Volume 3: Power*, London: Allen Lane.

Fowler, M. and Brenner, D. (1982), 'A marketplace approach to broadcast regulation', *Texas Law Review* 60, 207–57.

Fraser, N. (1989), *Unruly Practices*, Cambridge: Polity.

Fraser, N. (1997), *Justice Interruptus*, London: Routledge.

Frow, J. (1994), 'Timeshift: technologies of reproduction and intellectual property', *Economy and Society* 23, 291–304.

Gaines, J. (1991), *Contested Culture*, London: BFI.

Gallie, W. (1956), 'Essentially contested concepts', *Proceedings of the Aristotelian Society* 56, 167–98.

Gamson, W. (2001), 'Promoting political engagement', in W. L. Bennett and R. M. Entman (eds), *Mediated Politics*, Cambridge: Cambridge University Press, pp. 56–74.

Gamson, W. and Wolfsfeld, G. (1993), 'Movements and media as interacting systems', *Annals of the American Association of Political and Social Science* 528, 114–25.

Garber, M. (2001), *Academic Instincts*, Princeton, NJ: Princeton University Press.

Garnham, N. (1987), 'Concepts of culture: public policy and the cultural industries', *Cultural Studies* 1, 23–38.

Garnham, N. (1990), *Capitalism and Communication*, London: Sage.

Garnham, N. (1993), 'The mass media, cultural identity, and the public sphere in the modern world', *Public Culture* 5, 251–65.

Garnham, N. (1995), 'The media and narratives of the intellectual', *Media, Culture and Society* 17, 359–84.

Garnham, N. (1997), 'Political economy and the practice of cultural studies', in M. Ferguson and P. Golding (eds), *Cultural Studies in Question*, London: Sage, pp. 56–73.

Garnham, N. (1999), 'Amartya Sen's "capabilities" approach to the evaluation of welfare: its application to communications', in A. Calabrese and J.-C. Burgelman (eds), *Communication, Citizenship, and Social Policy*, Lanham, MD: Rowman and Littlefield, pp. 113–24.

Garnham, N. (2000), *Emancipation, the Media, and Modernity*, Oxford: Oxford University Press.

Gasché, R. (1999), 'On re-presentation', in R. Gasché, *Of Minimal Things*, Stanford, CA: Stanford University Press, pp. 242–59.

Giddens, A. (1981), *A Contemporary Critque of Historical Materialism, Volume 1*, London: Macmillan.

Giddens, A. (1984), *The Constitution of Society*, Cambridge: Polity.

Giddens, A. (1985), *Nation-State and Violence*, Cambridge: Polity.

Giddens, A. (1990), *The Consequences of Modernity*, Cambridge: Polity.

Gilroy, P. (1996), 'British cultural studies and the pitfalls of identity', in J. Curran D. Morley and V. Walkerdine (eds), *Cultural Studies and Communications*, London: Arnold, pp. 35–49.

Gitlin, T. (2000), *Inside Prime Time*, Berkeley, CA: University of California Press.

Gregory, D. (1989), 'Presences and absences: time-space relations and structuration theory', in D. Held and J. Thompson (eds), *Social Theory of Modern Societies*, Cambridge: Cambridge University Press, pp. 185–214.

Gregory, D. (1994), *Geographical Imaginations*, Oxford: Blackwell.

Greimas, A. (1990), *The Social Sciences: A Semiotic View*, Minneapolis: University of Minnesota Press.

Habermas, J. (1983), 'Hannah Arendt: on the concept of power', in J. Habermas, *Philosophical-Political Profiles*, Cambridge, MA: MIT Press.

Habermas, J. (1987), *The Theory of Communicative Action, Volume 2*, Cambridge: Polity.

Habermas, J. (1988), *The Philosophical Discourse of Modernity*, Cambridge MA: MIT Press.

Habermas, J. (1989), *The Structural Transformation of the Public Sphere*, Cambridge, MA: MIT Press.

Habermas, J. (1990), *The New Conservatism*, Cambridge, MA: MIT Press.

Habermas, J. (1992), 'Further reflections on the public sphere', in C. Calhoun (ed.), *Habermas and the Public Sphere*, Cambridge, MA: MIT Press, pp. 421–61.

Habermas, J. (1994a), 'Struggles for recognition in the democratic constitutional state', in A. Gutman (ed.), *Multiculturalism*, Princeton, NJ: Princeton University, pp. 107–48.

Habermas, J. (1994b), *The Past as Future*, Lincoln, NE: University of Nebraska Press.

Habermas, J. (1996), *Between Facts and Norms*, Cambridge: Polity.

Habermas, J. (1998), *The Inclusion of the Other*, Cambridge: Polity.

Habermas, J. (2001), *The Postnational Constellation*, Cambridge: Polity.

Hadley, P. and Samarajiva, R. (1997), 'Regulation of on-line content in the new trade environment: NAFTA and communication policy', *Communication Review* 2, 207–33.

Halcli, A. (1999), 'Aids, anger and activism: ACT UP as a social movement organization', in J. Freeman and V. Johnson (eds), *Waves of Protest: Social Movements Since the Sixties*, New York: Rowman and Littlefield, pp. 135–50.

Halcli, A. (2000), 'Social movements', in G. Browning, A. Halcli and F. Webster (eds), *Understanding Contemporary Society*, London: Sage, pp. 463–75.

Halperin, D. (1995), *Saint Foucault*, Oxford: Oxford University Press.

Hancher, L. and Moran, M. (1998), 'Organizing regulatory space', in R. Baldwin, C. Scott and C. Hood (eds), *Regulation*, Oxford: Oxford University Press, pp. 148–72.

Hannah, M. (1998), 'Space and the structuring of disciplinary power: an interpretative review', *Geografiska Annaler* 79B:3, 171–80.

Harcourt, A. J. and Raedelli, C. M. (1999), 'Limits to EU technocratic regulation?' *European Journal of Political Research* 35, 107–22.

Hartley, J. (1996), *Popular Reality*, London: Arnold.

Hartley, J. (1999), *Uses of Television*, London: Routledge.

Harvey, D. W. (1982), *Limits to Capital*, Oxford: Blackwell.

Harvey, D. W. (1989), *The Condition of Postmodernity*, Oxford: Blackwell.

Harvey, D. W. (1990), 'Between space and time: reflections on the geographical imagination', *Annals of the Association of American Geographers* 80, 418–34.

Harvey, D. W. (1996), *Justice, Nature and the Politics of Difference*, Oxford: Blackwell.

Harvey, D. (2000), *Spaces of Hope*, Edinburgh: Edinburgh University Press.

Harvey, D. (2001), 'The art of rent: globalization, monopoly and the commodification of culture', in L. Panitch and C. Leys (eds), *A World of Contradictions: Socialist Register 2002*, London: Merlin Press, pp. 93–110.

Heidegger, M. (1977), *The Question Concerning Technology and Other Essays*, New York: Harper and Row.

Heins, M. (2001), *Not in Front of the Children: 'Indecency', Censorship, and the Innocence of Youth*, New York: Hill and Wang.

Held, D. (1989a), 'Citizenship and autonomy', in D. Held and J. Thompson (eds), *Social Theory of Modern Societies*, Cambridge: Cambridge University Press, pp. 162–84.

Held, D. (1989b), *Political Theory and the Modern State*, Cambridge: Polity.

Herbst, S. (1993), *Numbered Voices*, Chicago: University of Chicago Press.

Hillis, K. (1998), 'On the margins: the invisibility of communications in geography', *Progress in Human Geography* 22:4, 543–66.

Hills, J. and Michalis, M. (1999), 'Is convergence a purely European obsession?', paper presented at CCIS/Euricom Colloquium on the Political Economy of Convergence, University of Westminster.

Hindess, B. (1991), 'Imaginary presuppositions of democracy', *Economy and Society* 20, 173–95.

Hindess, B. (1996), *Discourses of Power*, Oxford: Blackwell.

Hindess, B. (1997), 'Politics and governmentality', *Economy and Society* 26, 257–72.

Hoffmann-Riem, W. (1996), *Regulating Media*, New York: Guilford Press.

Hohendahl, P. U. (1979), 'Critical theory, public sphere and culture: Jürgen Habermas and his critics', *New German Critique* 16, 89–118.

Hohendahl, P. U. (1987), *The Institution of Criticism*, Ithaca, NY: Cornell University Press.

Hohendahl, P. U. (1995), 'Recasting the public sphere', *October* 73, 27–54.

Honig, B. (1991), 'Declarations of independence: Arendt and Derrida on the problem of founding a republic', *American Political Science Review* 85, 97–113.

Honig, B. (1992), 'Toward an agonistic feminism: Hannah Arendt and the politics of identity', in J. Butler and J. W. Scott (eds), *Feminists Theorize the Political*, London: Routledge, pp. 215–35.

Honneth, A. (1995), 'The other of justice: Habermas and the ethical challenge of postmodernism', in S. White (ed.), *The Cambridge Companion to Habermas*, Cambridge: Cambridge University Press, pp. 289–323.

Honneth, A. (1999), 'The social dynamics of disrespect: situating critical theory today', in P. Dews (ed.), *Habermas: A Critical Reader*, Oxford: Blackwell, pp. 320–37.

Horton, D. and Wohl, R. (1956), 'Mass communcation and para-social interaction', *Psychiatry* 19, 215–29.

Horwitz, R. (1989), *The Irony of Regulatory Reform*, Oxford: Oxford University Press.

Horwitz, R. (1991), 'The First Amendment meets some new technologies', *Theory and Society* 20, 21–72.

Horwitz, R. (1993), 'Begging the question: consistency and "common sense" in First Amendment jurisprudence of advertising and begging', *Studies in Law, Politics, and Society* 13, 213–47.

Horwitz, R. (1996), 'Broadcast reform revisited: Reverend Everett C. Parker and the "standing" case' *Communicaton Review* 2, 311–48.

Horwitz, R. (1997), 'Telecommunications policy in the new South Africa: participatory politics and sectoral reform', *Media, Culture and Society* 19:4, 503–34.

Horwitz, R. (2001), *Communication and Democratic Reform in South Africa*, Cambridge: Cambridge University Press.

Howell, P. (1993), 'Public space and the public sphere', *Environment and Planning D: Society and Space* 11, 303–22.

Howell, P. (1994), 'The aspiration towards universality in political theory and political geography', *Geoforum* 25, 413–27.

Hunter, I. (1988), *Culture and Government*, London: Macmillan.

Hunter, I. (1993), 'Subjectivity and government', *Economy and Society* 22, 122–34.

Hunter, I. (1994), *Rethinking the School*, Sydney: Allen and Unwin.

Iosifides, P. (1999), 'Pluralism and media concentration policy in the European Union', *Javnost* 4:1, 85–104.

Jachtenfuchs, M., Diez, T. and Jung, S. (1998), 'Which Europe? Conflicting models of a legitimate European political order' *European Journal of International Relations* 4, 409–25.

Jacobs, S. (1999), 'The media and the elections', in A. Reynolds (ed.), *Election '99 South Africa*, Cape Town: David Philip, pp. 147–58.

James, W. (2000), *Pragmatism and Other Writings*, London: Penguin.

JanMohamed, A. (1995), 'Refiguring values, power, knowledge; or Foucault's disavowal of Marx', in B. Magnus and S. Cullenberg (eds), *Whither Marxism?*, London: Routledge, pp. 31–64.

Johnson, J. (1997), 'Communication, criticism, and the postmodern consensus: an unfashionable interpretation of Michel Foucault', *Political Theory* 25, 559–83.

Kaitatzi-Whitlock, S. (1996), 'Pluralism and media concentration in Europe', *European Journal of Communication* 11, 453–83.

Kalven, H. (1965), 'The concept of the public forum', in P. B. Kurland (ed.), *Supreme Court Review 1965*, Chicago: University of Chicago Press, pp. 1–32.

Kant, I. (1970), *Political Writings*, Cambridge: Cambridge University Press.

Katz, J. and Aakhus, M. (2002), *Perpetual Contact: Mobile Communication, Private Talk, Public Performance*, Cambridge: Cambridge University Press.

Katznelson, I. (1996), 'Social justice, liberalism and the city', in A. Merrifield and E. Swyngedouw (eds), *The Urbanization of Injustice*, London: Lawrence and Wishart, pp. 45–64.

Keane, J. (1984), *Public Life and Late Capitalism*, Cambridge: Cambridge University Press.

Keane, J. (1991), *Media and Democracy*, Cambridge: Polity.

Keane, J. (1995), 'Structural transformation of the public sphere', *Communication Review* 1, 1–22.

Keenan, T. (1993), 'Windows of vulnerability', in B. Robbins (ed.), *The Phantom Public*, Minneapolis: University of Minnesota Press, pp. 121–41.

Kirsch, S. (1995), 'The incredible shrinking world: technology and the production of space', *Environment and Planning D: Society and Space* 13, 529–55.

Klandermans, B., Roefs, M. and Olivier, J. (2001), *The State of the People: Citizens, Civil Society and Governance in South Africa, 1994–2000*, Pretoria: Human Sciences Research Council.

Lacey, K. (1996), *Feminine Frequencies: Gender, German Radio, and the Public Sphere, 1923–1945*, Ann Arbor: University of Michigan Press.

Laclau, E. (1993), 'Power and representation', in M. Poster (ed.), *Politics, Theory, and Contemporary Culture*, New York: Columbia University Press, pp. 277–96.

Laclau, E. and Mouffe, C. (1985), *Hegemony and Socialist Strategy*, London: Verso.

Lacombe, D. (1996), 'Reforming Foucault: a critique of the social control thesis', *British Journal of Sociology* 47, 332–52.

Lazarus, E. (1998), *Closed Chambers: The Rise, Fall, and Future of the Modern Supreme Court*, Harmondsworth: Penguin.

Le Duc, D. (1969), 'The FCC v. CATV et al.: a theory of regulatory reflex action', *Federal Communcations Bar Journal* 23: 2, 92–109.

Le Duc, D. (1987), *Beyond Broadcasting*, London: Longman.

Le Duc, D. (1988), 'Unbundling the channels: a functional approach to cable television', *Federal Communications Law Journal* 41, 1–16.

Lee, B. (1992), 'Textuality, mediation, and public discourse', in C. Calhoun (ed.), *Habermas and the Public Sphere*, Cambridge, MA: MIT Press, pp. 402–18.

Lee, B. (1997), 'The performativity of foundations', in B. Lee, *Talking Heads*, Durham, NC: Duke University Press, pp. 321–46.

Lefort, C. (1986), *The Political Forms of Modern Society*, Cambridge: Polity.

Lefort, C. (1988), *Democracy and Political Theory*, Cambridge: Polity.

Lefort, C. (2000), *Writing: The Political Test*, Durham, NC: Duke University Press.

Lessig, L. (1996), 'The zones of cyberspace', *Stanford Law Review* 48, 1403–11.

Lessig, L. (2000), *Code and Other Laws of Cyberspace*, New York: Basic Books.

Levy, D. A. (1999), *Europe's Digital Revolution*, London: Routledge.

Leyshon, A. (1995), 'Annihilating space? The speed-up of communications', in J. Allen, and C. Hamnett (eds), *A Shrinking World*, Oxford: Oxford University Press, pp. 9–54.

Libertus, M. (2000), 'To protect and to serve pluralism and the public service mission: comments on the European Commission's communications review 1999', *International Journal of Communications Law and Policy* 5.

Lippmann, W. (1925), *The Phantom Public*, New York: Harcourt Brace.

Lodge, T. (2001), 'South African politics and collective action, 1994–2000', in B. Klandermans, M. Roefs and J. Olivier, *The State of the People: Citizens, Civil Society and Governance in South Africa, 1994–2000*, Pretoria: Human Sciences Research Council, pp. 1–26.

Louw, P. (ed.) (1993), *South African Media Policy*, Johannesburg: Anthropos.

Low, M. (1997), 'Representation unbound', in K. Cox (ed.), *Spaces of Globalization*, New York: Guilford Press, pp. 240–80.

Low, M. (1999), 'Their masters' voice: communitarianism, civic order, and political representation', *Environment and Planning A* 31, 87–111.

Lury, C. (1993), *Cultural Rights*, London: Routledge.

Lyon, J. (1999), *Manifestoes: Provocations of the Modern*, Ithaca, NY: Cornell University Press.

Lyotard, J.-F. (1991), *The Inhuman*, Stanford, CA: Stanford University Press.

Macherey, P. (1992), 'Towards a natural history of norms', in T. Armstrong (trans.), *Michel Foucault: Philosopher*, London: Harvester Wheatsheaf, pp. 176–91.

MacCormick, N. (1997), 'Democracy, subsidiarity, and citizenship in the "European Commonwealth"', *Law and Philosophy* 16, 331–56.

MacKinnon, C. (1993), *Only Words*, Cambridge, CA: Harvard University Press.

Majone, G. (1996), *Regulating Europe*, London: Routledge.

Manin, B. (1997), *The Principles of Representative Government*, Cambridge: Cambridge University Press.

Mann, M. (1993), *The Sources of Social Power, Volume 2*, Cambridge: Cambridge University Press.

Marks, G. (1993), 'Structural policy and multilevel governance in the European Community', in A. Cafruny and G. Rosenthal (eds), *The State of the European Community*, New York: Lynne Rienner, pp. 391–410.

Marston, D. and Mitchell, K. (forthcoming), 'Citizens and the state: contextualising citizenship formation in space and time', in C. Barnett and M. Low (eds), *Spaces of Democracy*, London: Sage.

Martin-Barbero, J. (1993), *Communication, Culture, and Hegemony: From Media to Mediations*, London: Sage.

Marx, K. and Engels, F. (1979), *Collected Works, Volume 11, 1851–1853*, New York: International Publishers.

Massey, D. (1994), 'A place called home?', in D. Massey, *Space, Place and Gender*, Cambridge: Polity, pp. 157–73.

Massey, D. (1995), 'Thinking radical democracy spatially', *Environment and Planning D: Society and Space* 13, 283–8.

Massey, D. (1999), 'Spaces of politics', in D. Massey, J. Allen and P. Sane (eds), *Human Geography Today*, Cambridge: Polity.

Matsuda, M. J., Delgaslo, R. Lawrence, C. and Crenshaw, K. (eds) (1993), *Words that Wound*, Boulder, CT: Westview Press.

McAdam, D. (1996), 'The framing function of movement tactics: strategic dramaturgy in the American civil rights movement', in D. McAdam, M. Zald and J. McCarthy (eds), *Comparative Perspectives on Social Movements*, Cambridge: Cambridge University Press, pp. 338–55.

McChesney, R. (1993), *Telecommuncations, Mass Media, and Democracy*, Oxford: Oxford University Press.

McChesney, R. (1999), *Rich Media, Poor Democracy*, Urbana, IL: University of Illinois Press.

McGuigan, J. (1998), 'What price the public sphere?', in D. K. Thussu (ed.), *Electronic Empires*, London: Arnold, pp. 91–107.

McLaughlin, L. (1993), 'Feminism, the public sphere, media and democracy', *Media, Culture and Democracy* 15, 599–620.

McLuhan, M. (1964), *Understanding Media*, New York: McGraw-Hill.

McNay, L. (1994), *Foucault*, Cambridge: Polity.

McNay, L. (1998), 'Michel Foucault and agonistic democracy', in A. Carter, and G. Stokes, (eds), *Liberal Democracy and its Critics*, Cambridge: Polity, pp. 216–37.

McQuail, D. and Siune, K. (eds) (1998), *Media Policy: Convergence, Concentration and Commerce*, London: Sage.

Meehan, E. (1986), 'Conceptualizing culture as commodity', *Critical Studies in Mass Communication* 3, 448–57.

Meiklejohn, A. (1961), 'The First Amendment is an absolute', in P. B. Kurland (ed.), *The Supreme Court Review*, Chicago: University of Chicago Press, pp. 245–66.

Meredyth, D. and Minson, J. (eds) (2001), *Citizenship and Cultural Policy*, London: Sage.

Meyer, C. (1999), 'Political legitimacy and the invisibility of politics: exploring the EU's communication deficit', *Journal of Common Market Studies* 37, 617–39.

Miège, B. (1987), 'The logics at work in the new cultural industries', *Media, Culture and Society* 9, 273–89.

Miller, J. H. (1991), 'The critic as host', in J. H. Miller, *Theory Then and Now*, London: Harvester Wheatsheaf, pp. 143–70.

Miller, P. and Rose, N. (1990), 'Governing economic life', *Economy and Society* 19, 1–31.

Miller, T. (1991), 'Splitting the citizen', *Continuum* 4:2.

Miller, T. (1993), *The Well-Tempered Self*, Baltimore, MD: Johns Hopkins University Press.

Miller, T. (1996), 'The crime of Monsieur Lang: GATT, the screen and the new international division of cultural labour', in A. Moran (ed.), *Film Policy: International, National and Regional Perspectives*, London: Routledge, pp. 72–84

Miller, T. (1998), *Technologies of Truth*, Minneapolis: University of Minnesota Press.

Mitchell, D. (1997), 'The annihilation of space by law: the roots and implications of anti-homeless laws in the United States', *Antipode* 29, 303–35.

Mitchell, J. (1998), 'New audiovisual and information services and the protection of children: the European dimension', *Journal of Consumer Policy* 21, 3–44.

Montgomery, K. (1989), *Target: Prime Time: Advocacy Groups and the Struggle Over Entertainment*, Oxford: Oxford University Press.

Moores, S. (1993), 'Television, geography and "mobile privatization"', *European Journal of Communication* 8, 365–79.

Moreira, J. (2000), 'Cohesion and citizenship in the EU cultural policy', *Journal of Common Market Studies* 38, 449–70.

Morley, D. (1998), 'Media Fortress Europe: geographies of exclusion and the purification of cultural space', *Canadian Journal of Communication* 23: 2.

Morley, D. and Robbins, K. (1995), *Spaces of Identity*, London: Routledge, pp. 341–58.

Morris, M. (1998), *Too Late, Too Soon*. Bloomington, IN: Indiana University Press.

Morrow, J. and Puren, N. (1998), 'Law and culture', in K. McGowan (ed.), *The Year's Work in Critical and Cultural Theory, 1995*, Oxford: Blackwell, pp. 274–304.

Mosco, V. (1996), *Political Economy of Communications*, London: Sage.

Mouffe, C. (1994), *The Return of the Political*, London: Verso.

Mouffe, C. (2000), *The Democratic Paradox*, London: Verso.

Murdoch, J. (1998), 'The spaces of actor-network theory', *Geoforum* 29, 357–74.

Murdock, G. (1992), 'Citizens, consumers, and public culture', in M. Skovmand and K. Christian-Scholder (eds), *Media Cultures*, London: Routledge, pp. 17–41.

Murdock, G. (1993), 'Communications and the constitution of modernity', *Media, Culture and Society* 15, 521–39.

Nancy, J. L. (1991), *The Inoperative Community*, Minneapolis: University of Minnesota Press.

Napoli, P. (1999), 'The marketplace of ideas metaphor in communications', *Journal of Communication* 49, 151–69.

Negt, O. (1978), 'Mass media: tools of domination or instruments of liberation?', *New German Critique* 14, 61–82.

Negt, O. and Kluge, A. (1993), *Public Sphere and Experience*, Minneapolis: University of Minnesota Press.

Nixon, R. (1994), *Homelands, Harlem and Hollywood*, London: Routledge.

Oliver, K. (2001), *Witnessing: Beyond Recognition*, Minneapolis: University of Minnesota Press.

O'Malley, P. (1996), 'Indigenous governance', *Economy and Society* 25, 310–26.

O'Neill, J. (2001), 'Representing people, representing nature, representing the world', *Environment and Planning C: Government and Policy* 19, 483–500.

O'Neill, O. (2000), *The Bounds of Justice*, Cambridge: Cambridge University Press.

O'Neill, O. (2002a), *A Question of Trust*, Oxford: Oxford University Press.

O'Neill, O. (2002b), *Autonomy and Trust in Bioethics*, Cambridge: Cambridge University Press.

O'Neill, P. (2000), 'Organized citizen action and media accountability', in D. Pritchard (ed.), *Holding the Media Accountable*, Bloomington, IN: Indiana University Press, pp. 90–108.

Ong, A. (1999), *Flexible Citizenship*, Durham, NC: Duke University Press.

O'Regan, T. (1992), 'Mistaking policy: notes on the cultural policy debate', *Cultural Studies* 6, 409–23.

Ouellette, L. (1999), 'TV viewing as good citizenship: political rationality, enlightened democracy and PBS', *Cultural Studies* 13, 62–90.

Page, B. (1996), *Who Deliberates?*, Chicago: University of Chicago Press.

Patton, C. (1993), 'Tremble, hetero swine!', in M. Warner (ed.), *Fear of a Queer Planet*, Minneapolis: University of Minnesota Press, pp. 143–77.

Pauwels, C. (1999), 'From citizenship and consumer sovereignty: the paradigm shift in European audio-visual policy', in A. Calabrese and J.-C. Burgelman (eds), *Communication, Citizenship and Social Policy*, Lanham, MD: Rowman and Littlefield, pp. 49–76.

Peters, J. D. (1993), 'Distrust of representation: Habermas on the public sphere', *Media, Culture and Society* 15, 541–71.

Peters, J. D. (1999), *Speaking into the Air: A History of the Idea of Communication*, Chicago: University of Chicago Press.

Phillips, A. (1991), *Engendering Democracy*, Cambridge: Polity.

Phillips, A. (1992), 'Universal pretensions in political thought', in M. Barrett and A. Phillips (eds), *Destabilizing Theory*, Cambridge: Polity, pp. 10–30.

Phillips, A. (1995), *The Politics of Presence*, Oxford: Clarendon Press.

Pitkin, H. (1967), *The Concept of Representation*, Berkeley, CA: University of California Press.

Pitkin, H. (1981), 'Justice: on relating public and private', *Political Theory* 9, 327–52.

Pitkin, H. (1998), *The Attack of the Blob: Hannah Arendt and the Concept of the Social*, Chicago: University of Chicago Press.

Popper, K. (1966), *The Open Society and its Enemies, Volume 1*, London: Routledge, Kegan and Paul.

Post, R. (1990), 'The constitutional concept of public discourse: outrageous opinion, democratic deliberation, and *Hustler Magazine v. Falwell*', *Harvard Law Review* 103, 601–86.

Post, R. (1993), 'Managing deliberation: the quandary of democratic dialogue', *Ethics* 103, 654–78.

Post, R. (1995), 'Recuperating First Amendment doctrine', *Stanford Law Review* 47, 1249–81.

Post, R. (ed.) (1998), *Censorship and Silencing*, Oxford: Oxford University Press.

Preuss, U. (1998), 'Citizenship in the European Union: a paradigm for transnational democracy?', in D. Archibugi, D. Held and M. Kohler (eds), *Re-imagining Political Community*, Cambridge: Polity, pp. 138–51.

Price, M. E. (1995), *Television, the Public Sphere, and National Identity*, Oxford: Oxford University Press.

Price, M. E. and Duffy, J. F. (1997), 'Technological change and doctrinal persistence: telecommunications reform in Congress and the Court', *Columbia Law Review* 97, 976–1015.

Prinsloo, J. (1999), 'South African media education in the late twentieth century: rising phoenix or dying swan?', in C. Von Feilitzen and U. Carlsson (eds), *Children and Media*, Göteborg: Nordicom, pp. 163–88.

Prinsloo, J. and Criticos, C. (eds) (1991), *Media Matters in South Africa*, Durban: Media Resource Centre, University of Natal.

Putnam, R. (1995), 'Bowling alone: America's declining social capital', *Journal of Democracy* 6:1, 65–78.

Raedelli, C. (1999), 'The public policy of the European Union: whither politics of expertise?', *Journal of European Public Policy* 6, 757–74.

Rawls, J. (1972), *A Theory of Justice*, Oxford: Oxford University Press.

Rawls, J. (1993), *Political Liberalism*, New York: Columbia University Press.

Ricoeur, P. (1965), 'The political paradox', in P. Ricoeur, *History and Truth*, Evanston, IL: Northwestern University Press, pp. 247–70.

Ricoeur, P. (1981), *Hermeneutics and the Human Sciences*, Cambridge: Cambridge University Press.

Robins, K. (1997), 'The new communications geography and the politics of optimism', *Soundings* 5, 191–202.

Robbins, B. (1993), 'Introduction: the public and phantom', in B. Robbins (ed.), *The Phantom Public*, Minneapolis: University of Minnesota Press, pp. vii–xxvi.

Robbins, B. (1999), *Feeling Global*, New York: New York University Press.

Rodriguez, A. (1997), 'Commercial ethnicity: language, class, and race in the marketing of the Hispanic audience', *Communication Review* 2:3, 283–309.

Rose, N. (1994), 'Expertise and the government of conduct', *Studies in Law, Politics, and Society* 14, 359–97.

Rose, N. (1996), 'The death of the social? Re-figuring the territory of government', *Economy and Society* 25, 327–56.

Rose, N. (1999), *Powers of Freedom*, Cambridge: Cambridge University Press.

Ross, S. D. (1998), 'First Amendment trump? The uncertain constitutionalization of structural regulation separating telephone and video', *Federal Communications Law Journal* 50, 282–309.

Saccamano, N. (1991), 'The consolations of ambivalence: Habermas and the public sphere', *Modern Language Notes* 106, 685–98.

Samarajiva, R. and Shields, P. (1990), 'Integration, telecommunications, and development: power in the paradigms', *Journal of Communication* 40, 84–105.

Samarajiva, R. and Shields, P. (1997), 'Telecommuncation networks as social space: implications for research and policy and an exemplar', *Media, Culture and Society*, 19, 535–55.

Sandel, M. (1996), *Democracy's Discontent*, Cambridge, MA: Harvard University Press.

Scannell, P. (1989), 'Public service broadcasting and modern public life', *Media, Culture and Society* 11, 135–66.

Scannell, P. (ed.) (1991), *Broadcast Talk*, London: Sage.

Scannell, P. (1992), 'Media and democracy', *Media, Culture and Society* 14, 325–8.

Scannell, P. (1996), *Radio, Television, and Modern Life*, Oxford: Blackwell.

Scannell, P. (2000), 'For-anyone-as-someone structures', *Media, Culture and Society* 22, 5–24.

Scannell, P. (2001a), 'Media events', *Media, Culture and Society* 23, 699–705.

Scannell, P. (2001b), 'Music, radio, and the record business in Zimbabwe today', *Popular Music* 20:1, 13–27.

Schauer, F. (1982), *Free Speech*, Cambridge: Cambridge University Press.

Schauer, F. (1994), 'Judicial review of the devices of democracy', *Columbia Law Review* 94, 1324–47.

Schauer, F. (1998a), 'Deference to legislative fact determinations in first amendment cases after Turner broadcasting', *Harvard Law Review* 111, 2312–29.

Schauer, F. (1998b), 'Principles, institutions, and the First Amendment', *Harvard Law Review* 112, 84–120.

Schauer, F. and Wise, V. (2000), 'Nonlegal information and the delegalization of law', *Journal of Legal Studies* 29, 495–515.

Scheuerman, W. (1998), *Between the Norm and the Exception*, Cambridge, MA: MIT Press.

Schiller, D. (1996), *Theorizing Communication*, Oxford: Oxford University Press.

Schiller, D. (2000), *Digital Capitalism*, Cambridge, MA: MIT Press.

Schlesinger, P. (1990), 'Rethinking the sociology of journalism: source strategies and the limits of media centrism', in M. Ferguson (ed.), *Public Communication*, London: Sage.

Schlesinger, P. (1993), 'Wishful thinking: cultural politics, media, and collective identities in Europe', *Journal of Communication* 43, 6–17.

Schlesinger, P. (1997), 'From cultural defence to political culture: media, politics and collective identity in the European Union', *Media, Culture and Society* 19, 369–91.

Schlesinger, P. and Doyle, G. (1995), 'Contradictions of economy and culture: the European Union and the information society', *European Journal of Cultural Policy* 2:1, 25–42.

Schmitt, C. (1996), *The Concept of the Political*, Chicago: University of Chicago Press.

Schmitter, P. (1999), 'The future of democracy: could it be a matter of scale?', *Social Research* 66, 933–57.

Schudson, M. (1992), 'The limits of teledemocracy', *American Prospect* 3: 11, (1 September).

Schudson, M. (1995), *The Power of News*, Cambridge, MA: Harvard University Press.

Schudson, M. (1997), 'Why conversation is not the soul of democracy', *Critical Studies in Mass Communication* 14, 297–309.

Scott, A. and Sharpe, J. (2000), 'From media protest to e-protest: the use of popular culture and new media in parties and social movements', *Information, Communication and Society* 3, 215–40.

Sedgwick, E. (1990), *The Epistemology of the Closet*, Berkeley, CA: University of California Press.

Seekings, J. (1996), 'The decline of South Africa's civic organisations', *Critical Sociology* 22:3, 135–57.

Sen, A. (1999), *Development as Freedom*, Oxford: Oxford University Press.

Shields, P. (1995), 'Theorising the "policy moment": the example of US telecommunications policy', *Media Information Australia* 76, 82–91.

Shields, P. and Muppidi, S. (1996), 'Integration, the Indian state and Star TV: policy and theory issues', *Gazette* 58, 1–24.

Shore, C. (1993), 'Inventing the "People's Europe": critical approaches to European Community cultural policy', *Man* (NS) 28, 779–800.

Shore, C. (1996), 'Transcending the nation-state? The European Commission and the (re-)discovery of Europe', *Journal of Historical Sociology* 9, 473–96.

Siedentop, L. (2000), *Democracy in Europe*, London: Allen Lane.

Silk, J. (1998), 'Caring at a distance', *Ethics, Place and Environment* 1, 165–82.

Silverstone, R. (1994), *Television and Everyday Life*, London: Routledge.

Silverstone, R. (1999), *Why Study Media?*, London: Sage.

Simons, J. (2002), 'Governing the public: technologies of mediation and popular culture', *Cultural Values* 6, 167–181.

Sinclair, J., Jacka, E. and Cunningham, S. (1996), *New Patterns in Global Television*, Oxford: Oxford University Press.

Sinfield, A. (1992), *Faultlines: Cultural Materialism and the Politics of Dissident Reading*, Oxford: Oxford University Press.

Slater, D. (2002), 'Other domains of democratic theory', *Environment and Planning D: Society and Space* 20, 255–76.

Smith, A. and Minson, J. (1997), 'See under: Discipline', *Economy and Society* 26, 191–210.

Smith, D. J. (1997), 'Stay the course: a history of the FCC's response to change in the cable industry', *Journal of Law and Politics* 13, 705–46.

Smith, R. (2001), '*Yizo Yizo*: this is it? Representations and receptions of violence and gender relations', unpublished MA Dissertation, University of Natal.

Smythe, D. (1977), 'Communications: blindspot of western Marxism', *Canadian Journal of Political and Social Theory* 1:3, 1–28.

Spivak, G. C. (1988), 'Can the subaltern speak?', in C. Nelson and L. Grossberg (eds), *Marxism and the Interpretation of Culture*, London: Macmillan, pp. 271–313.

Splichal, S. (1999), *Public Opinion: Development and Controversies in the Twentieth Century*, Boston: Rowman and Littlefield.

Splichal, S. (2002), 'The principle of publicity, public use of reason and social control', *Media, Culture and Society* 24, 5–26.

Staeheli, L. (1996), 'Publicity, privacy, and women's political action', *Environment and Planning D: Society and Space* 14, 601–19.

Staeheli, L. (1999), 'Globalization and the scales of citizenship', *Geography Research Forum* 19, 60–77.

Staeheli, L. and Mitchell, D. (forthcoming), 'Spaces of public and private', in C. Barnett and M. Low (eds), *Spaces of Democracy*, Sage: London.

Stephens, S. (2000), 'Kwaito', in S. Nuttall and C.-A. Michael (eds), *Senses of Culture: South African Culture Studies*, Cape Town: Oxford University Press, pp. 256–73.

Streeter, T. (1996), *Selling the Air*, Chicago: University of Chicago Press.

Streeter, T. and Wahl, W. (1995), 'Audience theory and feminism: property, gender, and the television audience', *Camera Obscura* 33/34, 243–61.

Sunstein, C. R. (1992), 'Preferences and politics', *Philosophy and Public Affairs* 20, 3–34.

Sunstein, C. R. (1995a), *Democracy and the Problem of Free Speech*, New York: Free Press.

Sunstein, C. R. (1995b), 'The First Amendment in cyberspace', *Yale Law Journal* 104, 1757–804.

Sunstein, C. R. (1996), *Legal Reasoning and Political Conflict*, Oxford: Oxford University Press.

Svendsen, N. V. (2001), 'Reporting air pollution in South Durban: a case study of environmental journalism in Durban newspapers', unpublished MA Dissertation, Graduate Programme in Cultural and Media Studies, University of Natal, Durban.

Tarrow, S. (1998), *Power in Movement* (2nd edition), Cambridge: Cambridge University Press.

Teer-Tomaselli, R. (1995), 'Moving towards democracy: the SABC and the 1994 election', *Media, Culture and Society* 17, 577–601.

Teer-Tomaselli, R. (1996), 'DEBI does democracy: recollecting democratic voter education in the electronic media prior to the South African elections', in G. Marcus (ed.), *Connected: Entanglements with the Media*, Chicago: University of Chicago Press, pp. 375–422.

Thompson, J. B. (1995), *The Media and Modernity*, Cambridge: Polity.

Thompson, J. B. (2000), *Political Scandal*, Cambridge: Polity.

Tilly, C. (1990), *Coercion, Capital and European States*, Oxford: Blackwell.

Tilly, C. (1994), 'Social movements as historically specific clusters of political performance', *Berkeley Journal of Sociology* 38, 1–30.

Tomaselli, K. (1997), 'Ownership and control in the South African print media: black empowerment after apartheid, 1990–1997', *Ecquid Novi* 18:1, 21–68.

Tomaselli, R., Tomaselli, K. and Muller, J. (eds) (1989), *Broadcasting in South Africa*, London: James Currey.

Tomlinson, J. (1994), 'A phenomenology of globalisation?', *European Journal of Communication* 9, 149–72.

Tushnet, M. (1993), 'The Supreme Court and its First Amendment constituency', *Hastings Law Review* 44, 881–99.

Tushnet, M. (1999), 'The new constitutional order and the chastening of constitutional aspirations', *Harvard Law Review* 113, 29–109.

Unger, R. (1983), 'The critical legal studies movement', *Harvard Law Review* 96, 561–675.

Venter, L. and Van Vuuren, D. (2000), 'Out-of-home television viewing: a cross-cultural comparative study', *Ecquid Novi* 21:1, 98–119.

Ward, D. (2001), 'The democratic deficit and European Union communication policy: an evaluation of the Commission's approach to broadcasting', *Javnost* 8:1, 75–93.

Warner, M. (1990), *The Letters of the Republic*, Cambridge, MA: Harvard University Press.

Warner, M. (1993), 'The mass public and the mass subject', in B. Robbins (ed.), *The Phantom Public*, Minneapolis: University of Minnesota Press, pp. 234–56.

Warner, M. (2002), *Publics and counterpublics*, New York: Zone Books.

Weber, M. (1970), 'Politics as vocation', in *From Max Weber*, H. H. Gerth and C. Wright Mills (eds), London: Routledge, pp. 77–128.

Weber, S. (1996), *Mass Mediauras*, Stanford, CA: Stanford University Press.

Weintraub, J. (1997), 'The theory and politics of the public/private distinction', in J. Weintraub and K. Kumar (eds), *Public and Private in Thought and Practice*, Chicago: University of Chicago Press, pp. 1–42.

West, C. (1989), *The American Evasion of Philosophy*, London: Macmillan.

Wiener, A. (1997), 'Making sense of the new geography of citizenship: fragmented citizenship in the European Union', *Theory and Society* 26, 529–60.

Wiley, D., Root, C. and Peek, S. (2002), 'Contesting the urban industrial environment in South Durban in a period of democratisation and globalisation', in B. Freund and V. Padaychee (eds), *(D)urban Vortex: South African City in Transition*, Pietermaritzburg: University of Natal Press, pp. 223–55.

Williams, R. (1974), *Television: Technology and Cultural Form*, London: Fontana.

Williams, R. (1989), *Resources of Hope*, London: Verso.

Wolin, S. (1997), 'What time is it?', *theory and event* 1:1 <http://muse.jhu.edu/journals/theory_&_event>.

Young, I. M. (1990a), *Justice and the Politics of Difference*, Princeton, NJ: Princeton University Press.

Young, I. M. (1990b), *Throwing Like a Girl and Other Essays in Feminist Philosophy and Social Theory*, Bloomington, IN: Indiana University Press.

Young, I. M. (1993), 'Justice and communicative democracy', in R. Gottlieb (ed.), *Radical Philosophy*, Philadelphia: Temple University Press pp. 123–43.

Young, I. M. (1997), *Intersecting Voices*, Princeton, NJ: Princeton Univeristy Press.
Young, I. M. (1998), 'Harvey's complaint with race and gender struggles: a critical response', *Antipode* 30, 36–42.
Young, I. M. (2000), *Inclusion and Democracy*, Oxford: Oxford University Press.
Young, I. M. (2001), 'Activist challenges to democracy', *Political Theory* 29, 670–90.
Zolo, D. (1992), *Democracy and Complexity*, Cambridge: Polity.

Index